The Human Web

Gerard O'Donnell BA, ACP, FRAI, FRSA
Principal, Rockingham College of Further Education (Rotherham)

John Murray   Albemarle Street   London

Acknowledgements

The diagrams drawn from *Social Trends* are reproduced by permission of the Controller of Her Majesty's Stationery Office. My thanks are also due to the editors of *New Society*, the *Daily Telegraph*, and the *Journal of Moral Education* for permission to reproduce diagrams; to Mr K. Chafey, the Librarian at Wellington Public Library, for his help (librarians often seem to be taken for granted!); to my wife Sara for her invaluable assistance in preparing the manuscript; and to my sons, Duncan and Rory, who numbered the pages.

Gerard O'Donnell 1974
Wellington, Somerset

Further reading suggestions listed at the end of each chapter fit into the following categories:
* Books suitable for the general reader.
† Books that are not particularly difficult and are about O-level standard.
Other books are suitable for students who wish to develop their study of particular topics or for reference.

Filmset in Lumitype Meridien and printed in Great Britain by Butler & Tanner Ltd, Frome and London

0 7195 3389 9

The Human Web is intended for a wide variety of students following general and liberal studies courses in secondary schools and Colleges of Further Education. It will be particularly suitable for those students who are engaged in work with a social-service bias or who hope to be employed in work of this kind in the future; but it is hoped that it will assist all students to understand the influences that affect them as individuals in our society.

The book also provides a framework for students following GCE O-level Sociology courses. All the topics in the Associated Examining Board and Oxford Local Board syllabuses for this subject are dealt with, and background information on related matters is also provided. The single textbook approach is inappropriate for courses in sociology and this book should be used in conjunction with the reading suggestions to be found at the end of each chapter; it is also hoped that students will follow up at least some of the wide range of texts included in the text sources section at the end of the book.

At the end of each chapter there are suggestions for additional discussion, written work, and research; but these should not be regarded as exclusive, as the repetition of questions from easily available past GCE papers has been avoided. A wide range of graphs and statistical tables is included to provide an opportunity for the student to become adept at interpreting material of this kind and to stimulate discussion on the issues raised by the statistics given.

The non-technical approach adopted in the book will make it an ideal textbook for classes in which a proportion of the students wish to take an examination and will wish to do the extra work involved, while others will not have an examination as their objective. It will also prove suitable for many adult non-vocational discussion and liberal studies courses.

In this second edition the facts and figures have been updated where these are significant and where current information is available. Footnotes have been appended to tables where relevant. Some information, however, cannot be brought up to date until the 1981 census takes place.

Cover: from a photograph by Colin Davey, Camera Press, London

'Will he ever get out?'
(comment by author's son, aged six)
Photograph: Nick Hedges, Shelter

Contents

Introduction

This book aims to provide a systematic outline of the society in which we live, and is intended to place the student clearly within the context of that society.

Human beings are notoriously unwilling to criticize their own behaviour, and so it is not surprising that the scientific study of our behaviour is, perhaps, the last of the sciences to become accepted. Long after men had worked out complicated laws of mathematics they still thought that bodily illness was the punishment for sin; later still they believed mental abnormality to be the result of demoniacal possession or personal failing—imprisoning and torturing those who were so afflicted. The first belief gave way as the study of medicine advanced; the second has crumbled under the onslaught of both medical science and psychology.

Yet in many ways we still remain in the past so far as the study of society, the organization within which we live, is concerned. Social behaviour different from our own is condemned as immoral and bestial, or as the personal fault of those who practise it, just as, in days gone by, the epileptic was condemned to the mad house to have the demons whipped out of him.

Why do people commit crimes, have illegitimate babies, commit suicide, or otherwise transgress our social code? The sociologist believes that the answer often lies within the society in which they live, and that only by finding the cause can one effect a cure—if indeed a cure is desirable.

It would not be true to say that sociology is entirely new, any more than it would be to claim psychology as a modern innovation. Both have been understood by many philosophers throughout the ages, but they were not studied scientifically. However, it is as well to remember that if, in natural science, you take hydrogen and react it with oxygen in the correct proportions you always get water. Whereas in social science, if you take a Swiss Protestant, friendless and unemployed, living in a bed-sitting room in Paddington, you do not always get suicide!

Part One
Ourselves

Chapter 1

The Family

The family is the most important and basic group in our society today. It always has been and (despite the soothsayers in our Sunday papers) it probably always will be. We are not unique in this because nearly every other society in history has been based on family groups. The family group may not be the one we are familiar with—father, mother, two or three children, and, perhaps, a grandparent or two—but it will consist of two or more adult people who have established a stable relationship with each other, a relationship which enables them to live together while the children in their charge are young.

Just as societies differ, so do family systems, and it usually happens that a particular society gives its 'sanction' (or approval) to one kind of family system. In other words, a society generally makes rules laying down which people will be allowed to live together and the society will usually have some sort of ceremony by which it shows that the men and women who intend to live together are obeying the rules; we call this marriage.

But marriage alone does not mean that a family has been brought into existence, for the essential feature of a family is that it includes children, and the fundamental function of the family is to enable children to grow up ready to play their parts in the society.

Some people have suggested that we are moving towards a 'neuter future', and that men's perfume and flamboyant clothes are an indication of this—a future symbolized by the New York judge who looked at the newly wed hippies and said mildly: 'Will one of you kiss the bride?' However, the hippies were getting married and so do most people! We can assume for all practical purposes that heterosexual attraction is natural and that most people desire to mate, have children, and rear them. Obviously any society which failed to arrange for the production and rearing of new members would disappear and although new members could be produced without a family system it would be difficult in most societies to arrange for these new members to be reared in a satisfactory way if a family system did not exist. A secondary function of the family is the regulation of the sexual behaviour of its members so that children who cannot be reared are not produced.

Even in societies which have advocated free love the family has re-emerged as the basic unit (often with some new form of marriage) once the initial enthusiasm has worn off. This happened in Russia, which abolished the family as a bourgeois institution after the revolution of 1917 but which now has families protected apparently by an even stricter marriage morality than our own.[1]

The essential role which the family plays in the rearing of children has been illustrated by the work of John Bowlby and others[2] who have found that if infants and young children are deprived of a warm, intimate, and continuous relationship with a mother (or 'mother substitute'), although it does not affect their biological growth, it does affect their social growth and very serious damage is done to a person's personality if he does not have a close relationship with a 'mother figure' (not necessarily a woman) during the first few months of his life. For children of three to five the damage is not so serious, as the child can conceive of the passage of time, but to an infant a week's absence from its mother is what an apparently unending prison sentence is to an adult. There is a need, too, for an environment which is not constantly changing, for a stable background in which to establish a relationship with the mother figure, a relationship which includes both love and hate.

For these reasons it is important that children should not be removed from their families without the most serious thought. Where children are living in loving but slum conditions it is usually better for them to remain in these conditions rather than to be removed to hygienic institutions. Although, of course, one should seek to improve the conditions under which they are compelled to live! We should remember the love which children have even for bad parents who beat and ill-treat them.

In a survey of the results of evacuating children during World War II the then Ministry of Health found that these results emphasized 'the importance of the family in a child's development and the impossibility of providing children with any completely adequate substitute for the care of their own parents'. Their report went on to say, 'this has led to an increased awareness in some quarters of the importance of improving home conditions in order to keep families together instead of removing children from unsatisfactory homes'.[3]

[1] Small numbers throughout the text refer to text sources listed at the end of the book.

This was home for a London family in 1971. *Do many people still live in conditions like these?*
Do you think it is better to grow up in a large or a small family?
How can big families be protected from poverty and poor housing like this?
Photograph: Nick Hedges, Shelter

Some of the effects on children of being deprived of this early social contact are illustrated by Bowlby's study, which found that one-third of the children who had spent five years or more of their childhood in institutions became inadequate parents and their children were likely to be neglected and deprived in turn; that many prostitutes are such because of the lack of warmth in their early lives; and that children reared in institutions were likely to fall far below the standards of others with similar heredity but reared in foster homes, particularly in intelligence, social maturity, and speech.[4]

The experts do not all agree.[5] Some have pointed out that there are children who have been deprived yet have not apparently suffered. Others claim that the most important period of a child's development comes at a later age. But although they disagree on details, they all agree that this early social contact is very desirable.

Nowadays great concern is felt by local authorities in this country that children in their care should feel this sense of family warmth. This is provided by the 'cottage home' system of a group of a dozen or so children of varying ages brought up by a 'house-mother' as a family. The cottage home system emphasizes the vital importance to a child of a mother's love. It is because of this importance of a close personal relationship that children are personally and not collectively reared in a society. But if the child is to be personally reared there must be some division of labour between its father and mother. It would be grossly unfair, and in many situations impossible, for the woman to have the sole responsibility for caring for herself and her child while the father went off and made merry elsewhere! The child's need for close personal attention obviously gives an excellent cultural basis for marriage—the sensible refusal of women to cohabit with men unless they enter into a contract to keep both their offspring and their wives. It may also be true that man, like some other animals and birds (for example the rhinoceros, white whale, orang-utan, eagle, and swan), actually and instinctively desires to stay with the same mate.

The fact that the family is not primarily concerned with sexual relationships may also be supported by the observed behaviour of some animals. For example some monkeys will stay with the same mate and guard their family jealously for most of the time, but during the mating season these same monkeys will indulge in indiscriminate copulation.[6] It is interesting to note that most divorced men in our society accept a great deal of responsibility for their ex-family, even although the sexual relationship has ceased.

There are, then, sensible social reasons for the existence of families, the formation of which is usually approved by marriage. It is not, however, always a question of one man marrying one woman in order to form a family. There are three ways in which a family may be constituted: *monogamy*—one man married to one woman; *polygyny*—one man married to several women; *polyandry*—one woman married to several men.

To understand why these different forms of marriage exist it is important to realize that in a society in which, for example, one man marries six women there are probably not five unmarried men for every married one. This is partly because a polygynous society usually has a surplus of women, a polyandrous one a surplus of men, and a monogamous society about even numbers of both sexes. However, the surplus of men or women in polygamous (that is either polygynous or polyandrous) societies is usually not large enough for all men or all women to have more than one partner and the imbalance is sometimes artificially increased; for example in polygynous societies girls are usually married as early as possible while men must usually wait until they are thirty or so. Additionally, polygyny is mainly a privilege of the wealthy as a dowry must usually be paid to the father of each of the brides. Most men, even in a polygynous society, have only one wife and only a very small proportion have more than two, although the pastoral Turkana in Uganda have been recorded as having 28 per cent of men with three or more wives.[7] Polygyny also assists a man to become richer because his wives provide sons to herd cattle or work in his fields, while the wives themselves provide him with a work force. Also, marriage to more than one woman is a means of forming alliances with a number of other families, thus gaining power and influence.

Polyandry, too, may assist the economy of a particular society. For example, in Tibet, where brothers jointly marry a single wife, the conditions of life are harsh and the resources limited. The fact that brothers are all married to a single wife means that the division of property between brothers is unnecessary and that the number of their descendants to share their inheritance is limited.[8]

Although economic considerations are probably paramount in influencing the development of a particular family system within a society the sexual and social function of the family should not be overlooked.

The family system would have difficulty in surviving in a society with large numbers of unmarried women or men. The biological need to breed could result in large numbers of uncared-for children and the breakdown of the society. The social acceptance of homosexuality may also be a factor in permitting a polygynous society to function where there is not a great excess of females. However, it seems to be possible for a society to absorb a greater number of unmarried women than unmarried men, as women generally find it easier to find other outlets for their sexual drive. This is illustrated by the results of a survey for the National Institute of Mental Health in the United States which found that the single male was three times as likely to put himself in an 'unhappy' category as the single woman, and four times as likely to hate his job. This does not really fit in with the popular view of marriage as a triumph for women and a defeat for men!

The reasons why societies vary in the proportion of males to females are rather complicated. Generally, more boys are born than girls, but boys are weaker at birth than girls (in many ways they remain so and end up with five years less life expectancy) and therefore in a society where the standards of hygiene are low, and the infant death rate correspondingly high, one finds that more boy babies than girl babies die—which outweighs the greater male birth rate and increases the number of females in the society. This tendency was increased in the past by the fact that larger numbers of men than women were likely to be killed in time of war. Nowadays, the more 'advanced' nations of the world kill both indiscriminately.

Many countries in the Middle East, for example Saudi Arabia, still have polygyny. The people there are no less moral than we are, they just have a different society from ours. As societies (for example, Turkey) become westernized, polygamy tends to disappear—not, basically, because they accept western morality, but because westernization has improved hygiene and medical care and therefore altered the proportion of the sexes within the society; while at the same time it becomes more difficult in a modern wage economy for a man to acquire more than one wife, as additional wives are likely to be more of an economic liability than an economic asset.

There are a few societies where physical conditions, and isolation from the rest of the world and its diseases, have meant that for thousands of years there have been more men than women in the society. For example, in the Marquesas, a group of tiny islands in the Pacific Ocean more than 3000 miles from the nearest mainland, most women had several husbands. The imbalance between the sexes also seems to have affected the distinctive youth culture. Adolescents dressed in special yellow clothes, dyed themselves with saffron, and spent most of their time enjoying themselves, and while all adolescents had considerable sexual freedom, girls were actually denigrated if they were not promiscuous—an exaggerated reversal of the double standard that tends to operate in our society.[9]

It is interesting to note that the family system necessary in any society is backed by its religion. Judaism was polygamous while the Jews were primitive nomads. It gradually became monogamous as the people settled down to an orderly life governed by strict rules which encouraged hygiene.

The Hindu concept of women as inferior beings to men, whose sole purpose was to bear sons, led to child marriage so that child-bearing

The position of women in Great Britain

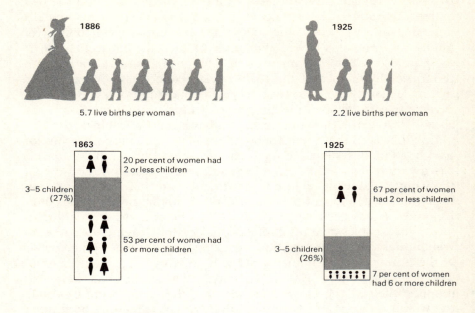

1886

1925

5.7 live births per woman

2.2 live births per woman

1863

20 per cent of women had 2 or less children

3–5 children (27%)

53 per cent of women had 6 or more children

1925

67 per cent of women had 2 or less children

3–5 children (26%)

7 per cent of women had 6 or more children

The legal position of women

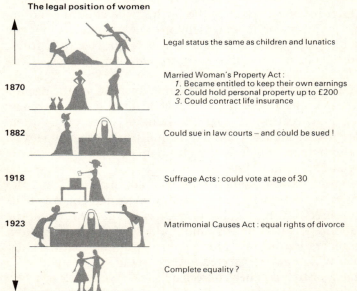

Legal status the same as children and lunatics

1870

Married Woman's Property Act :
1. Became entitled to keep their own earnings
2. Could hold personal property up to £200
3. Could contract life insurance

1882

Could sue in law courts – and could be sued !

1918

Suffrage Acts : could vote at age of 30

1923

Matrimonial Causes Act : equal rights of divorce

Complete equality ?

From an examination of these charts, what changes would you expect to have taken place in the behaviour of men and women in Great Britain during this century? How far have these expectations been realized?

activities could be carried out over the maximum length of time. Divorce was made easy so that a wife could be disposed of if she was barren; and Suttee, the practice of burning the wife on her husband's funeral pyre, disposed of the wife when her duties were completed. (Suttee was prohibited in 1829 but cases were recorded up to 1936.)[10]

Islam also relegates women to an inferior position and ensures the continued dominance of the male by inheritance laws which order that males must benefit by twice as much from family assets as females. Divorce is easy for men though not for women, while the Koran has been interpreted as allowing a man four wives plus concubines.[11]

It will be seen that there are both biological and cultural reasons for having a family system, but the organization of most family systems is based mainly on sex differences. The structure is based on the fact that the woman bears the child and has to nurse and care for it for a relatively longer period of time than any other animal needs to look after its young. It has been suggested that this is because we are all born as 'premature' babies as a result of our predecessors leaving their trees to walk upright on the ground, thus reducing the size of the human pelvis at the time when the human head was growing bigger to accommodate our larger brains. Natural selection favoured those mothers who dropped their young early, thus allowing the head to grow outside the womb rather than inside it, so that human babies are born in an 'unfinished' state. Immediately after the birth of the child the mother was occupied in caring for it and therefore was unable to join the menfolk in hunting and other tasks, and it was reasonable to continue this division of labour as the child grew up, with the man providing for the family.[12]

It has also been suggested that the male human accepted the responsibility of staying with the mother of his child during this unusually long period of child rearing because the human is the only animal whose sexual activities are not confined naturally to a seasonal pattern, and because the human female is the only female who is capable of sexual activity at almost any time.

Families exist so that the human race shall continue, and societies adapt themselves to allow men and women to mate and children to be reared in an ordered and reasonable way. It is in the family that the process of handing on the 'norms' and 'values' of the society from generation to generation begins, and it is in the family that the child learns the 'role' which he is expected to play in the society. The child learns the behaviour that is expected from a little boy or a little girl—by being dressed in an appropriate way, by being given different toys to play with, and by being encouraged to engage in activities which are considered appropriate to a male or a female. The approved sex differentiation within the society is also learnt by watching how mother

10

and father behave and by the children acting out the expected behaviour of male and female in their play. This process of 'socialization' of children is the prime function of the family, particularly in the early years before the school and other children start to take part in the process.

Not all families within a society follow the same cultural pattern and so the socialization of all the children within the society will not be identical. For example, middle-class parents are more likely to explain to their children why the child must or must not do something—this will improve the child's verbal reasoning (which will be beneficial in a society which regards this skill as important). However, the superior skill of the parent in argument means that the child is inevitably forced to accept defeat and this may make the child feel inadequate. It may also make the child feel guilty, as his desires can be made to appear self-centred when they are compared to the parents' 'logical' wishes. The working-class child may just be ordered not to argue back, and may do as he is told because he has to; this will not improve his verbal reasoning, but allows him to continue to regard his attitude as correct and that of his parents as unreasonable.

The difference in family situations will also influence differences in the socialization process—the working-class child in Britain will be less likely than the middle-class child to have facilities such as a garden or a play area in the home and therefore more likely to play on the street and clash with authority. Frequent confrontations with the police, park attendants, and the general public will mean that the child's attitude towards authority develops along different lines from that of the middle-class child.

Differences in the socialization of children will also arise because of variation in the behaviour and personalities of the parents: some will be more permissive than others; some will be anxious and others calm; some will lack emotional response; others will be over-protective. The attitudes of the parents may not help the children to integrate into our society: cultural patterns in some homes may actually encourage 'deviant' behaviour. But overall the family will play a vital part in the socialization of children.

We have seen that the form which the family takes varies considerably from society to society: it may be monogamous, polygynous, or polyandrous. It may further be classified as 'patriarchal' if the main authority in the family rests with the father or the father's kinsmen, or 'matriarchal' if the main authority lies with the mother or her kinspeople. Should authority in the family be more or less equally divided the family system is called 'equalitarian'. If inheritance passes through the male line we call the family 'patrilineal'; if through the mother we call it 'matrilineal'. If a married couple set up house near the man's family we further classify the family as 'patrilocal', and if they go to live near the woman's family the family is 'matrilocal'; if the married couple live away from both sets of parents their family is known as 'neolocal'.

Structurally, however, there are two basic types of family—the 'nuclear' family and the 'extended' family. The nuclear family consists of a husband, a wife, and their children; while an extended family also includes additional relatives, such as grandparents, uncles, and aunts.

The extended family usually operates as a unit in all primitive societies and in Britain it is most common in working-class areas. The advantage of the extended family is that at times of crisis there are additional resources to call upon: at childbirth the wife's mother may be at hand; if the family is large there may be unmarried sisters to assist the hard-pressed mother; if the husband is unemployed because of economic recession or injury at work he may have brothers who can assist him financially. The extended family then brings an element of security and it is not surprising that it is normally strongest where the world outside the family is most hostile.

However, in Britain during the last hundred years the nuclear family has become more and more the typical family structure. Improvements

Families in Great Britain (1971)

Source: Social Trends 4, HMSO 1973

1   *What sort of people compose the 51.2 per cent of families without dependent children?*
2   *Why are large families rare nowadays?*
3   *What sort of people have large families?*

12

in transport have made it easier for people to move about, while changing job opportunities have meant that such movements are often essential if people are to find work or improve their promotion prospects. The nuclear family can move more easily than the extended one. The development of the Welfare State has removed some of the uncertainties from which people were previously shielded by the extended family and contraception has led to smaller and more manageable families. The development of education has meant that children are less likely to go into occupations similar to those of their parents and have to be more mobile as a result; while the need to find satisfactory housing has driven the young family into the relative isolation of new housing estates.

The nuclear family is now the usual operating unit among the middle class and is gradually becoming more general among the working class. It brings greater freedom and opportunity for the young but throws new strains upon the family relationship and at the same time may bring uncertainty, loneliness, and lack of purpose to the old.

The family is universal and apparently essential. Among advanced societies the family is most restricted in its operation within the Israeli kibbutz: in the kibbutz the family is not a unit of production or consumption; meals are eaten in the common dining hall of the settlement, and the children sleep in a separate establishment from their parents.[13] The kibbutz is the result of an idealistic attempt to establish a completely communal life, but even here arrangements are made for parents and children to have some social contact, and there seems to be evidence that some kibbutz women are now seeking to re-establish motherhood as their primary role.[14]

Among primitive societies, the Nayar people of Malabar in India is an example of a society in which the mating of men and women and the upbringing of children would in fact have been hindered rather than helped by the existence of a normal family system.[15] When the first detailed descriptions of the Nayars were written in the eighteenth century the Nayars were a people in which the men provided for the women and children mainly by raiding their neighbours. The able-bodied men would all be away for considerable periods of time, such absences often resulting in casualties—as is likely to happen if people make their living by fighting! If a normal family system had existed the wives would often have been left alone while their menfolk were away. This happens to a small percentage of wives in our society, or to a large number for a limited period in wartime, but in the case of the Nayars it would have happened to all of the wives most of the time. In addition there would have been frequent cases of the society having to absorb the dependants of a man killed during a raid.

The Nayars did not have the institution of marriage, although just before puberty a woman would have a gold ornament tied around her neck by a man who would then spend three days privately with her. However, she might have no further contact with him, but when he died she and her children would observe a purification ritual.

Nayar brothers and sisters lived together in one house, although the brothers were not often at home, with the sisters' children and their daughters' children. A woman could have intercourse with any men she wished, providing they were not of a lower caste than herself, and as a result little Nayars arrived, but as the sexes mingled freely there was no way of knowing who was the father of a child. This was not important as it was the responsibility of the mothers' brothers to look after their sisters' children—and where this was not possible they were provided for by the nearest male relatives on the mother's side.

This system may well sound strange to us, but it achieved similar ends to our own family system and it allowed the peculiar warrior society of the Nayars to function smoothly. The women were together to assist each other during the frequent absences of the men, and in the event of one male relative being killed there would still be several left to provide for the woman and her children. Just as we may declare that we do not see why we should provide for our sisters' children, so the Nayar male would have been amazed at the suggestion that he should care for his own sons and daughters. Again, just as most men do not abandon their wives and children in our society, so most male Nayars would accept the responsibility of caring for their sisters and their sisters' children—jointly with their brothers, of course!

The Nayar system is possibly unique, but many of the family systems adopted by other societies have been even more complicated; for example the Iroquois Indians in the area now occupied by New York State had a system in which a man might belong to a different clan from his wife but had to remain in his mother's home visiting his wife only on approved occasions, the male regarding himself as the father of his brothers' children as well as his own, his wife regarding herself as mother of her sister's children as well as her own.[16]

But all family systems whether simple or complicated have one object in common—the absorption of children into the society.

More discussion or written work

1   What are the advantages and disadvantages of being an 'only' child?

2   Under what circumstances is the State justified in taking a child away from its mother?

3   If the number of males in proportion to the number of females continues to rise in Great Britain would you accept polyandry?

4   Do you think that changing fashions in personal appearance and dress reflect a change in the attitudes and roles of the persons involved?
5   Children in the Manus tribe of New Guinea are disciplined by their father beating their mother if the children do anything wrong. What do you think are the best methods of disciplining children?

Research

1   Find out the people you are not permitted to marry by English law and in each case give as many reasons for this as you can.
2   Discover as many people with different family systems to ours as you can. Give what you consider are the main reasons for their methods of organizing their family systems.

Imagination

In the year 2001 the family has been abolished. How did this happen and what was the result?

Reading suggestions

* M. Mead, *Coming of Age in Samoa*, Penguin
† J. Bowlby and M. Fry, *Child Care and the Growth of Love*, Penguin
† F. George Kay, *The Family in Transition*, David & Charles
† J. and E. Newson, *Patterns of Infant Care in an Urban Community*, Penguin
† M. Young and P. Willmott, *Family and Kinship in East London*, Penguin
  M. Anderson (ed.), *Sociology of the Family*, Penguin
  M. Rutter, *Maternal Deprivation Re-assessed*, Penguin

For an explanation of the symbols next to the reading suggestions at the end of each Chapter see the Acknowledgements page at the beginning of the book.

Chapter 2

Education

Education is the process by which people develop their faculties in order that they may play their part in society. The form this education takes will depend upon the society, and the more complex the society the more complex will be the educational process.

The term 'education' can be used to describe the whole process of socialization which continues, formally or informally, from the cradle to the grave. However, this chapter will be concerned mainly with education as a formal process, preparing people for their place in the wider society outside the home. Although, when children go to school, the family continues as a socializing agency, its relative importance will gradually diminish as the child grows up. When the child reaches adolescence the focus for even informal socialization is likely to shift from the family to the 'peer group', that is to the adolescent's companions of the same age and status as himself.

As our society becomes increasingly specialized the formal teaching that the child receives is likely to become more and more remote from the family context. A child's awareness that his parents lack knowledge in certain fields may make him more likely to assume that the knowledge, and therefore the opinions, of his parents are suspect in other areas where he could benefit from their advice.

In a complex industrial society there is often little that a family can do to prepare a child for its future occupation. The educational component of the socializing process is, therefore, becoming increasingly important.

Without the right kind of socialization, people would not be human. This can be illustrated by the case of the two children found living with wolves near Midnapore, India, in 1920. They were unable to walk upright, ate raw meat, lapped their food like dogs, refused to wear clothes, and howled like wolves. They had been socialized but they had been socialized as wolves. There have been many similar cases of children who have been found living with animals: for example a 'gazelle child' in 1961 and a boy aged about twelve who was found living with monkeys in Sri Lanka in 1973. Some of these children may well have been mentally deficient or autistic, and abandoned by their parents for these reasons, but others appear to have been normal

16

children whose behaviour is actually the result of having lived with wild animals and of having been deprived of human socialization.

This does not mean that education can make men out of animals. The importance of heredity is illustrated by the baby chimpanzee raised by Professor Kellog in 1931, alongside his own child.[1] It received the same treatment as his own child in every particular and yet, although it became very intelligent for a chimpanzee, it remained very decidedly an ape! We know that the difference in heredity between man and ape results in man being more intelligent. But it is by no means certain that heredity has much influence on the difference in intelligence between one normal man and another. Many experiments have been made to try to determine the relative importance of heredity and environment in deciding intelligence.

Some experts have taken rats and put them in a maze, so that the rats have to work out the quickest way to the food in the middle. Those rats that learnt how to get to the food quickly were then bred with other 'bright' rats, while the slower rats were bred with other 'dull' rats. The offspring of 'bright' rats which also proved 'bright' were then bred together; in the end there were two groups—some very clever rats, some very stupid ones. This, said the experts, proved that heredity did influence intelligence within a given species. But they have not yet been able to breed a 'bright' man because of man's dislike, as a species, for such experiments and because people cannot reproduce as quickly as rats. (A rat can start to reproduce at the age of about five months, has a gestation period of twenty-one days, and has seven to eight young rats in each litter!) Many authorities, such as A. R. Jensen[2] and H. J. Eysenck,[3] have regarded heredity as a major factor in the production of intelligence; Richard Herrnstein goes so far as to say that 'our society may be sorting itself willy-nilly into inherited castes', so that as with the rats in the maze there will be one group of people of very high intelligence and a 'residue that may be unable to master the common occupations, cannot compete for success and achievement, and are most likely to be born to parents who have similarly failed'.[4]

In 1973 Professor William Shockley claimed that intelligence was governed 80 per cent by heredity and 20 per cent by environment, and suggested a 'voluntary sterilization bonus plan' whereby people of low intelligence (and those suffering from diabetes, epilepsy, and so forth) would receive substantial sums of money if they agreed to be sterilized so that they could not reproduce. Professor Shockley believed that if 'genetically disadvantaged' people reproduced more than intelligent people, then the human race would go into 'retrogressive' evolution and gradually become less intelligent.

However, these are extreme views even for those who support the view that intelligence is mainly inherited. H. J. Eysenck, for example,

17

claims that environment contributes only about half as much as does heredity to individual differences in intelligence; but he has gone on to say that mankind is not splitting into two groups of people, one dull and the other intelligent. Professor Eysenck's research showed that there is a tendency for the children of very bright parents to be brighter than average but less bright than their parents; similarly, children of very dull parents are duller than the average but not as dull as their parents. There is then a tendency for the majority of children to approximate towards an average and a genetic class system is therefore prevented.[5]

An equally strong group, however, hold that intelligence is not hereditary in man or that heredity has so little comparative influence that, for all practical purposes, it may be discounted.[6] This school of thought cites as evidence the many extremely intelligent people born of apparently dull parents.

Some recent research has shown that the human brain develops earlier than the rest of the body: at birth it is about 25 per cent of its adult weight and by five nearly 90 per cent.[7] During these early years the protein requirements of the brain are considerable and it would appear that severe malnutrition before two years of age can cause a permanently lowered IQ as the nerve cells will not branch out properly. Experiments also seem to indicate that the first five years provide a once and for all opportunity to develop the potential for future learning and that if certain stimuli are not provided during these years the effect is likely to be permanent.

Some cynics have suggested that psychologists, with their vested interest in the importance of the mind's internal influence, favour the importance of heredity in determining intelligence; while sociologists, who have a vested interest in the importance of society's external influences, tend to emphasize the influence of the environment. The probable answer is that intelligence is hereditary up to a point, but that so few human beings have been given an opportunity to develop to the limit of their capacity, that in most cases it is impossible to tell which have the best intellectual heredity. The argument that one can choose the best sort of school for a child by considering its genetic background is therefore not valid, although it underlies many of the more socially acceptable arguments put forward in favour of selective education.

Education does reflect the sort of society that people are being educated to be part of. For example, America was mainly colonized by

A back alley in Manchester serves as a playground as well as a rubbish tip.
What effect do play facilities have on a child's development?
What are the advantages and disadvantages of growing up in a town rather than in the country?
Photograph: Nick Hedges, Shelter

19

people who wanted everyone to have an equal opportunity in life: we find that the State of Massachusetts passed a law in 1647 making the support of schools compulsory, and education free and universal. This egalitarian character has remained in the American educational system despite the development of the privileged 'Ivy League' colleges.

It was not until 1870 that a national system of elementary education was established in England and secondary education did not become general in this country until after the Education Act of 1902. Yet hundreds of years before, Winchester and Eton had been established (1387 and 1441 respectively), while the expansion of trade, and consequent growth of a large middle class, led to the opening of many grammar schools in the sixteenth century. In the nineteenth century the public schools reached the peak of their power as an indispensable part of the process of producing administrators for the far-flung British Empire. The rule of the British Empire was far from being glamorous or enjoyable for most of its administrators. Straight from their public schools, they might find themselves at twenty-five in charge of a vast area of India having perhaps a population of four million under their direct control. When their children were four or five years old they would be sent back to school in England, and from then on would only be seen rarely by their fathers. Usually, the administrator's wife would follow the children after a time, and the administrator would be left alone in an alien land, surrounded by dust and flies, doing his 'duty' until he returned home to die. Not a particularly pleasant prospect, and one that proved the need for the nineteenth-century public schools' rigid code of obedience, discipline, and austerity. The history of Britain as a colonial power whose public schools influenced later educational development may also help to explain why corporal punishment has survived in British schools long after most countries have abandoned it.

The industrial developments of the nineteenth century also established a need for skilled workers in the factories and these could not be provided by the charity schools on which the great majority of children depended for a basic education. The upper and middle classes were worried about extending education to the mass of the working class; they had seen the revolution in France and thought that education would encourage dissatisfaction and lead to revolution by the workers of England. However, the Government took the first step towards state intervention in education by making grants to the charity schools in 1833. Towards the end of the nineteenth century the British lead in the industrial and economic fields began to be challenged by such countries as the United States and Germany, and the need to keep pace with these countries led to the Education Acts of 1870 and 1902.

The need for more administrators, clerical workers, and professional people led to the extension of the grammar schools, designed on the lines of the existing public schools; while the demand for technicians and semi-skilled workers led to the development of the elementary schools for children aged between five and fourteen. However, the elementary schools seemed to be inadequate for the task of providing a satisfactory secondary education for the bulk of the population and a campaign for reform began. The pressure for reform grew during World War II and may have been increased by the fact that many people who would not normally have met children from the slum areas of the large cities came into contact with those who had been evacuated, and were shocked by their low standard of education; it may also be that those in authority in the armed forces were surprised to discover so many people of high ability who had had little formal education.[8]

The division of education into two main sectors continued after the Education Act of 1944. The Act required universal secondary education, but left open the question of how it should be organized. It did, however, retain religious instruction as the one compulsory subject that must be taught in all schools. The Act raised the school-leaving age to fifteen (1947) and made many other reforms aimed at raising both the standard of education and the standard of health of the pupils.

The 1944 Act envisaged that all children in state schools would receive a similar education up to the age of eleven and would then proceed to a school which would provide an education suited to the ability and potential of each child. The system which developed from the Act was a secondary modern school for those who required a practical sort of education, a grammar school for those who needed an academic education, and a secondary technical school for those whose potential could best be stimulated by a vocationally inclined education. The secondary technical school was never much favoured and never became widespread. Very soon the grammar school was seen as the best agency for social advancement and career opportunity, and the selection procedure at eleven became a question of 'passing' or 'failing' to pass into a grammar school. Although there was a theoretical possibility of transfer from a secondary modern school to a grammar school (or vice versa) at a later stage in the pupil's life this transfer rarely occurred and a child's future career possibilities were effectively decided at the age of eleven. Some local authorities introduced alternatives to the once and for all 'eleven-plus' examination, such as continuous assessment of the child's potential by his teacher, but gradually dissatisfaction with the 'bipartite' or 'tripartite' system grew.

The system of separate schools was seen by some people as 'socially divisive', that is it was seen as perpetuating a class structure in which children were made to see themselves as belonging to one of two distinct types of people: a comparatively small group, containing about 20 per cent of the population mostly with middle-class parents, who were being educated in the grammar schools, saw themselves as part of the future middle class; while the majority of future citizens saw themselves as 'failures' and destined to be part of the future working or lower-middle classes. The increasing demand for experts also led some people to claim that the nation could not afford to lose the services of any of its most able members and it was felt by some that the talents of many children were not being fully developed by the secondary modern school. For both these social and economic reasons some local authorities began to develop new sorts of schools which would educate all children of secondary school age together, and the name 'comprehensive' was given to schools of this kind. This development was strengthened by a circular issued by the Labour Government in 1965 directing local authorities to prepare plans for a completely comprehensive system of state education. The Conservative Government, however, withdrew this circular when they gained control in 1970 as they claimed that it limited the freedom of local authorities to decide the

Pupils in public-sector secondary schools by region (January 1972)*

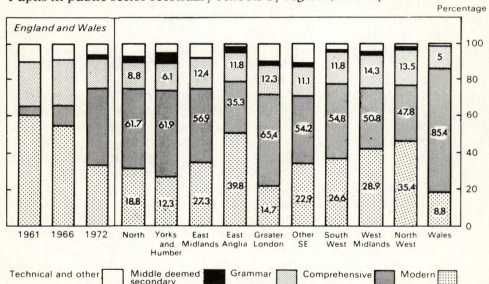

* 1974 percentages for Grammar, Comprehensive, and Modern Schools are printed on the 1972 percentage columns in the chart; in most areas these now represent almost all schools.
Source: adapted from Social Trends 4 and 6, HMSO 1973, 1975

1 *Which area has the best ratio of comprehensive and grammar schools to modern schools?*
2 *If you wanted to choose an area to live in based on the 'best' education for your children, which area would you choose from the chart, and why?*

22

kind of education most suited to local needs and desires. However, comprehensive education continued to develop, and in 1974 the newly returned Labour Government ordered all local authorities to proceed with the establishment of comprehensive schemes.

These comprehensives do not conform to one pattern: the National Foundation for Educational Research identified twelve different types of school and seven different systems of comprehensive education when it issued its first report in 1968.[9] By 1973 three main forms of comprehensive education were easily identifiable and were attended by a third of the maintained secondary school population. One form consists of a primary education, followed by membership of a school dealing with everyone in the eleven to eighteen age range—'all-through comprehensives'. These schools are usually large and may have 2000 or more pupils, although 1000 or so pupils is a more usual size. Alternatively, primary education may be followed by education at a 'middle school', taking pupils from eight or nine to the age of twelve or thirteen, and then at an 'upper school'—these schools being sometimes called 'Junior' and 'Senior' High Schools. Or the comprehensive system may be on the basis of primary education to eleven or twelve followed by education at a senior school to the age of fifteen or sixteen, and then a transfer to a sixth-form college or in a few cases to a college of further education, for those who wish to continue their education on a full-time basis. The sixth-form colleges are sometimes combined with technical colleges in one institution, thus allowing young people of differing aptitudes to meet, and helping to break down the barrier which may exist between academic and applied studies. For example, it gives students the opportunity to take Ordinary National Diploma and Ordinary National Certificate courses as well as A-levels and O-levels. This development is another indication of the way that education adapts to assist in the running of the society in which the educational system exists. For there is no doubt that our technological society increasingly requires technicians of a high intellectual calibre.

This last form of comprehensive education has increased in popularity in recent years as it allows the educational authorities to concentrate their specialist teaching staff and equipment more economically, and allows young people to work in a more adult atmosphere.

Some people, such as Tyrell Burgess, claim that comprehensive education has almost no disadvantages, that bright children do as well as they would at grammar schools, and that children who would otherwise go to secondary modern schools do much better. They claim that intelligence cannot be accurately measured at the age of eleven, that it develops differently in different children between the ages of eleven and sixteen, and that there are *not* two fundamentally different categories of children needing different sorts of education in different schools.[10]

Some supporters of comprehensive education also oppose 'streaming' in schools.[11] This is the selection of children for different classes according to their ability, which some people feel is harmful to those children placed in the classes for the lower ability range.

Many people, however, oppose comprehensive education and feel that the bright individual will be held back by less intelligent pupils in the same class and that we shall end up with a general mediocrity and lowering of academic standards. Some claim that the comprehensive schools will be less successful than the grammar schools in overcoming class distinction, as they will draw all their pupils from one neighbourhood—unlike the grammar schools which have traditionally drawn their pupils from a wide area—and that the quality of the 'neighbourhood comprehensive' will reflect the social class of the area from which all their pupils come. It certainly seems that some forms of comprehensive education will indeed reduce the opportunity for children from a 'deprived' area to receive an academic education.

The aim of the comprehensive school is to eliminate class distinction from education, but some distinctions cannot be altered merely by creating new institutions in which education takes place. The child from a home which has given him a good linguistic ability will be at an advantage in the literate environment of the school, among middle-class teachers using elaborate language (and often not being conscious of doing so). Children who may not have been 'programmed' to receive such elaborate linguistic communication will not fully understand the teacher, and may make up for their shortcomings by making a nuisance of themselves, not paying attention, and playing truant, which will in turn reduce their ability to achieve success within the school context.

The attitudes of parents will have a considerable influence on the attitude of the child to the school: if the parents (perhaps 'under-achievers' themselves at school) tend to dismiss school as a waste of time the children are likely to adopt this approach as well and will not make the maximum use of their abilities.

It is even possible for comprehensives to increase social distinctions if there is an obvious process of streaming which puts the literate (often middle-class) children in a group with a high ability level, and the less literate (often working-class) children in a low ability stream. Although streams may be disguised, the top and bottom streams are usually quickly recognized and become associated with 'status'. It is interesting to note that some studies have shown that the children in the top streams, irrespective of their original ability level, seem to increase their IQ score, while the IQ of children placed in the lower streams appears to be reduced still further.

In England and Wales boys and girls are generally taught together in primary schools and about two-thirds of pupils in maintained

Reading comprehension score at age eleven by social class of parents (Great Britain, 1969)

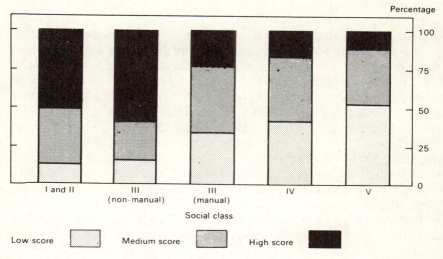

Source: adapted from Social Trends 6, HMSO 1975, from National Child Development Survey

1 *Are the results of the comprehension score study what you would expect?*
2 *Suggest some reasons for the results shown in the chart.*

secondary schools attend mixed schools; this 'coeducation' does have advantages in making the sexes more realistic and open towards each other. However, some studies have shown that as girls mature physically and emotionally (and perhaps intellectually) more quickly than boys, coeducation may give some girls an exaggerated view of their abilities, and some boys a pessimistic view of theirs.

In 1971 in England and Wales there were 8.5 million children in state schools and 128 000 in schools receiving grants directly from the Department of Education and Science; there were also 408 000 children in 2636 independent schools. About 270 of the largest and most important of these independent schools are known as 'public schools'; most of these are boarding schools usually with fees of more than £1500 a year. (In Scotland the term public schools is used for state-supported schools.) The proportion of children being educated privately fell from 10.5 to 8.5 per cent between 1961 and 1971.

Independent schools, and public schools in particular, have attracted a great deal of criticism in recent years from those who feel that they help to perpetuate the class structure in British society. The opponents of these schools claim that parents who pay for their children's education are buying their children a superior position in society, and that if those in positions of power and influence had to educate their children in state schools they would ensure that resources were made available to improve the standards of these schools.

It is claimed by some people that the accents and mannerisms acquired in public schools will assist the children to obtain the best positions in their future occupations when they leave school and that those in positions of authority who were themselves educated in public schools will favour those with a similar background; this favouritism is called 'the old school tie network'. It is certainly true that the universities of Oxford and Cambridge have always accepted a high proportion of former public school boys and that many senior civil servants and army officers were educated at public schools. The supporters of the public school system contend that all parents should have the right to buy a better education for their children and that it is because the public schools provide such a superior education that their product is likely to be successful in later years.

There are also 1600 'special' state schools in Britain, both boarding and day, for children who require special educational treatment for reasons such as blindness, delicate health, maladjustment, or educational subnormality, although there is a growing movement which wishes to integrate these children into normal schools whenever possible. An organization called the National Association for Gifted Children claims that the number of gifted children, that is children with outstanding intellectual powers, in the population is about the same as that of mentally handicapped children, and therefore the same amount of money should be allocated to the gifted as is given to the mentally handicapped so that gifted children can also be provided with special schools. The NAGC argues that gifted children who are frustrated in school react in one of four ways: they may become classroom clowns or partial drop-outs spending more time outside the classroom than in it; they may become apathetic and do just the minimum amount of work to get by; they may become maladjusted and need psychiatric treatment; or they may become delinquents and, later, organizers and planners of crime—more intelligent than the police.

The same sort of arguments are used against the continued expansion of our universities as are used against comprehensive schools. It is claimed that many people now going to university cannot benefit from the education given there and that the standards of the lecturers are declining. It is also suggested that there will not be sufficient suitable jobs for our future output of graduates, who will be forced to take work which does not measure up to their ability. This situation might produce in our society a large number of highly intelligent, frustrated, and discontented people—a potentially revolutionary situation. On the other hand, it is argued that the purpose of education is to provide the

26

maximum opportunity for self-fulfilment, and that education should not be career-orientated. Holders of this opinion maintain that everyone with the ability to profit from a university education should be able to receive one.

We are told that Britain is not producing enough highly educated people, that we only have 8.5 per cent of the age range twenty to twenty-four at university—about one-third of the figure for the United States—which means that in Europe only Italy, Spain, Rumania, Iceland, and Austria are behind us. However, there has been a tremendous increase in the rate of growth of further education in Britain during the last twenty years. In the autumn of 1971 there were 313 489 full-time and sandwich-course students and 1 551 633 part-time students in vocational further education. Compulsory part-time education up to the age of eighteen in Colleges of Further Education approved by the Fisher Act of 1919 has, however, not materialized, although some people would have preferred a system of compulsory part-time education to the raising of the minimum school-leaving age from fifteen to sixteen in September 1972.[12]

Education is certainly a 'growth industry': in 1971–72 total public expenditure on education was almost £3000 million, which was 13 per cent of all public expenditure and nearly three times the expenditure in 1961–62. But it would appear that Fidel Castro in Cuba is looking a long way into the future when he says that universities will ultimately have to be abolished, since the whole population will eventually be up to university standard, and would need—because of the expansion of knowledge—to be at university all the time. However, the successful establishment of the Open University in this country is an indication of the demand for a much more general provision of education of university standard for people of all ages. Adult education, which is mainly concerned with non-vocational education for those over school-leaving age, has also been expanding rapidly, and although facilities in most areas are still poor, especially for day-time work, the old Evening Institute image is fast disappearing. The Russell Report in 1973 recommended a considerable expansion and improved facilities for this branch of education.

It may be to this last field that we should look when considering the future of British education. At the beginning of this chapter we saw that education is the process by which members of a society learn formally to play a useful part in that society—and the society of the future is likely to be more leisure-orientated as manual and routine clerical work are increasingly automated. Less time spent in obligatory work will provide a marvellous opportunity for greater creativity and personal satisfaction, so long as members of the society have learnt how to use and benefit from their greater leisure.[13] But the mere withdrawal of work, without the compensation of more rewarding activities, will lead to boredom and eventual chaos. The increased emphasis on education for leisure may mean that education in our society has started off in a new direction—as it must do when a society alters if that society is to survive and flourish.

More discussion or written work

1   Do you think that parents have a right to decide to which school their child should go and what sort of education he or she should receive there?
2   Some people think that examinations should be abolished—do you?
3   Should pupils and/or students have more control over their schools or colleges?
4   Is there too much discipline in schools and colleges in this country?
5   What advantages or disadvantages have boarding schools compared with day schools?

Research

1   Find out as much as you can about the present education system in any country other than Great Britain.
2   Find out how many different *kinds* of schools and colleges there are in this country, and discover a few details of the purpose of each of them.

Imagination

Imagine that you have been appointed head or principal of a newly built school or college and can organize its students and courses in any way you choose. Organize them and contrast your scheme with schools or colleges you have known.

Reading suggestions

† T. Burgess, *Inside Comprehensive Schools*, HMSO
† P. Goodman, *Compulsory Miseducation*, Penguin
† B. Jackson and D. Marsden, *Education and the Working Class*, Penguin
† R. Pedley, *The Comprehensive School*, Penguin
† G. Pickering, *The Challenge to Education*, Penguin
† W. Van der Eyken, *The Pre-School Years*, Penguin

Chapter 3

Morality

Morality is behaviour which a society recognizes as good; immorality is behaviour which a society regards as bad. Many people will say that a society recognizes as good, behaviour which helps the society to run smoothly, whereas immorality is behaviour which damages that society. If this is the case, then morality will clearly vary from one society to another. On the other hand, many people believe that there is an unchangeable code of morality, summarized perhaps in the Ten Commandments. It may be that morality is a changeable code of conduct which alters according to the needs of the society, or it may be that it is a 'natural law' which never alters, although some societies may obey it and others not. In order to make a decision it will be useful to examine one 'moral' rule, see how far it is followed in different societies, and then try to decide why differing societies behave in the way they do.

If we take one of the Ten Commandments, 'Thou shalt not kill', we find that no society has ever allowed its members to kill at random but that sometimes killing outside the tribe is regarded as harmless, even praiseworthy—as among the Mundugumor of New Guinea.[1] Blood revenge for murder is often positively insisted on ('an eye for an eye, a tooth for a tooth') and may be continued from generation to generation as with the vendetta in Sicily, Corsica, and Crete.

Killing is, of course, not restricted to murder: it may occur in the forms of war, infanticide, suicide, euthanasia, or as a punishment for crime. Generally, only the killing of human beings is regarded as wrong; but sometimes this attitude is extended to cover certain animals as well, perhaps because the animal is the totem of the tribe and is believed to contain the tribe's spirit. For Hindus, to kill a cow is a deadly sin. Some Buddhists regard all killing as sinful, and the Jains of Southern India wear masks over their mouths and carry brushes to sweep the ground in front of them as they walk, in case they should crush an insect or breathe one in. These people believe in reincarnation and for them all life has value.

Killing in war has sometimes been condemned, as by Buddhists, while other faiths have put the military high in the social scale. For example, Hinduism placed the Kshatriyas, the warriors, second in the caste system, perhaps because Hinduism developed among the 'Aryan' settlers, who displaced the original dark-skinned inhabitants of India, and violence was necessary to maintain this supremacy. The Old Testament prophets were pacifists—they lived in the eighth and seventh centuries BC when Israel was a little border state surrounded by powerful neighbours, where a submissive policy seemed most sensible. But earlier, when the Jews were an advanced pastoral people seeking the Promised Land, their warrior-heroes were believed to be assisted by God.

Christianity has interpreted killing in two ways. At first sight, the teaching of Christ seems to condemn all war. This was the attitude taken by the early Christians, and it is a view which has had supporters in most ages, notably among the Quakers. (Some people have claimed that the Quakers were pre-eminently capitalists, and that therefore anything which had a bad effect on trade—such as war—was repugnant to them.) When Christianity became the official religion of the Roman Empire in the fourth century the general tendency was to support the State; and it has been suggested that the Emperor Constantine became a Christian with an eye to Christian support both in politics and in the army. Saint Augustine laid down the conditions of a 'just' war, and these conditions are still quoted to justify any particular war. It should be remembered that at that time the Teutonic migrations had put the Christian Empire in peril.

After the Reformation, and during the religious wars that followed, it was inevitable that the reformers should support war: if they had not, they would have been crushed. Calvin took the view that rebellion was justified: 'It is no breach of the command "thou shalt not kill".² The slaying of the authors of the unjust war is an execution; the judge is God, and the fighting men who defend the right are merely God's instruments.' In England, Calvin's view meant that it was lawful for the Puritans to rebel against Charles I, for Calvin had had no support from princes. Luther's main strength, on the other hand, was based on the support of German princes. Hence he was equally sure that rebellion was always immoral, since, in his view, tyranny was God's punishment of the people for their sins. He said that tyrants would be punished adequately in the next life, and ordinary men had no right to interfere.

Islam was founded when the followers of Mohammed were in much the same position as were the Jews when fighting for the promised land of Canaan. They were a nomadic people seeking land for settlement; and the Koran, their holy book, promised paradise to anyone who was killed fighting unbelievers. Later the Crusaders were promised heaven if they died fighting the Mohammedans!

More recently, in the nineteenth century, the Western European countries, with their expanding industries, found it necessary to pursue

The terror of war—children flee from an accidental aerial napalm strike in South Vietnam.
Photograph: Associated Press

Is war ever acceptable?
The Geneva Convention bans the use of certain weapons—what weapons would you ban?
Is the bombing of non-combatants ever justifiable?

The boy on the right in a Vietnam refugee camp has never known peace.
Photograph: Central Press

a policy of colonialism in order to establish markets for their products. This colonialism was justified by philosophers at the time, who took the view that an aggressive war was justified when its object was to replace a lower civilization by a higher one.[3]

Capital punishment is another modification of the general rule prohibiting the killing of human beings. Judaism, with its strong emphasis on family solidarity, prescribed the death penalty for cursing one's father or mother. While the Romans, whose society was also based on the family unit, tied up people who had killed their father or mother, put them in a sack with a dog, a cock, a viper, and an ape, and threw them into the river or the sea. In the Middle Ages the law was particularly severe on witches and heretics, and suspects were often burnt to death. The Old Testament order, 'thou shalt not suffer a witch to live', was quoted as justification. In those days, the main pillar of society was the Church, and anything that undermined the Church was regarded as damaging society as a whole. The importance of the Church in the structure of society is emphasized by the fact that attacks on the Church were punished by the State. It would appear that, once it is felt that good order can be maintained without capital punishment, it is generally abolished—as under the Empress Elizabeth in Russia in 1754, and now in most of Europe and parts of the United States.

Another example of the needs of a society overcoming what we might regard as normal human feelings is the practice of killing children (infanticide). While most societies have regarded the killing of children as utterly immoral, others have regarded it as perfectly moral and have insisted upon it as a social duty. On islands in the Pacific, where the soil is very meagre on the coral or volcanic rock, the food supply is strictly limited. In the past, the great distance from any mainland prohibited the emigration of any surplus population, and so the population had to be rigidly controlled. Some islands had a local 'law' limiting the number of children that parents might raise. For example, on Vaitupu, in the Gilbert and Ellice Islands, a couple were allowed only two children; any children born subsequently were smothered immediately after birth. Yet, far from disliking children, these people are said to have been extremely fond of them. In the warrior society of ancient Sparta where physical fitness was regarded as the supreme virtue (some 30 000 men having the task of holding down about 600 000 slaves), all children were examined by the senior citizens, and those regarded as unfit to live were left in the open to die.

Abortion, although sometimes insisted upon in cases of incest or rape, has usually been condemned: first, because abortion has been used to conceal illicit intercourse; and secondly, because it endangers the mother's life. In the past, among Christians, abortion has earned the death penalty if the embryo was formed, as a formed embryo was then

Abortions in Great Britain[1]

Figures in thousands	1968 Apr.–Dec.[2] All women	1970 All women	1971 All women	1972 All women	1972 Married	1972 Unmarried[3]
Total number of abortions	25.2	91.8	133.1	167.5	73.0	94.3
Age of mother:						
Under 16 years[4]	0.6	1.8	2.8	3.5	—	3.5
16 to 19 years[4]	3.5	15.2	24.0	30.6	1.1	29.5
Under 20 years	4.3	18.0	26.7	34.1	1.1	33.0
20 to 34 years	15.4	55.6	81.0	102.5	47.0	55.4
35 to 44 years	4.8	16.0	22.4	27.6	23.1	4.5
45 years and over	0.2	0.5	0.6	0.7	0.6	0.1
Age unknown	0.6	1.8	2.4	2.6	1.2	1.4
Place of abortion:						
NHS hospitals	16.1	52.9	60.0	64.6	33.6	30.9
Private hospitals and clinics	9.1	39.0	73.2	102.9	39.4	63.5
Grounds for abortion:						
Risk to or to save life of woman	1.3	2.5	2.7	4.0	2.3	1.7
Risk to or to save physical or mental health of woman	18.2	70.9	102.6	127.7	42.9	84.8
Risk to physical and mental health of existing children with or without other factors	4.3	16.2	25.2	33.3	25.9	7.4
Risk of child being abnormal with or without risk to health of woman	1.4	2.2	2.6	2.4	1.9	0.5
Percentage of patients from abroad [5]	*4.9*	*11.2*	*23.8*	*30.1*	—	—

[1] 174 600 abortions were performed in 1973 and in 1974 the total was 170 700.

[2] These figures relate to notifications of abortions carried out during the period 27 April to 31 December 1968 under the provisions of the Abortion Act, 1968, and include abortions in private hospitals and clinics.

[3] Includes single, widowed, divorced, and separated women.

[4] Prior to 1971 figures are for England and Wales only.

[5] Including Northern Ireland.

Source: Adapted from *Social Trends* **4**, HMSO 1973

1   *(a) What was the total number of abortions performed in Great Britain in 1972?*
(b) Which age group shows the greatest percentage increase in abortions during the past three years? Why?
(c) What factors make it difficult to compare the figures given for 1968 with those given for 1972?
2   *Under what conditions would you permit legal abortions to be carried out?*
3   *Do you think that this table proves that 'immorality' is increasing in Great Britain?*

believed by theologians such as St Augustine to have a soul. The punishment, however, was only a fine if the abortion took place soon after conception, when, incidentally, the risk to the mother is much less. In Britain and in some other countries the changing attitude to extra-marital intercourse, and the improvements in hygiene which have removed much of the danger to the mother, have led to an acceptance of abortion by some people. Others claim that such an attitude attacks the sanctity of life and, applied in other areas, would lead to the killing of the mentally handicapped, the old, the maimed, and anyone else who is an embarrassment, and thus ultimately destroy society itself.

Its attitude to the sanctity of life is only one of many 'attitudes' prevailing in a society, which will be the basis for the morality of that society. These attitudes will be more firmly fixed as elements of the society than the more changeable views and beliefs that we call 'opinions'; they will carry emotional overtones and an element of approval or disapproval. Our attitudes, as we have seen, will depend upon both the period and the place in which we live; and although there are many firm attitudes in our society, it is probable that the attitudes of western societies today are the most fluid that have ever existed. This is largely because we are more aware of the values and customs prevailing in other societies, as a result of improved communications.

A society's morality would appear to coincide with the needs of the society, and it has been found that most individuals behave in the way that people expect them to behave. If Johnny is constantly told by his parents that he is a nasty, dirty boy, there is a tendency for him to follow this expected pattern of conduct and become a nasty, dirty boy. Or if Jane is trained to expect 'good' behaviour from herself, she will tend in time to become a 'naturally good girl'. As children meet various situations and adapt to them they come gradually to expect to react to a given situation in a particular way—they have started to act a part, their 'role'.

As Jane gets older she will assume various 'status' positions: she may have the status of a mother or the status of an employee; she will have the status of a teenager and the status of an old age pensioner. Each status will demand a particular cultural pattern, and it is this cultural pattern which will be Jane's 'role' in that situation. Jane will act many roles at the same time and some of these may require contradictory behaviour. Her role as a mother may conflict with her role as an employed person and her attempt to reconcile these roles may cause tension; sometimes Jane will be unsure of her role. She may be promoted from typist to supervisor and be uncertain whether she should identify with her former workmates or the management, and this uncertainty will also cause tension.

Although different people act different roles—the role of the employer will be quite different from that of the prospective employee whom he is interviewing—it is clear that in a particular culture the same basic needs are generally felt and the same situations have to be faced. It is therefore to be expected that a person will act in much the same way as the other members of the community.

This socially acceptable behaviour is called a 'norm' and is enforced by 'social control'. The most basic form of social control is the individual's own acceptance of 'norms' so that he will act out his expected roles; however, his acceptance is reinforced by 'negative' and 'positive' sanctions. Positive social control is composed of the rewards available in a society which encourage acceptable behaviour. This positive control may be formal and give specific rewards: religion may promise heaven for acceptable behaviour; the State may dangle a knighthood. Or the control may be informal, and operate through such channels as public opinion. Negative social control is made up of the penalties which a society inflicts on those who do not abide by its norms. This negative control may be formal—religion may threaten hell for sin, and the law may threaten imprisonment for crime—or it may be informal and operate through disapproval and ridicule.

Generally speaking the religious sanction attaching to 'sin' may relate to any breach of the moral code of the society that the religion reflects. Sin is personal to the sinner and may even extend to thoughts, so that the concept of sin may be an even more effective instrument of social control than the formal crime instituted by the legal code which can only deal with overt actions.

We call the degree to which a person acts in the accepted way, his 'character'. Of course no-one is completely predictable and everyone has the potentiality for quite different 'selves' from those exposed to the world under ordinary circumstances. However, while in most people such deviation takes place only occasionally, others will adopt a deviant role. It is this deviation from 'normal' behaviour that gives us our leaders, our inventors, our poets, and artists—and our criminals. Our criminals, however, may also be people who have fully accepted the roles expected of them by a deviant society within the main society; such a deviant society is called a 'sub-culture' and may exist, for example, in a particular area of a big town.

As the society changes because of mechanization, a change in food supply, contraception, education, new medicines, or for any other cause, it is to be expected that the behaviour of the people will also change. Sometimes their behaviour may change more quickly than the accepted code of conduct changes, and we may find virtually everyone behaving in a way which runs counter to public morality.

It is interesting to note that in our 'permissive' society the value set on virginity is still high and that in 1971 Geoffrey Gorer found that 46 per cent of men and 88 per cent of women did not have intercourse other than with the person whom they subsequently married (26 per cent of men and 63 per cent of women actually were virgin at marriage, although virginity was less likely in the younger members of his sample).[4] Gorer's survey illustrates the double standard of morality which operates for men and women: 27 per cent of men and 49 per cent of women were against sexual experience before marriage for a young man, but 43 per cent of men and 68 per cent of women were against such sexual experiences for a young woman. It is perhaps not surprising that such a double standard should prevail—the risks involved in pre-marital intercourse are much greater for women than for men as it is they who risk bearing illegitimate children and having to cope with all the consequent economic and social problems. This may also be an example of a moral code reflecting a need within a society.

Although this survey shows an increase in sexual permissiveness since Gorer's earlier survey, *Exploring English Character,*[5] in 1955, it also shows less inconsistency between what people say and what they do. In the earlier study Gorer found 75 per cent of men were opposed to pre-marital intercourse but that 40 per cent claimed to have had such intercourse, while in his more modern work he found that those who had had pre-marital intercourse were more likely to feel that it was acceptable behaviour.

Moral rules are not always enforced by fear of punishment: people obey them because they expect to do so, in the same way that children obey the rules of the games which they play, although there may be no adult supervision or any other obvious reason why they should do so. On the other hand, people may obey the rules because of the threat of punishment in this life or fear of punishment in the next; or they may be influenced by the fear of hurting someone else. In New Guinea an Arapesh will punish someone who wrongs him by hacking at one of his *own* trees, trees being highly prized by the Arapesh.[6] In our own society industrial workers who stage a 'sit down' strike in their factories bring discomfort, loss, and inconvenience primarily on themselves as do prisoners on hunger strike, but they hope that in the process they will influence, through guilt, the persons who were responsible for arousing the aggression.[7]

The ever-changing nature of morality may be illustrated by the fact that a man admired by one generation may be despised by another; while a man ignored or persecuted in one age may be honoured in years to come.

What factors do you think account for the apparent trends shown by the charts at right?

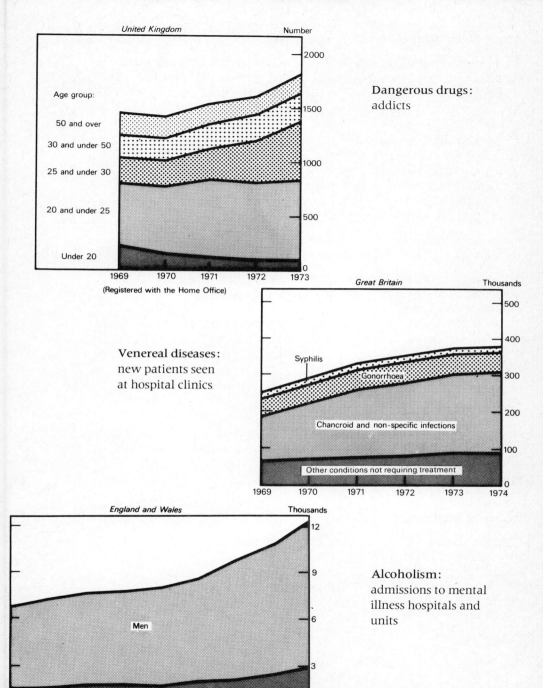

United Kingdom

Number

Age group:

50 and over

30 and under 50

25 and under 30

20 and under 25

Under 20

(Registered with the Home Office)

Dangerous drugs:
addicts

Venereal diseases:
new patients seen
at hospital clinics

Great Britain

Thousands

Syphilis

Gonorrhoea

Chancroid and non-specific infections

Other conditions not requiring treatment

England and Wales

Thousands

Men

Women

Alcoholism:
admissions to mental
illness hospitals and
units

Source : Social Trends 6, HMSO 1975

More discussion or written work

1   Is morality just another word for self-interest? In other words, do we adhere to a particular code of behaviour because we think that it will pay us to do so—either in this life or the next? Or does our behaviour reflect a feeling that we owe certain duties to other people—or a God?
2   Should different moral rules apply to men than apply to women?
3   What examples are there of men who were despised or admired in their own time, but who are now regarded quite differently?
4   Is there any action which is wrong in all circumstances?
5   Would you prefer to live in a society with a rigid set of moral rules or in a society where people can do much as they please?

Research

1   Take one of the Ten Commandments, other than 'thou shalt not kill', and find out the way in which this particular rule has been followed in different societies.
2   It is often said that we live in a permissive society. Find out the ways in which we are more restricted in our activities than people were one hundred years ago, and in what ways we have more freedom of action.

Imagination

Imagine that you are in a country in which food supplies are rapidly dwindling and that in the future there is no prospect of the situation improving unless drastic changes are made. Think of changes in our present moral code which might help to remedy the situation.

Reading suggestions

* M. Mead, *Growing Up in New Guinea*, Penguin
† N. Polsky, *Hustlers, Beats and Others*, Penguin
† M. Schofield, *The Sexual Behaviour of Young People*, Penguin
† K. Walker and P. Fletcher, *Sex and Society*, Penguin
  G. Vickers, *Value Systems and Social Process*, Penguin

Chapter 4

Marriage

Marriage is a system by which a society recognizes the right of a man and a woman to live together and have a stable sexual relationship. It also enforces a system of taboos which ensures that certain people do not mate, for if parents mate with their children, or brother mates with sister, recessive genes (those from previous generations) may be accentuated, and over several generations this could lead to weaker people, perhaps with impaired intelligence, if these traits were present in the recessive genes. Primitive man probably became aware of the dangers of inbreeding when deaf-mutes, albinos, and babies with additional fingers, all the results of recessive genes, were born to closely related people. The incest taboo was also socially valuable in that it increased the likelihood of harmony in the home by eliminating competition among father and sons for the sexual favours of their mother and sisters. One of the functions of marriage was to ensure the observance of the taboo on inbreeding and this taboo is still part of our marriage laws: its observance is ensured by such customs as 'calling the banns'. However, this biological function of marriage is less important in large urban societies where there is a wide choice of marriage partners and it is the social function of marriage which is most important in our society today.

Just as the family is not primarily concerned with sexual relationships, neither is sex the primary force driving people into matrimony. One study found that out of 250 societies, 65 allowed unmarried and unrelated people complete sexual freedom while others gave a qualified approval to such freedom. Obviously, people marrying in societies where complete sexual freedom outside marriage is approved of cannot be motivated primarily by sex when they enter into a marriage agreement.[1]

There may be only one man and one woman involved in the marriage agreement, or there may be one man and many women, or one woman and many men. The partners may be chosen by each other, they may be chosen by parents or tribal elders, they may be bought, or they may be captured. The number of people involved in the marriage itself, and the method by which the partners are chosen, will obviously influence the husbands' and wives' attitudes to each other and therefore the whole structure of the family.

The religion of the society will also have a marked effect upon marriage relationships. For example, the coming of Christianity to Britain reduced the status of the wife and as a result enhanced that of the husband. The Christian reaction against the degeneracy of the later Roman Empire and St Paul's anti-feminist propaganda ('It is good for a man not to touch a woman') led to a situation where by AD 585 the Christian bishops assembled at Mâcon could solemnly discuss whether women were human! Sexual pleasure was regarded as evil and intercourse was held as being allowable only for the procreation of children. Intercourse was sinful during the hours of daylight, during pregnancy, during Lent, the nights before and after attending Mass, and for a number of days after childbirth! In the circumstances a man was likely to feel guilty about his attraction towards his wife and was likely to despise her as inferior to himself. In addition, the pre-Christian custom of the bride being bought by the husband's family by payment of a dowry continued. Under the influence of these factors the female was subordinate to the male, and the emotional relationship was weak.[2]

Gradually the Mediaeval view of a wife as a mere belonging changed, but by the nineteenth century the husband and wife relationship was still based on the idea of male dominance. Slowly the concept of love as the main basis for marriage has become accepted; but the economic 'marriage of convenience' is still accepted to some extent in peasant societies and by royal dynasties.

Our own society is often compared unfavourably from a moral viewpoint with the society of Victorian England, but in 1887 the medical journal *The Lancet* estimated that (when the population of London was about one and a half million) one female in every sixteen (of all ages) was a prostitute and one house in every sixty was a brothel; certainly prostitution and hidden sexual immorality were prevalent, while the seduction of young girls by overseers in the factories and mills was the general practice.[3] When records were started in 1870 it was found that 6 per cent of all births in the United Kingdom were illegitimate. The decrease in prostitution in England today may be seen by some pessimists as due to increasing pre- and extra-marital relationships, and the fact that in the nineteenth century more women were desperately in need of money; but the more important factor may be the healthier outlook which we have to marriage.

In the nineteenth century marriage was postponed until people could afford to marry; now quite young men earn enough to keep a wife and children. The Victorians tended to have large families and it may be that they would have been even larger if the men had not married late and had recourse to prostitutes. But more important in comparing our attitudes to marriage with those of the Victorians is the fact that today marriage is not just an economic convenience but an erotic and friendly relationship as well. Today, moreover, facilities for divorce are more easily available, and although it may be claimed that divorce creates greater evils than it cures, in that a couple may resort to it before they can come to an understanding acceptance of each other and later a mutual dependence and love, it does introduce a more voluntary aspect to the marriage relationship and the possibility of greater mutual tolerance.

Divorce

	Rate per 1000 population				
	1963	1966	1968	1969	1970
United Kingdom	0.67	0.77	0.93	1.02	1.13
Belgium	0.56	0.61	0.63	0.67	0.68
Denmark	1.38	1.40	1.56	1.83	1.93
France	0.63	0.74	0.73	0.76	—
Germany (Fed. Rep.)	0.92	0.98	1.03	—	1.24
Canada	0.41	0.51	0.55	—	—
Japan	0.73	0.81	0.87	0.86	0.93
USA	2.27	2.55	2.93	3.17	3.51
USSR	1.30	2.77	2.72	2.56	2.63

The Divorce Law Reform Act 1966, came into effect in 1971. The Divorce (Scotland) Act was introduced in 1976 along the same lines—see page 42.

Approximate comparative rates for **1974**			
England and Wales	3.25	Germany	1.50
Scotland	1.35	USSR	3.00
France	1.00	USA	4.35

There was no provision for divorce in **ITALY** before 1970 except for annulment by the Church; since then it has been possible, though still difficult. In 1974 an attempt was made by referendum to make divorce illegal again, but this failed. **IRELAND** has no provision for divorce and as at 1978 there are no proposals for legalizing it.

Source: Adapted from *Social Trends* 4, HMSO 1973

1 *Which country in the chart has had the fastest growing divorce rate since 1963?*

2 *From the figures for the different countries, would you say that religion is likely to influence the number of divorces in a country?*

Is the increased divorce rate a sign that marriage as an institution is breaking up? It is certainly true that changes are taking place in the structure of marriage. Let us look at the facts: until 1857 a divorce was only possible in England by means of a private Act of Parliament; in 1923 women were given the same rights as men and the main grounds for divorce were desertion, cruelty, and adultery. In Britain in 1931 there were about 3700 divorces; by 1961 this had risen to 27 000 (representing two divorces for every thousand married people); in 1969 there were 55 000 divorces (representing four divorces for every thousand married people); and by 1975 this had risen to about 129 000 divorces (representing 10 divorces for every thousand married people).[4] These figures should be interpreted bearing in mind the more generous regulations regarding legal aid from 1961 onwards and the 1969 Divorce Reform Act (operational from 1971) which introduced a new and easier conception of divorce based on the 'irretrievable breakdown of marriage'.

By using the 'divorce rates', that is the proportion of marriages to divorces in a given year, the proportion of marital breakdowns to successful marriages can be made to seem greater than in fact they are, ranging from 0.5 per cent in 1910 to 12 per cent in 1969. However, even these rates seem comparatively small when compared with the rates in Muslim countries; for example, a rate of over 50 per cent was recorded in Malaya in 1952.[5] It is interesting to note that in Britain between two-thirds and three-quarters of all divorcees remarry—usually to other divorced persons. This seems to indicate that the divorced people themselves are not rejecting marriage as an institution.

The divorce rate may be increasing, not because the family is decreasing in importance, but because it is becoming *more* important as a unit. It is true that more women work nowadays, and equally true that most women expect to work for a time after marriage; but with the birth of a couple's first child the economic responsibility for the family is sharply focused on its one adult male member, and is no longer partially shared by the parents' fathers, grandfathers, and uncles! Whilst more responsibility is thrust upon the husband, the increasing isolation of the family in new housing estates and towns, away from parents and other relatives, focuses the responsibility of the mother role more sharply on the one adult woman, and cuts her off more and more from the help of her mother, sisters, and aunts. The husband's absence from home for a large part of the day leaves the wife to take the main responsibility for the children. Along with all this goes an increase in the emotional significance to the child of the parents as individuals, at first particularly the mother. This isolation emphasizes the partners' importance to each other, and therefore lays increasing stress upon love as a basis for marriage.

Attitudes to divorce—National Opinion Poll survey, 1965 (sample 1010 adults). Figures are percentages

Would you please tell me if you agree or disagree with the following statements?

	Agree	Disagree	Don't know
Nobody should be able to get a divorce	9	89	2
Nobody should be able to get a divorce if they have children under 16	33	62	5
Nobody should be able to get a divorce if they have children under 10	39	57	4
Divorce should always be possible if both husband and wife want it	80	17	3
A husband should always be able to get a divorce if his wife commits adultery	65	31	4
A wife should always be able to get a divorce if her husband commits adultery	64	31	5
Cruelty should always be a reason for divorce	81	14	5
Desertion for one year should be a reason for divorce	55	40	5

If a husband divorces his wife for adultery or some other offence, do you think he should always be the one to look after the children, or do you think it should sometimes be the wife?

Always husband	14
Sometimes the wife	75
Don't know	11

Which do you think is better for a child—to live with one divorced parent, or with two unhappily married parents?

With one parent	88
With two parents	6
Don't know	6

Do you think that you would tend to have a poor opinion of someone who had been the guilty partner in a divorce involving ...?

	Poor opinion	No	Don't know
Adultery	52	40	8
Cruelty	86	10	4
Desertion	62	29	9

Source: New Society

1 *What would your answers have been to the questions in this opinion poll? Can you give the reasons for your answers?*
2 *Do you think the questions are suitably phrased?*

These factors have led some sociologists, such as Parsons and Bales,[6] to conclude that the family is growing more important and stronger in our community today and that there is not a growing tendency towards free love; sexual relationships outside marriage, they claim, are taking place during pre-marital experimenting or because of dissatisfaction with present marital arrangements and with the hope of new ones— not because the people involved are rejecting marriage as an institution.

The rising divorce rate may not, therefore, be a sign of the break-up of our marriage system. The increase in the number of people being divorced may rather be a sign of the increasing importance of marriage and the family in our society. The isolation of the 'nuclear' family has made the tasks of the husband and wife more difficult; and as the difficulty of their tasks increases, so more people can be expected to fail to fulfil them until the necessary adjustments have been made.

The modern model family of a husband, a wife, and an average of two children is partially conditioned by the size of houses now being built and their availability, the fact that women wish to continue in employment, and the fact that children—as the school-leaving age rises—cannot go out to work so early and thereby add to the family income. These four people live a life isolated from most of their relatives, and the State has taken over many of the family functions. The use of state agencies increases as the family's connection with relatives decreases. A comparison which has been made of families in the old working-class area of Bethnal Green in London and families who moved to a new council housing estate on the outskirts of London demonstrates this change.[7]

It is also true that in the modern family husbands and wives are more likely to carry out tasks and enjoy their leisure together. John and Elizabeth Newson found in 1963 that both mother and father were becoming increasingly home-centred and concluded 'the modern father's place is in the home'.[8] This greater 'togetherness' is caused not only by their increased isolation from other relatives, and the fact that they chose each other, but also by the change in the position of woman in our society. They are better educated, work in the same spheres as men, have almost the same legal status as men, and are less likely to be worn out—or even dead—because of excessive childbearing in unhygienic conditions. In 1850, 50 per cent of women died before the age of forty-five; now only 10 per cent do. Women today are therefore better equipped mentally and physically to join with their husbands in work and leisure. In addition they can expect at least twenty years of married life after the children have grown up, to re-engage in their previous occupations, or to devote to their husbands, extended families, and leisure interests.

The position of women in our society could not have changed so much during the twentieth century if the size of the average family had remained as large as it was in the nineteenth century, and this decrease would not have been possible without the widespread use of birth control.

During the Middle Ages the artificial methods of birth control which had been used by the Greeks and Romans were largely unknown and the only means of birth control available were the use of the safe period, which could be discovered by experience, or restraint from intercourse; the withdrawal method could also be used, but this was condemned by the Church—and is still condemned by the Roman Catholic Church.

However, up to the sixteenth century the population of England was only increasing slowly, for although each woman bore an average of about six children less than half of these could be expected to survive and so the lack of an efficient means of birth control did not constitute a problem. Gradually, however, improvements in hygiene and medical knowledge led to more children surviving infancy, thus increasing the poverty of already poor families and increasing the necessity of putting children to productive work at the earliest possible moment.

These pressures led to a demand for birth control by social reformers, but this was opposed by the Government, who needed factory and cannon fodder for the expanding industries and Empire. Francis Place, who published a pamphlet on birth control in 1823, met with official hostility—a hostility which culminated, in 1875, in the prosecution of Charles Bradlaugh and Annie Besant for circulating a birth-control manual written by an American doctor. Although released on a technicality they were both first sentenced to imprisonment for obscenity and the publicity of the trial boosted the sales of the birth-control manual. Between 1870 and 1872, before the trial, the live births per thousand women in the United Kingdom had been 151.5, ten years later they had dropped to 145.7, and by 1890–92 they were 129.2.[9]

In 1968 it was estimated that between 70 and 80 per cent of all married couples used a method of birth control at some time. Without such controls the population would probably now be expanding at an even greater rate than during the population explosion of the nineteenth century, for infant mortality dropped from 129.4 per thousand live births in 1911 to 21.8 per thousand live births in 1960.[10]

In Britain, not only are people living longer but an increasing proportion are also getting married much younger, although the average age of men at marriage has remained at twenty-four for several years (24.4 in 1970 compared with 27.2 in 1901) and the average age of brides has also been fairly static at about twenty-two (22.7 in 1973 compared with 25.6 in 1901). However, an increasing number of people are getting married while they are still teenagers; the proportion of these to all other marriages is shown in the table, which is based on figures issued by the Government statistical service.

	Teenage bridegrooms	Teenage brides
1901	1.2%	5.9%
1931	1.3%	6.8%
1951	2.4%	15.5%
1961	5.4%	22.9%
1970	7.4%	24.4%

Marriage and illegitimate births in Great Britain

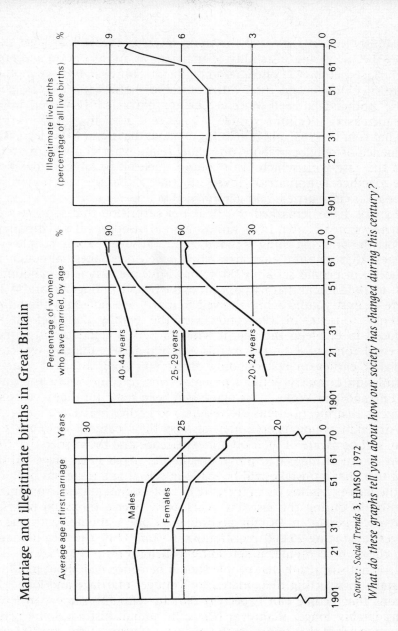

Illegitimate live births
(percentage of all live births)

%
9
6
3
0

70 61 51 31 21 1901

Percentage of women
who have married, by age

%
90
60
30
0

70 61 51 31 21 1901

40-44 years

25-29 years

20-24 years

Average age at first marriage

Years
30
25
20

70 61 51 31 21 1901

Males

Females

Source: Social Trends 3, HMSO 1972
What do these graphs tell you about how our society has changed during this century?

Just married—this couple met for the first time only a few hours before their wedding. According to Sikh custom their marriage in Swindon in 1970 was arranged by the bride's parents.
Do you think parents should choose a husband or wife for their child?
Photograph: Syndication International

47

Pessimists may suggest that the trend towards earlier marriages indicates the increasing instability of marriage as an institution and point to the fact that in 1971 one-quarter of the total births to teenage mothers were illegitimate and three-fifths of babies born within marriage to these mothers had been conceived before marriage.[11] However, despite the increasing illegitimacy rates (5.7 per cent of all live births in 1961, 8.2 per cent in 1968, and remaining at about that figure), the decreasing influence of religious taboos on sexual relationships outside marriage, and the ease with which birth control makes it possible for people to live together as unmarried 'lovers', the fact is that the vast majority of people do get married, and get married younger.

Experts have remarked that it is not surprising that some teenage marriages break down in an atmosphere of disapproval and disparagement: the amazing thing is that so many survive.[12] Some people even suggest that youthful marriages should be encouraged, although the majority of people certainly do not take this view. A national opinion poll in 1966 found that 64 per cent of the people in England and Wales were against youths being allowed to marry at eighteen without their parents' consent. In 1969, however, the Family Law Reform Act reduced to eighteen the age at which a person could marry without parental consent. Even before this Act, and despite the post-war trend towards earlier marriages, only about 600 applications a year for permission to marry without parental consent came before the courts in England and Wales. This figure had been static for many years and suggests that most parents are resigned to earlier marriage.

Although young people may dismiss their parents' opinions they may still be aware of their own inexperience and be worried that their own choice of mate will prove unsuitable; it has been suggested that this fear that a mistake will be made in selecting a mate has been one of the factors leading to an increase in professional marriage organizers in Britain during the last few years. Now over a thousand marriage bureaux operate in Britain according to one estimate, with the six largest averaging 25 000 registrations a year, while the idea of matching clients by computer is spreading to Britain from the USA.[13]

It is not surprising that people should be concerned about making a mistake in selecting their mates, for younger marriage and longer life means that people can expect to remain with the same partner for considerably longer than ever before in human history. Some people have suggested that to expect the majority of people to be satisfied with one partner for upwards of fifty years is unrealistic and claim that an examination of the present pattern of divorce suggests that in the future most people may expect to marry two or three times in their lives.

The peak period for divorce occurs consistently between five and nine years after marriage (33.1 per cent in 1970, 30.5 per cent in 1971).

There is also a higher risk of marital breakdown between ten to fourteen years after marriage (19.4 per cent in 1971) and after twenty years of marriage (24.2 per cent in 1971). The evidence suggests that marital failure occurs in phases.[14] The first is in the early years of marriage if basic physical and emotional relationships are not established. The second occurs a few years later when the personalities of the partners mature and new traits and needs may develop in the partners; if these needs are not met by the other partner divorce may be the solution. Finally, the marriage enters a new phase when the children grow up and leave home, leaving the married couple to redirect their emotional and social life—again if this reorganization fails marital breakdown may occur.

Trial marriages have also been suggested as a possibility for the future, as have group marriages.[15] Another possibility is some form of polygamy—it is interesting to note that in 1650 the city of Nuremburg decreed that every man could marry two women in order to increase the population which had been severely reduced by the Thirty Years' War.

By the year 2001 Government statisticians estimate that there will be rather more men than women in the twenty to twenty-four age group and a considerable excess of females in the age group over forty-four. Perhaps polyandry in early life and polygyny in later years might be a solution! However, most of us are probably happy to let monogamy continue.

Whatever future trends may be, most people regard marriage as essential to the stability of our society, an attitude which successive governments have adopted. Government grants are paid to such organizations as the National Marriage Guidance Council, the Catholic Marriage Advisory Council, and the Family Welfare Association, while family planning is now incorporated in the National Health Service.

More discussion or written work

1 Do women have an inferior, an equal, or a superior position to men in our society?

2 Do the advantages of marrying at an early age outweigh the disadvantages?

3 Do you think that it is preferable for the old to live with their sons or daughters or with other old people in a special home?

4 You are the prospective mother or father of an illegitimate child. Would you marry your partner in creating the child even though you had not previously intended to? Would you bring up the child yourself (in the case of the unmarried mother) or would you leave the rearing of the child to state agencies—through adoption, orphanage, foster home, etc.?

Research

1   Find out to what extent other countries allow divorce, and also the main requirements of the law as regards divorce in this country. Make any proposals for altering our laws that you think appropriate.
2   Find out the ways in which people get married in our own and other societies, noting in particular to what extent it is a religious or a civil ceremony.

Imagination

Imagine that in future all couples are to be selected for marriage by computer. You have been appointed to programme the computer for this purpose—to cross-reference those traits in the male partner and the female partner that may make a successful marriage, and to do the same with those traits that make marriage unfavourable.

Reading suggestions

* H. Gavron, *The Captive Wife*, Penguin
† J. Dominian, *Marital Breakdown*, Penguin
† R. Fletcher, *The Family and Marriage in Britain*, Penguin
  D. Beyfus, *The English Marriage: What it is like to be married today*, Penguin
  L. Mair, *Marriage*, Penguin
  D. Marsden, *Mothers Alone*, Penguin

Chapter 5

Occupation

Those of us who are working still spend more time doing our job than we do at any other activity—except perhaps sleep! A world run by slave robots and computers while we fulfil ourselves as human beings is still a long way off. For most of us this may well be a good thing, for without work we would probably either lie in bed and rot, or smash the place up out of sheer boredom. One of the unfortunate features of automation is that the *first* people it replaces are the unskilled workers doing repetitive and mentally undemanding work, and these workers are likely to be the least able to use their enforced leisure in a self-fulfilling way.

Although the normal working week in Britain in 1974 was in the range of thirty-nine to forty hours for manual work and thirty-seven to thirty-eight for non-manual work, the actual hours worked by men in manual occupations in October 1974 were 45.1.[1] (Comparatively little paid overtime is worked in non-manual occupations.) For, although the trade unions insist that they want a shorter working week so that their members may have more leisure to lead a fuller life, many of the members themselves want a shorter working week so that they can work more overtime at higher rates of pay. Consistent overtime working has disadvantages from both the employers' and the employees' points of view. As far as the employer is concerned, if overtime is available, there is no reason for any man to make an effort to get a day's work done during normal working hours. The employee suffers because in nearly all industries nominal wage rates are far below actual earnings, which leads to hardship when overtime is not available and men have to depend on the minimum wage without overtime. This is emphasized by the fact that standards of living rise to absorb overtime earnings and additional commitments are taken on. Yet one of the obstacles in negotiating realistic minimum rates is that known overtime pay is taken into consideration.

In the United States men often take on two jobs if their actual working week falls below forty hours: for example, New York policemen are often cab drivers. 'Moonlighting' has started to grow in this country, and there is always the danger that a particularly energetic and adaptable man may end up with two jobs, thereby displacing a less enterprising man who will thus be unemployed.

During the twenty years prior to 1967 the general unemployment rate

	Hours per week worked in manufacturing*				Annual averages %		
	1960	1970	1971		1969	1971	1972
United Kingdom	47.4	44.9	43.6		2.5	3.4	3.8
Belgium	41.4	37.9	37.5		3.6	2.9	3.5
France	45.7	44.8	44.5		—	—	—
Germany (Fed. Rep.)	45.6	43.8	43.0		0.8	0.8	1.1
Italy	8.0	7.8	7.7		3.4	3.1	3.6
Netherlands	48.8	44.2	43.8		1.4	1.6	2.7
Denmark	—	36.2	35.9		3.9	3.7	3.7
Irish Republic	45.4	42.7	42.3		6.4	7.2	8.1
Norway	39.3	35.3	—		1.0	0.8	—
Spain	43.5	44.1	—		—	—	—
Switzerland	46.1	44.7	44.6		—	—	—
USA	39.7	39.8	39.9		3.5	5.9	5.6
Canada	40.4	39.7	39.7		4.7	6.4	6.3
Japan	47.8	43.3	42.6		1.1	1.2	1.5

* Figures for Italy are hours per day.   *Source:* Adapted from *Social Trends* **4**, HMSO 1973

Average unemployment in the United Kingdom dropped to 2.3% in 1974 but rose thereafter to 8.8% in August 1976.

1   *How do the hours worked by people engaged in the manufacturing trades in the United Kingdom compare with those worked elsewhere?*
2   *It has been suggested that automation and mechanization will either increase unemployment or decrease the number of hours worked—or have a partial effect on both. Is there any evidence in the tables to support this view?*
3   *Compare the unemployment figures for Norway and Ireland—see if you can find any reasons for these differences.*

in Britain was among the lowest in the world, varying usually between 1 and 2 per cent. Since 1972 unemployment has tended to rise and by January 1976 was 6 per cent. Raising the school-leaving age, increasing numbers in higher education and earlier retirement in some industries have helped to keep unemployment down; but technological development and economic pressure to halt the growth of the service occupations, may mean a permanently higher unemployment figure, the dropping birth rate and plans for nursery education may increase the figures by releasing more married women for employment.

However, these low unemployment figures hide permanently high unemployment rates in certain areas. Northern Ireland, Scotland, and

Unemployed school leavers (in thousands)

1971	1972	1973	1974	1975	1976	
16.3	20.7	7.7*	15.1	48.6	88.4	*School leaving age raised to 16, in September 1972

Male unemployment by regions, Jan. 1972 (Aug. 1976 figures in brackets)

	Total male registered unemployed as percentage of all male employees	Percentage of wholly unemployed males by duration of registration (weeks):					Percentage of wholly unemployed males by age group					
		up to 2	3–8	9–26	27–52	over 52	under 20	20–29	30–39	40–49	50–59	over 59
North	9.3 (9.9)	9.0	19.2	33.1	15.9	22.8	11.9	25.0	16.3	16.3	15.2	15.3
Yorks and Humberside	6.7 (7.3)	11.4	18.6	33.5	17.4	19.1	10.7	25.8	17.2	16.2	15.0	15.1
North West	7.0 (9.6)	12.5	20.0	34.9	17.4	15.1	11.6	28.4	18.3	15.3	13.0	13.3
East Midlands	5.0 (6.5)	12.3	21.2	30.2	15.2	21.1	9.4	23.6	16.2	15.5	15.8	19.6
West Midlands	6.8 (7.8)	11.9	21.2	35.8	17.4	13.8	11.0	26.3	18.0	16.5	14.3	13.9
East Anglia	5.0 (6.5)	13.1	21.0	35.0	14.5	16.4	10.0	24.1	13.9	14.1	16.6	21.3
South East	3.4 (5.9)	18.6	25.3	33.2	12.2	10.7	9.0	24.8	16.8	14.7	15.3	19.4
South West	5.6 (8.5)	13.6	21.5	34.4	13.9	16.6	8.9	24.1	13.3	13.1	16.2	24.4
Wales	7.3 (9.4)	13.1	20.3	32.9	14.1	19.6	12.0	27.2	16.3	15.1	14.0	15.4
Scotland	9.5 (9.3)	9.5	20.7	32.5	17.4	19.8	13.7	27.1	19.6	16.3	12.9	10.4
Great Britain	5.9 (7.6)	12.9	21.3	33.6	15.6	16.7	11.0	26.0	17.2	15.5	14.5	15.8

Unemployment rates fell in 1973 and 1974 but rose rapidly in 1975 and 1976.

Source: Adapted from Social Trends 3, HMSO 1972; *Dept. of Employment Gazette,* Sept. 1976

On the basis of the figures in this table, compare the employment prospects of a twenty-five-year-old man in Sunderland with those of a forty-five-year-old man in London. Why do regional differences of this kind exist?

the North-East are traditional sufferers; and these areas suffer correspondingly more when there is more general unemployment throughout the country. For example, in January 1972 the number of unemployed men in Scotland was 9.5 per cent and in the North of England 9.3 per cent, compared with only 3.4 per cent in South-East England. These areas of under-employment are the areas where large numbers of people settled during the Industrial Revolution to work in heavy industries such as coalmining and shipbuilding which have since declined from 3.3 per cent of all employees in 1961 to 1.8 per cent of all employees in 1971. Rural areas have also suffered from static or declining populations as the number of people engaged in agriculture, forestry, and fishing continues to fall, from 2.6 per cent of the total working population of Britain in 1961 to 1.6 per cent in 1971.

Since the 1930s various Governments have tried to encourage industry to move to areas of under-employment, the most recent attempts being the Local Employment Act of 1970 and the Industry Act of 1972. These measures have included the refusal of Industrial Development Certificates for larger industrial developments unless they were sited in the development areas or in new towns planned to take population from the more congested areas, or could show good reason why they should not be sited in these areas. Office Development

Certificates have also been required since the Town and Country Planning Act of 1971 for office developments of over 10 000 square feet in South-East England. Other encouragements offered to those prepared to move or expand industry in the development areas have included a rent-free period in a government-built factory, grants to buy plant, loans, and grants towards the cost of the removal expenses of key personnel. The Government has also adopted a policy of decentralizing Government departments to the regions.

However, in some areas there is probably no long-term solution without continued subsidy, and British people may well have to become a great deal more ready to move about the country to where labour is required, as they do already in the United States. For although 33 per cent of the population of Great Britain changed their address between 1961 and 1966 most of these were probably just moving house; a better guide to those moving to new employment is that only 4.2 per cent had moved from one region to another during this period. One major deterrent to such mobility is the development of council housing, particularly in some of the 'depressed' areas. This means that the worker concerned cannot sell a house and buy elsewhere, but must give up a subsidized dwelling without any guarantee of suitable accommodation being available in the area to which he wishes to move. It is possible to be worse off working in an area with a severe housing shortage than unemployed and living on social welfare benefit but securely housed in another area.

Whatever the reason for the apparent failure to move sufficient industry to the depressed areas, it is certainly true that South-East England, the South Coast, and the more prosperous parts of the Midlands and Northern England have had high rates of population increase, but many of the older industrial towns and remote country areas have maintained more or less static populations. For example, the population of South-East England (10 584 square miles) went up between 1961 and 1971 by almost 1 million to a total of over 17 million people. While the population of the North region plus Yorkshire and Humberside (12 952 square miles) remained almost static at about 8 million.

There are some areas where unemployment has reversed the traditional roles in our society of the men working while the women look after the home. Northern Ireland has for many years had few jobs for male labour, but a high proportion of the female population has been engaged in the linen industry. The linen industry has now declined (although Northern Ireland still remains the greatest linen manufacturing region of the world), but the light industry (such as shirt-making) which has developed from it has continued to absorb female labour. The large number of unemployed men, and the resulting bitterness and sense of 'wasted manhood', has contributed substantially to Northern

Ireland's problems. A newcomer to the list of areas of 'role reversal' is Alfreton in Derbyshire, where the closure of four coal mines and an iron works has meant that the men have been displaced, while their wives have been able to find employment in the town's booming garment-making and hosiery factories.

Even in areas with a high level of employment there has been a merging of the roles of husband and wife as more married women decide to work while their children are still at school. (In 1971 nearly 63 per cent of working women were married and 54 per cent of all women of working age were in employment.) This has given rise to a fear that the children of working mothers will be neglected, but although children may suffer in a few instances (and these children may well have been neglected even if their mothers had not been working) there is no real evidence that the children of working mothers are more emotionally unstable, more likely to be delinquent, more prone to truancy, or worse cared for physically than the children of mothers who remain at home.[2] However, there may be ill effects on children under three if they are separated from their mothers for long periods, unless there is a stable mother substitute.[3]

One study has shown that most women work in order to give their families a higher standard of living, and not as an escape from family responsibilities, and that most women fitted their hours of work to these responsibilities.[4] Another study confirms that working mothers make arrangements for child care which compare favourably with what would have occurred had the mother stayed at home. It also suggests that the children from these 'career mother' families show greater independence and resourcefulness and that the necessity of helping in the home gives these children a sense of competence and social responsibility, helping to legitimize their right to share the family possessions.[5] Certainly the child of a working mother is likely to have a higher standard of living, with consequent greater educational and leisure opportunities. The working mother may also be a more interesting companion for her husband and children, and her employment may encourage greater cooperation from her family in the home—washing up, cooking, doing housework, shopping, and caring for babies may all become shared responsibilities.

It should be borne in mind that the bias against working mothers is mainly middle class in origin and that in many working-class communities it has always been considered normal that mothers should work, with grandmothers often sharing the responsibility for the children. The prejudice that has existed against working wives in some working-class groups is usually in areas dominated by industries in which women have been excluded from work opportunities, perhaps by law as in mining. As married women have not normally been able

to find employment in these communities the non-working wife has become the social norm and, as usual, any deviation from this norm has been criticized.

Although in some respects we may be returning to earlier attitudes in accepting the fact that married women will be employed, the social situation in which this is happening has changed dramatically. The breaking up of the extended family and the close-knit community means that adequate facilities for the care of the children of working mothers will have to be provided and employers may have to be more flexible in arranging their schedules to suit the working mother.

Perhaps the ultimate solution may be that all men and women will each work for some twenty hours per week and devote the rest of their time to their family, home, and leisure.

Not only has there been a reversal of roles between man and wife in certain areas, but there is a much more general reversal of roles between the age groups. By the age of seventeen more than 80 per cent of young people are in full employment and earning substantial incomes: the salary of a twenty-year-old shorthand-typist in London may sometimes reach comparatively astronomical heights. The significance of such an income lies in the fact that a large percentage of it is surplus to immediate requirements—a surplus which is really the true definition of 'wealth'. Not only are there young typists who earn more than their bus-driver fathers, but a far greater number of young people have more actual spending money than their parents. This has brought about a considerable change in the attitudes of the generations towards each other.

Generally speaking, the longer one lives the more one knows, and therefore in most societies responsibility is allocated partially by age. Responsibility carries power and, traditionally, the older generations are somewhat scornful of the younger ones and the younger age groups are hostile to the older. In many societies there is an initiation ceremony whereby the young become 'powerful' adults; every fifteen years the Nandi in Kenya have a ceremony in which the country is formally handed over by the older people to the younger. The fighting which is intended to be sham sometimes becomes very real![6] In our society the power seems to lie with hard cash and the roles seem to be reversing, the old are becoming hostile and the young contemptuous.

Two hundred cars a day roll off the highly mechanized Ford production line at Dagenham. In contrast, in the lower photograph, Chinese workers are laboriously planting rice—a very labour-intensive occupation.
What are the implications of a reduction in labour-intensive occupations throughout the world?
Photographs: Ford Motor Company and Camera Press

This may well be largely a question of surplus wealth and it is interesting to speculate by what means society will insist that the young become adult if adulthood becomes no longer a desirable state!

The type of work we do will obviously have a considerable impact on the way we live. There are some extreme cases like that of the men drilling for oil in Pridhoe Bay in the Arctic. These men are lured by salaries of more than £10 000 a year and spend their working time blanketed with clothes, only their eyes being visible; their leisure is passed in virtual imprisonment within their barracks. For most of us, however, the effect of our employment is less dramatic. We expect different jobs to have different financial rewards, which may result in different cars or houses. But the effects of our work can be much less tangible. A job may be so undemanding that it is forgotten immediately the worker leaves the factory; or it may so tax a person's physical strength and courage as to become the main topic of his conversation (like coalmining as described in *Coal is Our Life*[7]). But in every case the job we do will influence the way we spend our leisure.

In the fishing industry of Hull a man can expect to be away from home for three weeks at a time and will tend to have only two-and-a-half days at home before his ship sails again. He receives a low regular wage which is paid directly to his wife, if he has one. His income is then made up by a percentage of the catch and the cod-liver-oil money, which may vary from nothing to more than £100 a trip—depending on luck and the weather. While at sea the work is rough, tough, and risky: an average of one trawler a year goes down. The highest incomes are obtainable in middle age, and, as it is mainly his strength which the fisherman is selling, incomes decline rapidly in old age. The insecurity of income and occupation in fishing makes for a standard of living based on the basic wage: the remaining income is generally regarded as pocket money, to be spent in pubs, clubs, and betting shops. The search for enjoyment is all the more intense for the contrast between life aboard ship and time on shore.[8]

In the case of the coalminers of 'Ashton' in Yorkshire (*Coal is Our Life*), it was found by Slaughter that the discomfort, danger, and impersonality of the pit led to a demand for warmth, comfort, tidiness, and personal attention in the home—although the greater part of the miner's leisure was spent with his mates from the mine. The age groupings were the same as in the pit, and they went drinking and gambling together. There was a generally low standard of living because, as with the Hull fishermen, the traditional standard of living was set in early age on a low income: an increase of money meant an increase of pleasure.[9] The insecurity of mining decreased the incentive to save, not the reverse. Success and social acceptance were judged in the context of the miners' mates, the family having lost all functions of general social significance, except those of reproduction and of socializing the children. Home was reduced almost to 'the place where you fill in the pools on a Wednesday night'.[10] Women were no more allowed for in Ashton's leisure-time facilities than work was provided for them down the pit.

There still is, of course, a sex-barrier in some types of employment; few people would like to see women down the coal mines as they were early in the last century, and to employ women for work of this sort is illegal. There are, however, some jobs that belong traditionally to one sex for no immediately apparent reason: for instance, less than 2 per cent of the quarter of a million shorthand-typists in London are male! This is probably because the invention of the typewriter in 1873 and the introduction of shorthand in 1870 assisted in the emancipation of women by providing socially acceptable employment for middle-class girls. However, it is generally the woman who is discriminated against in employment rather than the man. An employer is reluctant to spend a lot of money training a woman for a skilled job, such as that of airline pilot, because of the likelihood that she will marry and leave. Men dislike having a woman put in authority over them, and it is said that women themselves often show a decided preference for a male boss. Girls often do not apply for jobs traditionally reserved for males, although there are women engineers and merchant navy captains. Only about 2 per cent of the members of the Institute of Directors are female, and not until 1973 were women admitted to the London Stock Exchange. Women claim that they have to be twice as able and twice as tough as a man to get to the top.

The principle of equal pay for equal work already applied in many occupations and became applicable to all in 1975 (Equal Pay Act, 1970). However, in 1971 the average earnings of women were only a little over half the average earnings of men. For example, in October 1972 the average earnings of full-time male adult manual workers were £35.82 a week and women in the same category earned an average of £18.30 a week (compared with £8.30 and £4.50 respectively in 1951).[11]

Many women are undoubtedly frustrated in the kind of employment available to them and by the rewards which they receive, but so are many men. There is still a great deal of truth in the statement: 'of all human troubles the most hateful is to feel that you have a capacity for power and yet you have no field to exercise it' (Herodotus).

More discussion or written work

1 Some jobs start with a fairly high income which is maintained for a time and then reduced; some start relatively low, get higher, and then get low again; while others start low and gradually increase with no reduction. Which sort of job comes into which category? Why? How

does this earning pattern affect the way people spend their time outside their working hours?

2   Do you think men and women should receive the same income if they do similar jobs?

3   It has been suggested that everyone should receive the same income irrespective of the job they do. Do you think this is a good idea?

4   Do you think it is easier to order or to obey?

5   A self-employed man pays more for his National Insurance stamp than an employed man, and does not get unemployment benefit, special pension, or industrial injuries benefit. Would you like to be self-employed? Why?

Research

1   Find out the average weekly income of men and women in this country, divided by age if possible. Then discover how this compares with incomes in other countries in real terms (that is, taking different costs of living into account). Compare the different amounts of leisure time in the countries concerned.

2   Find out the history of employment exchanges (Job Centres) and discover as much as you can about the employment services now available.

OR

Discover what proportion of married women with children go out to work (either full or part-time) in your area or street. Try to find out what these mothers feel has been the effect of this work on their children and family life, and compare these opinions with any formal research findings.

Imagination

Decide what job you would do if you could choose any occupation you wished. List all the good *and* all the bad facets of the job in detail.

Reading suggestions

* M. Powell, *Below Stairs*, Pan
* P. Toynbee, *A Working Life*, Peacock
† M. Carter, *Into Work*, Penguin
  S. Parker, *The Sociology of Industry*, Unwin Books
  W. Whyte, *The Organisation Man*, Penguin

Part Two
Our Choice

Chapter 6

Religion

One definition of religion is: 'a belief in spiritual beings'.[1] Another is: 'a method of appealing to powers superior to man which are believed to direct the course of nature'.[2] The first definition emphasizes the necessity of 'belief' in religion, the second emphasizes the necessity for some practice or ritual. Most religions have an element of both dogma and ritual. Generally speaking, the more primitive a society the more importance it attaches to ritual—until we reach the stage of 'magic' where the ritual will be all-important.

Magic is based on an idea that the Universe and all it contains is subject to unchanging laws and that if one has the appropriate 'key' one may manipulate these laws for one's own purpose. The necessary key may be a particular set of words or a particular ritual action; for example, one may have to pour water on the ground in order to produce rain. Supernatural beings need not enter into the magic at all, but if they do they are not omnipotent but are themselves subject to the laws; they may even be punished, as when the members of a tribe whip the images of their gods.

Even on a higher level of religious belief than that of magic, prayers often take a set form which must be repeated in order to obtain certain ends, such as the forgiveness of sin. The Buddhist prayer-wheel, one turn of which automatically repeats the prayer a thousand times, is an extreme example. The Catholic rosary is another, though it also serves to concentrate the mind. Most Christian groups, of course, also have set prayers. It is a comparatively modern idea that people may use their own words when speaking directly to God.

There does appear to be a real need for ritual among human beings. The ritual serves to provide a common identity for the people taking part and to register the importance of the life cycle in each human being. This is apparent in what are called 'rites of passage'. For example, many people who are not practising Christians will insist on their children being baptized and getting married in a church (in 1962 about 70 per cent of marriages were solemnized in a religious setting; in 1969 about 66 per cent were[3]). In the same way many people who do not normally attend a church will wish to receive a 'Christian' burial, while confirmation and first communion are basically initiation ceremonies.

In those societies which have rejected religion a considerable amount of ritual has been attached to the political creed itself and in many ways these creeds take on the form of a religion. They involve a belief in a superior power, a strict set of rules of conduct (and one sociologist, Durkheim, has defined religion as the 'affirmation of moral rules'[4]), a stated reason for the existence of the human being, and a 'priesthood'. In Nazism for example, the superior power was the State, the code of conduct included the immorality of marriage to 'inferior' races, the reason for the existence of the Aryan race was to form a superior civilization and eventually become dominant, and the priesthood was made up of the party officials. The ritual included the mass parade, the salute, and worship of 'the Leader'.

Among present-day religions it would appear reasonable to include Communism, which in theory includes many of the fundamental moral principles of Christianity and certainly includes many of the ritualistic aspects of religion. If one *does* include Communism it is probably true to say that the vast majority of mankind believes in a religion.

It is almost impossible to give exact numbers when dealing with religious groupings, but the most popular religion in the world is probably Christianity with some 950 million followers, about 55 per cent of whom are Catholics, 28 per cent Protestants, and 17 per cent Russian and Greek Orthodox. The next largest religion may be Islam, which has about 450 million believers; Hinduism may have 395 million adherents; Confucianism and Taoism could still have 440 million followers but conditions in China, its main home, make this unlikely; while Buddhism may account for 160 million people.

These five religions, with Communism, account for the vast bulk of the world's people, although there are many smaller religions. All five are fragmented within themselves, as indeed are most of the smaller ones, which is not surprising as men are thinking beings. It is interesting to note that many quite different religions have beliefs in common: one is the return of the prophet or god to Earth at some future time; the 'flood' appears in many, as do 'heaven and hell'; whereas others are exclusive and are restricted to a particular chosen race who alone can have a future life.

Some form of religion seems to be found in every society and this universal appeal of religion may stem partially from the wish of man to believe and partially from the desire of other men that he should believe.

Most people do not just accept things as they are; they look for a meaning. If they are rich they want to be convinced that they have a right to their good fortune, that they deserve to be in the position that they are in—'Good fortune thus wants to be "legitimate" fortune' (Max Weber).[5] This may imply that others who are less fortunate also deserve their positions and that they are therefore in some way inferior. Equally, the poor may wonder why it should be they who suffer starvation, disease, and brutality and may see a meaning for it as a preparation for a future life in which it is they who will be 'God's children' either in a heaven or in a world suddenly transformed. Norman Cohen describes how in Europe successive generations of poor people between the eleventh and sixteenth centuries were suddenly gripped by an expectation that the world was about to be suddenly and miraculously transformed in a struggle between Christ and the Antichrist who was responsible for their sufferings.[6]

Marx summed up this situation in a paragraph, part of which is often quoted: 'Religious distress is at the same time the expression of real distress and the protest against real distress. Religion is the sign of the oppressed creature, the heart of a heartless world, just as it is the spirit of a spiritless situation. It is the opium of the people.'[7] Marx felt, of course, that once the real enemy was faced 'the criticism of heaven would turn into the criticism of the earth'.

Some religions stress the need for diligence and hard work in this life if rewards are to be expected in the next—leading to what may be the unintended consequence of affluence, as among the Puritans. Or the religion may support the view that existence implies unrest and suffering and that the highest ideal is a complete withdrawal from it, as among the Buddhists. It is not surprising that the Puritans had their origin in prosperous sixteenth-century England and the Buddhists 2500 years ago in poverty-stricken India.

The wish fulfilment aspect of religion is not restricted to rationalizing economic positions. The death of those we love can be faced more readily if we can persuade ourselves to believe that the parting is temporary; we may be able to face the prospect of our own death more easily if we can accept the concept of a future life.

There is also what has become known as the 'social learning theory' of religion—that religious behaviour, beliefs, and experiences are simply part of our culture and are handed down from generation to generation in the same way as any other customs.[8] However, customs need a trigger to start them off, and need to continue to fill a need if they are to be maintained.

Man's desire for religious belief is reinforced by the desires of other men that he should believe. Religion may be the means of turning the dissatisfaction of the under-privileged into channels harmless to those in power—'The mortgage that the peasant has on heavenly possessions guarantees the mortgage that the bourgeois has on peasant possessions' (Marx).[9] It has been suggested that some groups actually create religious creeds to further their own ends; for example, it suited the Brahmins to institute a caste system in which they represented the head of the creator of the Universe and the original dark-skinned inhabitants (the 'Sudras') his feet! However, it is unlikely that any religion was callously invented with the sole purpose of keeping the underdogs down; early Christianity, in fact, was the religion of the underdog. It is more probable that such a charge can be made because a religion does tend to reflect the 'needs' of the society in which it exists; and most societies in the past have consisted of a vast labouring poor and a small rich elite. Even the minor details of a religion may reflect social needs: for example, the ban on eating pork among Mohammedans and Jews may well result from the fact that both religions have arisen in countries where pork is liable to go bad quickly; similarly, the recently abolished rule that Catholics should not eat meat on Friday was designed in the Middle Ages to encourage large fishing fleets that could be converted and used by Christendom as warships against 'the Turks' should the need arise. Only rarely is a religious doctrine harmful to a society, but the cow's sacredness to the Hindu prevents starving children being fed on milk and allows useless animals to feed on very limited grazing land.

Just as the religion reflects the needs of the society, so too does the Church usually come to reinforce the State, even though it may not do so in its early stages of development. Under primitive conditions religious and secular authority are often combined, and even in more developed societies the King has often been seen as a manifestation of God, as was the Inca in Peru and the Pharaoh in Egypt.[10] Although the ruler of China, among others, emerged as the supreme authority in both secular and religious matters this did not happen in Europe despite peaks of Papal power (as from 1198 to 1216). However, although the Church in England never became a mere adjunct of the State it has usually used its authority to maintain the *status quo*. This may be symbolized by the fact that twenty-six Archbishops and Bishops of the Church of England still have seats in the House of Lords.

Nearly everyone in Britain seems to think that religion is good for children because it is believed that religion teaches them morality; and it is children (and women over forty-five and those approaching the end of their lives) that appear to be the main source of church congregations. It is this teaching of morality that is sometimes claimed to be the main function of religion and it is said that church members are more likely to be moral than non-churchgoers, the evidence being that church members are less likely to become criminals than other people.[11] However, church membership may not be a sign of deep religious conviction; it may equally well provide that membership of a group which most people require and this church community is likely to have norms which will make it judge harshly someone who gets into trouble with the police. The church member, like other people, will conform to the expectations of his group in order not to be isolated from it. One study of Jews in Leeds showed that drunkenness and juvenile delinquency were less common among Jews than among other members of the community. However, this was probably as much a result of the Jews' desire to protect the good name of their group as it was of the moral code taught by their religion.[12]

It seems to be generally accepted in Britain that the influence of religion is declining; for example, a public opinion poll in 1973 showed that 70 per cent of the people interviewed felt that religion in Britain

Religion and age

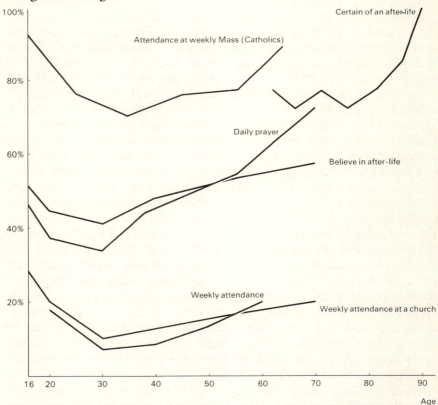

Note. The plots on the graph are taken from various surveys. The top two were carried out in the USA and the others in Great Britain.

Source: M. Argyle, *Religious Behaviour*, Routledge & Kegan Paul 1958

What reasons do you think may account for the decline and increase in religious activity shown in the graph?

was losing its influence.[13] However, it is important to realize that even before the Industrial Revolution a lot of people were indifferent to religion, and when people began to pour into the towns during the Industrial Revolution a lot of them were completely untouched by organized religion.

The only religious census that has ever been taken in England and Wales was in 1851 when it was found that out of a population of 17 927 609 only 7 261 032 people had attended a church or other place of worship on a specified Sunday.[14] At the beginning of this century, Charles Booth in his survey on religion in London found that the only group of people who were greatly influenced by organized religion were the Irish immigrants, and they were 'great beggars, as well as heavy drinkers'.

However, all the research that has been carried out does show that church attendance in Britain is declining. For example, Rowntree and Lavers found that adult attendance at places of worship in York was 35.5 per cent of the adult population in 1901, 17.7 per cent in 1935, and 13 per cent in 1948.[15] As one might expect, the decline seems to be greater in urban than in rural areas. Although there are about 27 million baptized members of the Church of England, about 5 million baptized Roman Catholics, and more than 1 million Nonconformists in England, only a small proportion of these attend a place of worship on a regular basis. In 1964, 94 per cent of those interviewed for ABC Television claimed to belong to a religious denomination but only 20 per cent claimed to go to church on Sundays.[16] More recently, in 1969, Geoffrey Gorer found that out of a nationwide sample of about 2000 people under the age of forty-five most claimed to have a religion, ranging from 72 per cent in South-East England to 81 per cent in the Midlands; most of these claimed to be Church of England (with a maximum of 63 per cent in the South-West) or Catholic (with a maximum of 21 per cent in the North-West).[17] The number of people claiming to have a religion went up steadily with age; from 64 per cent in the sixteen to twenty age range to 81 per cent among those aged between thirty-five and forty-five. However, more people in the sixteen to twenty group attended a place of worship once a week or more (16 per cent). Most people (90 to 94 per cent) attended a church sometimes, even if only for weddings and funerals.

Geoffrey Gorer found that social class made little difference: the lowest proportion of those claiming to have a religion was found in the working class (72 per cent); the highest in the lower middle class (81 per cent). However, a census of Roman Catholics attending mass in South-East England in 1968 showed that while the percentage of middle-class Roman Catholics attending mass was over 60 per cent, working-class attendance was under 40 per cent.[18]

Religion—National Opinion Poll survey, 1965 (systematic probability sample of England, Wales, and Scotland. 2160 people above 21 years)

A. What is your religion?

	%
Church of England	63.4
Nonconformist	10.5
Roman Catholic	10.1
Presbyterian and Church of Scotland	8.9
Jewish	1.3
Atheist/agnostic	1.1
Other religion	3.0
No religion	1.8

B. When did you last attend church?

Within 7 days %	Within 3 months %
6.2	24.1
2.7	5.3
5.4	6.7
1.6	4.1
0.2	0.8
—	0.1
0.8	1.5

Attendance at a place of worship would include occasional events such as baptisms, weddings, and funerals.

C. Religion and age

	21–24 %	25–34 %	35–44 %	45–54 %	55–64 %	65 + %
Base	134	394	435	420	378	399
Church of England	58	63	67	64	61	63
Nonconformist	6	8	7	13	12	16
Roman Catholic	17	15	12	7	9	5
Presbyterian	11	8	9	10	9	7
Jewish	1	1	1	2	2	1
Atheist/ agnostic	3	1	1	1	2	1
Other religion	1	2	2	3	3	6
No religion	3	3	1	1	2	2

Source: New Society

What would have been your answers to the questions in this opinion poll? Try to give an explanation for your answers to the questions in the tables D, E, and F.

D. Should instruction be comparative or Christian only?

Sex	All	Male	Female
Base	2160	1033	1127
	%	%	%
Compare	22.3	25	20
Concentrate	69.4	67	72
Don't know	8.2	8	9

Age	21–24 %	25–34 %	35–44 %	45–54 %	55–64 %	65 + %
Base	134	394	435	420	378	399
Compare	37	26	25	23	17	15
Concentrate	56	67	67	70	73	76
Don't know	8	7	8	7	10	9

E. Should the present school religious arrangements continue?

Age	21–24 %	25–34 %	35–44 %	45–54 %	55–64 %	65 + %
Base	134	394	435	420	378	399
Yes	86	87	91	93	88	93
No	11	11	8	6	10	6
Don't know	3	2	1	1	2	2

Sex	All	Male	Female
Base	2160	1033	1127
	%	%	%
Yes	90.0	87	93
No	8.3	11	6
Don't know	1.7	2	1

F. Is Britain a Christian country?

	%
Britain is a Christian country	79.7
Britain is not a Christian country	19.0
Don't know/no answer	1.3

Breakdown by religion

	C of E	RC	NC	Presby.
Base	521	145	115	88
	%	%	%	%
Is	85	78	70	82
Is not	15	21	29	15
Don't know	1	1	1	3

Although most people in Britain still claim to believe in Christianity, there is evidence of a continued decline in the beliefs associated with it; for example, a survey in 1973 showed that most people still claimed to believe in God (74 per cent) and in heaven (51 per cent), but that most people did not believe in the more unpleasant aspects of religion —only 20 per cent believed in hell, and only 18 per cent believed in

the Devil.[19] Belief in all four aspects of religion showed a decrease since a similar survey in 1967 (between 3 and 4 per cent of the population in each case). It is interesting to note that the belief in reincarnation was the only religious belief tested to show an increase, from 18 per cent in 1967 to 22 per cent in 1973. This belief in reincarnation may be associated with an apparent increase of interest in eastern religion generally. There also seems to be increasing interest in the occult and mysticism.

Just as Christianity was partially a reaction against the corruption of the Roman Empire, so the growing interest in the occult and mysticism may be a reaction against an increasingly materialistic age of which the established churches are seen to be a part. Factual evidence of such a trend, as opposed to sensational stories of witches in the more lurid Sunday papers, is difficult to provide, but one guide may be the increasing number of books on occultism that are being printed. Since 1968, the total number of non-fiction books published annually in Britain has remained fairly static but the number of books on the occult has risen annually—84 in 1968, 148 in 1969, 165 in 1970, 172 in 1971, and 205 in 1972.

Despite the evidence of decline in membership and belief in organized religion it cannot be assumed that the churches are no longer powerful influences in British society. In 1973 the Wells Fund Raising Organization estimated that there were 9 500 000 active members of 53 000 churches, congregations, and synagogues in the United Kingdom. These religious groups gave more than £64 million to their respective churches, but the total income of the churches amounted to £125 million (including £23 million from the Church Commissioners of the Church of England). The same survey found that the Church of England and the Roman Catholic Church were the largest in the United Kingdom with three million active members each and the Moravian Church was the smallest with two thousand members. The active membership and wealth of the churches supports vital social welfare work, as by the Salvation Army, the Society of St Vincent de Paul, the Jewish Welfare Board, Toc H, the YMCA and YWCA, and a host of others, including religious orders engaged in nursing, child care, and old people's homes. Church of England schools are attended by about 11 per cent of pupils in the state sector and there are also many Roman Catholic schools.

Followers of Krishna singing in a Paris street—a sight that is becoming increasingly common in Britain too as interest in Eastern religion, the occult, and mysticism appears to be spreading, particularly among the young.
Why do you think people are interested in these forms of religious expression while conventional church attendances in Britain continue to decline?
Photograph: Keystone

The churches can mount powerful pressure groups in Parliament and elsewhere when legislation on such issues as abortion, birth-control, or divorce is contemplated (39 Jews and 39 Roman Catholics were returned as Members of Parliament in the 1970 General Election). However, the political importance of religion in Britain is very much less than on the mainland of Europe and in America where religion and not class may still be claimed to be the main basis of the political parties, a situation which also applies in Northern Ireland.[20]

The future of religion in Britain is uncertain, although the evidence would suggest a continued decline. For example, the accepted view that women are more religious than men may well be a result of the social and economic situation of women rather than a reflection of a sexual inclination; it appears that working women tend to resemble men in their attitudes to religion and as women increasingly go out to work the church affiliations of this important source of congregations can be expected to decline.[21]

It has been suggested that Christianity has permitted a 'disinterested goodwill' to develop in western society and that this has resulted in our reasonably stable urban society, a stability lacking in non-advanced societies which have developed urban cultures in which bribery and corruption are rife. If this is so, it could be that these societies reflect our future as our residue of religious values and orientation wanes.[22]

On the other hand, it may be that the religious denominations will increasingly reflect secular needs and perform cultural, social, and psychological functions rather than spiritual ones—so that church attendance will become socially desirable. It has been suggested that this 'secularization' of religion accounts for the increasing church attendances in the United States.[23]

However, a movement away from the secular might also lead to more religious involvement, for it may be that if obedience to the social code is seen to depend less on religious beliefs, the churches will feel free to abandon their role of reinforcing the existing social structure and will be able to return to more spiritual objectives, which may in turn appeal to the increasing number of people who seem to be seeking a reason and objective for their lives.[24]

More discussion or written work

1   Does religion do more good than harm?
2   Should children be brought up and educated in a particular religious faith?
3   Nearly all religions claim miracles. How do you account for these?
4   Do you believe in (a) ghosts, (b) extra-sensory perception, (c) foretelling the future? If so, why? If not, why not?

5   What sort of functions does organized religion perform in Britain today?

Research

1   Find out as many examples as you can of religious beliefs seeking to influence social structures and thus causing conflict (for example, Muslim and Hindu in India, Catholic and Protestant in Ireland).
2   Find out what religions (and their denominations) exist in your own town or area. Discover their relative sizes in terms of membership and estimate the size of the non-church-going population, splitting this into age and sex groups if you can.

Imagination

Imagine that you have to found a religion to answer the needs of our society. Try to be entirely detached from your own real beliefs and draw up a suitable 'moral code' system of organization, ritual, and fundamental doctrines.

Reading suggestions

* For an outline of the basic beliefs and practices of the major world religions see *Living Religions* (series of nine booklets), Ward Lock
† J. Brothers, *Religious Institutions*, Longman (paperback)
  M. Argyle, *Religious Behaviour*, Routledge & Kegan Paul
  M. Marwick (ed.), *Witchcraft and Sorcery*, Penguin
  R. Robertson (ed.), *Sociology of Religion*, Penguin (particularly Chapters 9 and 10)
  R. H. Tawney, *Religion and the Rise of Capitalism*, Penguin
  B. Wilson, *Religion in Secular Society*, Penguin

Chapter 7

Politics

Politics is the means by which power is gained and exercised. In this chapter, politics is regarded as the pursuit of power, the stage in power formation where we have an opportunity to exercise our choice over who shall govern us. The exercise of power by those who gain it is examined in the chapter entitled 'Government'.

Power may be desired by a particular group or a particular individual in a society, merely because they enjoy exercising it or because it brings wealth (although wealth itself might be regarded merely as a means of wielding power over others); or it may be that a person or group seeks to gain power in order to put into effect certain ideals, misguided or otherwise.

In a static society, where the existing situation is generally accepted, politics is the pursuit of power for its own sake—as though the attainment of that power was the winning move in some weird adult game. In some societies the rules of this game are clearly laid down, for example by codes of chivalry: there may be a 'close season' in which the serious business of getting the harvest in is carried out before 'the time when Kings ride out to war'. In this sort of situation it may not matter to the vast majority of people who wins or loses the game of politics, just as it did not matter to the common people of England just who happened to be winning the Wars of the Roses at any given moment. Even in a static society there may be an outbreak of idealistic politics, as in the Peasants' Revolt of 1381, but such outbursts tend to be short-lived. The continuous attempt to gain power in order to change the society in which one lives is a fairly modern phenomenon and stemmed from changing ideas about religion during the Reformation, which in turn reflected a change in the structure of society itself.[1]

During the last 400 years, politics in the western world has been concerned mainly with people who wished to change their societies on the one hand, and people wishing to keep things as they were on the other, although the claiming of certain ideals may often be merely the cloak for the 'old-fashioned', power-hungry individual who just wants to get to the top of the human heap and stay there! Some people maintain that such a struggle for dominance is present in any organized group of mammals. Desmond Morris in *The Human Zoo* claims that this battle for dominance is emphasized in the unnaturally confined world of modern society.[2] He goes so far as to state 'ten golden rules' which must be obeyed by all leaders, from baboons to modern presidents and prime ministers:

'1. You must clearly display the trappings, postures, and gestures of dominance.
2. In moments of active rivalry you must threaten your subordinates aggressively.
3. In moments of physical challenge you (or your delegates) must be able forcibly to overpower your subordinates.
4. If a challenge involves brain rather than brawn you must be able to outwit your subordinates.
5. You must suppress squabbles that break out between your subordinates.
6. You must reward your immediate subordinates by permitting them to enjoy the benefits of their high ranks.
7. You must protect the weaker members of the group from undue persecution.
8. You must make decisions concerning the social activities of your group.
9. You must reassure your extreme subordinates from time to time.
10. You must take the initiative in repelling threats or attacks arising from outside your group.'

As with other European countries, politics in Britain changed from local feuding to a battle of ideas during the Reformation. The battle of ideas was probably even more bloody than the old selfish scramble to the top, and plenty of people used the new religious and social ideas for their own ends; but at last the argument was not merely who should rule but how they should rule.

The earliest recognizable political parties in Britain were called Whigs and Tories. The Whigs, named after a group of Scottish rebels, started in 1679, and wanted to limit the power of the monarch and give more power to Parliament; the Whigs became the Liberals with the appointment of Gladstone as Prime Minister in 1868. The Tories, whose name was taken from Irish outlaws, supported the monarchy, opposed the growing power of Parliament, and became known as Conservatives after the Reform Act of 1832. The Labour Party came into existence under its present name in 1906 (although the first Labour Members were elected to the House of Commons in 1892), and replaced the Liberal Party as one of the two biggest British parties in 1922.

Throughout the second half of the last century and for the first twenty years or so of this the battle was between the Liberals and the Conservatives. Many people say that the Liberals were supported by the new middle class of merchants, bankers, and manufacturers whose interests could best be served by change, while the Conservatives were supported by the landowners whose interests were best served by things remaining as they were. However, recent research by J. R. Vincent has suggested that the line-up was not quite so simple and that people tended to vote by occupation and not by class: butchers were predominantly Tory and grocers were predominantly Liberal; Church of England clergymen were Tory, and Methodists and Roman Catholics were Liberal.[3] It is probable that our own assumptions on how people vote today are also pretty inaccurate: there are certainly some very rich men in the Labour Party and some very poor ones among the Conservatives.

However, since 1872 when the secret ballot was introduced we have been unable to keep records as the earlier Victorians did and so we can never be absolutely certain how people vote. In Britain, interpreting voting behaviour has been more difficult than in some other countries because all the ballot papers for a constituency have to be mixed before being counted, so that it is only possible to compare constituencies and not specific areas within them. The detailed study of voting behaviour did not start until the 'scientific' survey by random sampling developed in the 1950s, and although such surveys can be inaccurate because of sampling errors, slanted questioning, incorrect interpretation, and the need for definite rather than qualified answers, they have been proven to have a fair degree of accuracy.

The political survey may be objective and seek definite information to such questions as 'who votes and who abstains?' or 'how do women vote as compared with men?' Or the survey may be subjective and seek to find out people's opinions on specific issues: for example, whether they think the Prime Minister is doing a good job, or whether they think that dog licences should be abolished. Views and voting behaviour may well be inconsistent; for example, in 1959 it was found that most Labour supporters opposed the re-nationalization of steel but still intended to support the Labour Party which was pledged to re-nationalize the steel industry.[4] Another survey in 1960 found that only 32 per cent of Labour voters and only 62 per cent of Conservative voters agreed with their party on seven or more items of policy out of a total of ten.[5]

It is often said that the 'don't knows' decide the results of General Elections.
Do posters like those in the top photograph help people to make up their minds?
The choice is especially difficult when big issues such as Common Market entry cut across party loyalties.
What sort of factors influence the way a person votes in a general election?
Photographs: upper, Keystone; lower, Popperfoto

It is generally assumed that working-class people vote Labour and richer people vote Conservative, with those vaguely in the middle voting Liberal. Although there is some truth in this, the Conservative Party would never be returned to power if it did not attract a large proportion of the votes of manual workers; conversely, the Labour Party attracts a substantial middle-class vote, although this is not so essential to the party's success as the manual workers' vote is to the Conservatives.

In 1958 the Conservative Political Centre published a survey which showed that about 32 per cent of the working class voted Conservative and about 62 per cent voted Labour; this was matched by about 77 per cent of the middle class voting Conservative and about 17 per cent Labour.[6] This finding has been substantiated by other surveys (the Liberal vote tends to be 'a mirror image of the nation').[7] A similar large working-class vote for conservative parties has been found in all Western European countries.

Tradition plays a part in voting behaviour: for example, the son of a manual worker who is now classified as middle class is more likely to vote Labour than someone doing the same kind of job who comes from a middle-class background. Equally a manual worker living in a working-class district is more likely to vote Labour than if he did the same job and lived in a middle-class district. This helps to explain the considerable regional differences in voting behaviour; in Wales, for example, in 1959 Labour received almost a quarter of the middle-class vote.

Women tend to be more right wing than men, perhaps because they are more likely to work in offices where the work may be more agreeable than in factories; older people are more likely to be right wing than the young, perhaps because the old in general find change more difficult to accept.

Religion has little impact on voting habits in England (in contrast with Northern Ireland), but the slight tendency for Roman Catholics to vote Labour is probably because Catholics are often Irish immigrants and Irish immigrants are often manual workers, a class rather than a religious influence.

Most British electors do vote in General Elections despite the fact that about half the Parliamentary constituencies are traditionally safe for one or other of the two larger parties. About 80 per cent of the electorate usually vote, either in the hope that their candidate will win or as a private act of allegiance to a particular party. Some 5 to 8 per cent of electors will no longer be on the voting register or will be prevented from voting, and about 12 to 15 per cent will abstain, possibly because they dislike the policies or personalities of all the candidates that are available, but more probably because they are just not interested. The abstainers are likely to be the old, the young, and poorer people. 'Floating voters' probably only represent about 15 per cent of total voters but they are conclusive in deciding the results of elections.

It would not be correct to assume that the present voting patterns are here to stay: there could well be a swing away from traditional loyalties as the number of white-collar workers increases as a proportion of the population, people move from the centre of urban areas, and the number of owner-occupiers grows.

It has been stated that two-party partisanship reached a peak in 1951, when about three-quarters of the electorate had a strong affinity with one or other of the two largest parties, but that it has been decreasing since as shown by higher abstention rates, increased votes for minor parties, and greater regional variations.[8] This movement away from the two-party system continued in the February 1974 Election when more than 7.5 million people, representing about 25 per cent of those voting, voted for alternative parties or independent candidates. Most of these votes went to the established alternative groups— Liberals, Nationalists, and Ulster political groupings: fringe candidates continued to do badly. All these trends continued in October 1974.

It should be remembered that when political change comes it can come quite quickly; for example, the Labour Party had only twenty-nine Members of Parliament in 1906 yet sixteen years later it had won 142 seats and replaced the Liberals as the second largest party. Some people would claim that the Labour Party represents concrete interests, whereas the Liberal Party is more concerned with general principles than the welfare of one particular group in the society. This difference in approach is said to mean that the changes brought about by the Labour Party have been much less fundamentally radical than those brought about earlier by the Liberal Party. Others, on the contrary, see the Liberal Party as representing conscience-stricken Conservatives and believe that the Labour Party represents the only possibility of radically altering the social structure of British society. Much smaller groups would in turn reject the Labour Party as too bound by the conventions of our society and would advocate some form of communism on the one hand, or fascism on the other. It is probable that there will always be some form of conservative party in British politics and at least one party of change, because these are the two major opinion groups into which people can be split.

Each party represents a wide spread of opinions, but there are so many possible solutions to the problems of society that even three major parties cannot represent everyone's views. Yet minority parties in Britain tend to be small, partly because the big parties give such a wide scope for disagreement within themselves, and partly because the British system of voting makes it very difficult for a small party to get representation in Parliament. The British system of voting, which returns to Parliament the candidate in each constituency who has the most votes regardless of how small the majority may be, has certain advantages—it is simple and it tends to prevent coalition governments which can sometimes be unstable. It does, however, lead to results which some people feel are unfair, and many would say that proportional representation, which has worked well in other countries, notably Canada, the Irish Republic, and Australia, could be equally successful in Britain. In individual constituencies, where there are more than two candidates in an election, it is often found that the candidate returned to Parliament has received less votes than the total votes for his opponents and therefore cannot fairly claim to represent the majority of people in his constituency. One recent result was Liberal 12 489, Conservative 12 432, Labour 6178, and other candidates 198 ;[9] here a Liberal Member of Parliament was returned, although only 12 489 people had voted for him while 18 808 people had voted for his opponents.

Obviously, if a lot of MPs are returned on a minority vote there can easily be a Government which does not represent the majority of voters; indeed, this usually happens! Sometimes there may even be more people voting for its nearest rival party, as happened in 1951 when 13 949 105 people voted for the Labour Party and only 13 718 069 people voted Conservative; the Conservatives formed the Government with 320 out of 630 MPs. In February 1974 the situation was reversed: 11 928 677 people voted Conservative and only 11 661 488 voted Labour; yet the Labour Party ultimately formed the Government with 301 MPs, against the 296 returned for the Conservatives. The Liberals obtained only 14 Members of Parliament for the 6 056 713 votes cast for their party.

Many proposals for proportional representation have been put forward to remedy this situation, including multi-member constituencies, as in Ireland, electing candidates on a quota system (the single transferable vote). One of the simplest systems suggested is the 'alternative vote' which allows the voter to number the candidates in order of preference, as in Australia. Should one candidate obtain an overall majority of votes on the first ballot he is declared elected. If the candidate at the top of the poll does not have an overall majority, the candidate at the bottom of the poll is removed and the second preferences of those who have voted for him are redistributed; the candidate who then has the majority of votes is declared elected. In the example given earlier the second preferences of the voters supporting independent candidates would not have altered the result as an overall majority would still not have been available, but if these second preferences and those supporting the Labour candidate had been redistributed the result

		Labour	Conservative	Liberal	Others	Result
General Election 1945	votes	11 985 733	9 894 851	2 253 197	848 459	Labour
	seats	396*	213	12	16	majority
		(* inc. 3 ILP)				(155 MPs)
General Election 1950	votes	13 318 325	12 149 649	2 621 489	380 495	Labour
	seats	315	298	9	2	majority
						(8 MPs)
General Election 1951	votes	13 949 105	13 718 069	730 552	198 969	Conservative
	seats	296	320	6	2	majority
						(16 MPs)
General Election 1955	votes	12 405 246	13 311 938	722 395	321 175	Conservative
	seats	277	344	6	2	majority
						(59 MPs)
General Election 1959	votes	12 195 765	13 750 965	1 661 262	255 346	Conservative
	seats	258	365	6	1	majority
						(100 MPs)
General Election 1964	votes	12 205 581	11 980 783	3 101 103	368 682	Labour
	seats	317	303	9	—	majority
						(5 MPs)
General Election 1966	votes	13 064 951	11 418 433	2 327 533	452 689	Labour
	seats	363	253	12	1	majority
						(97 MPs)
General Election 1970	votes	12 179 166	13 144 692	2 117 638	903 311	Conservative
	seats	287	330	6	6	majority
						(31 MPs)
General Election 1974 (February)	votes	11 661 488	11 928 677	6 056 713	1 695 315	Labour
	seats	301	296	14	23	minority
						Government
General Election 1974 (October)	votes*	11 468 646	10 429 020	5 345 271	1 944 700	Labour
	seats	319	276	13	26	majority
						(4 MPs)

The Speaker seeking re-election is not included.
* The voting figures for October 1974 are provisional.

could have been different. In 1976 the Hansard Society Commission for Electoral Reform Report advocated proportional representation and tended to favour an 'Additional Member System' under which the Commons would have three-quarters of the members elected under the present system, the remaining seats being allocated to the parties to redress the distorted result produced by the directly elected constituencies.

Alternatively, there could be a mixture of the single transferable vote in urban areas and the alternative vote in rural areas, as unanimously recommended by all three political parties in the 1917 Speaker's Conference. This would obviate huge rural constituencies, but prevent the major loss that the Conservative Party would suffer if the alternative vote was introduced everywhere. (The alternative vote would mainly have the effect of reducing Conservative strength in the rural areas, while the single transferable vote would reduce Labour representation in the urban areas from which the party draws its main support. In most recent General Elections the Liberal Party would have been likely to benefit most from proportional representation.

However, the actual voting for Members of Parliament is only the last step in a process of selection which may be open to more general criticism. Prospective Members of Parliament for the various parties are effectively chosen by local selection committees in each constituency. The selection committees are drawn from the very limited number of political activists who support the party concerned in the constituency. In some cases the committee may be controlled by one powerful local personality.

Although the names that the political parties give to their committees vary, the usual procedure is that a committee of the local political party chooses from a pool of 'approved' candidates when they draw up their short list. These approved candidates will already have been interviewed and vetted by the headquarters of the party concerned. The aspiring applicants who have reached the short list will then be interviewed and ultimately a selected candidate will be recommended for adoption at a meeting of party members. The party members usually accept the recommendation, and the candidate chosen by a handful of people (out of an electorate of 50 000 or so) becomes the 'prospective parliamentary candidate'.

More than two-fifths of all the parliamentary constituencies in Great Britain have not changed their political representation since 1935 (in Wales the proportion rises to more than half), and in these 'safe' seats the MP has, in effect, been chosen by the selection committee of the locally predominant party—even in the seats that are not 'safe' the voters' choice is usually restricted to two or three candidates nominated by the local party organizations. Thus the members of the House of Commons are chosen only partially by election and to a major extent by the process of selection of candidates.

Political parties undoubtedly carry out a vital job in our present constitutional system; ideally, they:

1. seek to overcome the apathy and indifference of citizens
2. seek to educate and inform
3. set a priority scale of values to fulfil the wishes of the many small groups that make up our society
4. select spokesmen and leaders to represent the various branches of national interest
5. undertake the responsibility of election campaigns.[10]

In England only the Labour, Conservative, and Liberal Parties have exercised any powerful parliamentary influence during the last fifty years. A number of new parties have been formed and have returned a few Members to Parliament, but they have either quickly withered and died, like the Common Wealth Party founded in 1943; remained small, like the Communist Party founded in 1920; or have become absorbed in one of the three major parties in the way the Cooperative Party has merged completely with the Labour Party and the National Liberals with the Conservative Party.

In order to stand a chance of election in Britain (and in most other countries) it is essential to be nominated by a political party, for although anyone may stand for Parliament, provided he is not a convicted felon, a lunatic, or a lord, and can find the required deposit and a handful of local electors to sign his nomination papers, it is extremely rare for an 'independent' candidate to be elected and unless there are exceptional circumstances they usually attract a derisory share of the poll. The bulk of any candidate's vote will be for the political party he represents and in normal circumstances the number of personal votes he attracts is unlikely to be more than 500.

Although political parties are a comparatively new arrival on the political scene they have been the backbone of the British system of democracy for over a hundred years. However, some people now suggest that the present political parties are outdated as they stem from the economic interests, political ideas, and nationalism of the nineteenth century. Some countries have turned to a one-party system of government, but this usually endangers personal freedom, although it may actually be a means of extending choice: if one party is in the position of always being assured of a huge majority, at least the electors may have the choice of several candidates from one party instead of one political nominee assured of victory in any case. With increasing specialization all countries will have to find an effective way of controlling 'the expert'; one man with all the information to hand on a specialized subject is likely to get his own way when dealing with others in a superior social position but with less knowledge.

If there is a demand for change in a society and there appears to be no means by which this change can be accomplished by constitutional methods, there may be an attempt to alter the Government by force; most people would accept that there may be circumstances in which such force would be justified. Crane Brinton compared revolution to a kind of fever in the State that destroys wicked people and harmful and useless institutions, just as a fever in the human body is a symptom of a battle that, if successful, will restore the body to health.[11]

The sociologist will look for common factors in revolutionary situations—one such factor is that the society is 'unhealthy' with a large number of its members in a state of misery. There is a theory that revolution occurs as conditions begin to improve—as though in conditions of abject subjugation and poverty people accept their positions as inevitable. A slight easing of the situations seems to be the light at the end of the tunnel; a new vista of a better life is opened, and then that better life is required quickly.

A second common factor in revolution is the need for leadership and support from the middle classes. Rebellion (unsuccessful revolutions) have been attempted without middle-class support, but they are nearly always unsuccessful and remain mere rebellions (for example, in England, Wat Tyler's Peasants' Revolt in 1381 and Jack Cade's rising in 1450). There are occasional exceptions to this rule in situations where there is no real middle class: for example, Toussaint L'Ouverture became the leader of the successful slave revolution in Haiti (St Domingo) in 1791. However, although he was a slave he could read and write and was the 'superintendent' of his estate; he could also call upon the support of the Spanish who occupied a portion of the island. Normally revolutions require a degree of alienation from the government by the middle, and preferably also the upper, classes in a society. The Russian Revolution had middle-class leaders such as Lenin, while the French Revolution had bourgeois leaders like Robespierre.

A successful revolution tends to be led by a charismatic figure who can act as a symbol of unity, drawing the divergent strands of the revolution together. Although the successful revolution is usually directed against a weak government, even a weak government will control a more or less disciplined army and police force and it is therefore essential for the revolutionaries to be well organized and preferably have some support in the armed services. Spontaneous uprisings without prior preparation rarely work, although such a spontaneous uprising may be the signal for a well-disciplined corps of revolutionaries to swing into action.

The frustrated power-seeker will have his greatest chance of success in a well-organized revolution aimed against a weak government in a country where injustice and poverty are rampant. He will launch his offensive as conditions begin to improve and he will have substantial middle-class support with some well-educated leaders (although the charismatic hero figure will not always be in this category). These conditions existed for Fidel Castro in Cuba; they were not all present for Che Guevara in Bolivia.

More discussion or written work

1   'The State the enemy'—how much truth is there in this statement?
2   Do you foresee the present political groupings continuing in Britain unchanged? Suggest alternative arrangements and say why you consider these likely or unlikely to come about.

3 'All power corrupts and absolute power corrupts absolutely.' Do you think this is always so?

4 How important are party politics in local government? Do you think local government is a legitimate field for the activities of political parties?

5 How fair is our system of electing MPs? Do you think any other system would be desirable?

Research

1 Find out the various systems of voting that exist in European countries. Say which you favour and why.

2 Discover what you can about the American system of 'primaries'. Suggest ways in which this system might be adopted in Britain.

Imagination

Imagine that you wish to become an important politician. Describe the steps that you would take in order to achieve your aim.

Reading suggestions

† J. Blondel, *Voters, Parties and Leaders*, Penguin

† G. Roberts, *Political Parties and Pressure Groups in Britain*, Weidenfeld & Nicolson

D. Butler and D. Stokes, *Political Change in Britain: Forces Shaping Electoral Choice*, Penguin

H. Laski, *An Introduction to Politics*, Allen & Unwin

Chapter 8

Trade Unions

A trade union is an organized group of workers in a particular trade or industry who band together to protect and promote their common interests. Sometimes the qualification to join a union depends on the type of job a person does and everyone following a particular occupation may join wherever they are employed; in other cases the qualification is industrial and the union will try to persuade all the employees in a particular industry to join regardless of the job they do. This can cause some friction if more than one union is trying to recruit the same people.

There have been trade unions of a kind for at least two thousand years; the first time a Government in England stepped in to regulate their activities was in 1350 when a great plague had killed off large numbers of the workers and the survivors took advantage of their scarcity value to demand increased wages. However, it was not until the eighteenth century, when the Industrial Revolution had greatly increased the number of workers and concentrated industry into large units, that trade unions as we know them today started to develop, first among skilled craftsmen and then gradually among the unskilled workers.

At first the trade unions encountered harsh opposition from employers who feared that these groups would demand higher wages and who also saw a resemblance between these organized workers and the revolutionary groups in France. A series of Acts of Parliament (beginning in 1799) first prohibited these 'combinations' of workers, with serious penalties for those workers who did combine, and then grudgingly permitted them. At last, in 1875, picketing was made legal; and in the following year it became legal for a body of men to withhold their labour. At the same time the old Master and Servant Act was repealed; this had provided prison sentences for a workman in breach of his contract and only a fine for an employer guilty of exactly the same offence.

In 1887 a Mr Burnett produced a report on trade unions in which he said, 'The trades organizations of Britain have gradually achieved complete emancipation; and there can be no doubt that the freedom which, in this respect, they now enjoy, tends to make them the most contented industrial community in the world.' The grinding misery of the industrial masses of Britain at the turn of the century could hardly have made them contented, but British trade unionism has never experienced the bitter violence of its American counterpart. However, the groundwork was prepared for the mass movement which was to be largely responsible for the changes in the social conditions of the great majority of people in Britain over the next hundred years. In 1910 there were 2.5 million trade unionists; fifty years later there were 10 million. By the end of 1970 there were 481 unions with a total membership of about 11 million. In spite of this increase in membership the actual number of unions has decreased considerably in the last twenty years; although some unions are still very small, over 75 per cent of all trade unionists are in the twenty-three largest unions, more than half being in the largest nine unions (each with a membership of over 250 000). These large unions effectively control the trade union movement because of the 'block voting' system at the Trades Union Congress, whereby the delegates of a particular union have the right to one vote for each member of their union.

The TUC does not itself negotiate over wages and conditions: this is done by individual unions. It is the 'general staff of labour' and is

Trade union membership (United Kingdom)

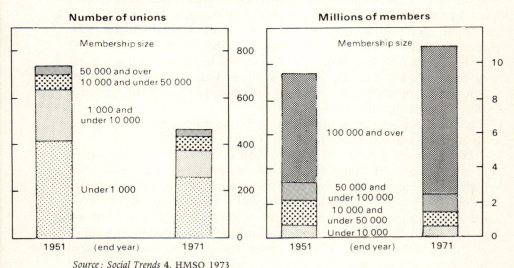

Source: Social Trends 4, HMSO 1973

1   What have been the main changes in the structure of the trade union movement during the period 1951 to 1971?

2   If this trend continues what sort of effects would you expect?

not affiliated to any political party. In 1951 the TUC General Secretary said, 'It is our long-standing practice to seek to work amicably with whatever Government is in power, and, through consultation jointly with ministers and with the other side of industry, to find practical solutions to the social and economic problems facing the country.' However, since the foundation of the Labour Party in 1906 the trade unions have been closely associated with it and contribute the greatest proportion of Labour Party funds. Some people claim that this has meant that the Labour Party has had to do what the unions wish and others think the connection is undesirable because many trade unionists do not support the Labour Party. Most unions include a political levy in their subscription and if a member does not wish to pay it he must 'contract out', that is, sign a document stating that it should not be included in his subscription. Some people feel that most workers are 'afraid' to make this gesture and suggest that the old scheme of 'contracting in' should be reintroduced.

Many Labour MPs are 'sponsored' by a trade union, such as the National Union of Railwaymen, the Transport and General Workers' Union, or the National Union of Mineworkers, and the union will give financial assistance to the Member in paying his constituency organization and fighting General Elections. It may also pay him a retainer to look after the union's interests in Parliament. A few non-manual unions, such as the National Union of Teachers, may sponsor candidates from any of the three major parties but such union nominees have no particular significance in the Conservative or Liberal Parties. The National Farmers' Union which was founded in 1908 with 20 000 members, and now has about 200 000 members, sponsors many Conservative MPs, but the title 'union' is misleading as this is more of an employers' association, farm workers being catered for by the National Union of Agricultural Workers.

The growth of the trade unions has been accompanied by problems, both internal and external.

1. *Demarcation disputes.* These are disputes over 'who does what', and often involve friction between rival unions. Normally it is obvious which jobs should be done by each category of worker, but sometimes it is not clear and then each group of workers tries to protect its own work opportunities. An example of this was the 1968 dispute between the Associated Society of Locomotive Engineers and Firemen (ASLEF) and the National Union of Railwaymen (NUR), who disagreed as to which group should do the job of the second man in the driving cab of the newly introduced diesel engines where firemen were unnecessary.

2. *Closed shop.* The system whereby a union or unions insists that everyone in a particular workplace must belong to them or to one of a number of named unions. It is claimed that this is necessary in order

that the union may represent all the workers in negotiations with the management and it is further claimed that it is unfair for workers who make no contribution to union funds to benefit from agreements made by the union on behalf of its members.

3. *Unofficial strikes.* These are strikes which are not supported by a trade union. Usually official union 'stoppages' take place after lengthy negotiations and after all other methods of reaching a settlement have failed. The unofficial or 'wildcat' strike is often a result of some trivial incident which could have been settled by a display of common sense on both sides. Unofficial strikes are not usually recognized by the general public as in any way different from official stoppages and they give the official trade unions a bad reputation, as well as damaging the national economy and making the workers concerned, and their families, suffer unnecessary economic hardship. The trade unions themselves do their best to prevent wildcat strikes and in June 1969 the TUC General Council undertook to use its authority to deal with 'unauthorized and unconstitutional' stoppages of work; these strikes usually result in more lost working hours each year in Britain than are lost by the official stoppages.

4. *Official strikes.* Official strikes are less frequent than unofficial ones, but when they do occur they are often more prolonged and cause more intensive harm to particular sections of the economy. Although most people agree with the principle that workers may withhold their labour, many people feel that the frequent use of strike action results in the well-organized and comparatively well-off members of the craft unions continually improving their positions relative to the unskilled, less-organized section of the labour market. It is also felt that the majority of workers would not strike as frequently if all strike action had to be ratified by secret ballot—others reply that this is nonsense.

Over the past ten years the number of working days lost in Britain as a result of industrial disputes has been considerably less than the number of days on account of sickness, accidents, and absenteeism. A yearly average of 5.4 million days lost works out at less than a quarter of a working day per worker each year. However, the proportion of working days lost through strike action has been increasing. In 1966 almost 2.5 million working days were lost through strikes, but 20 million were lost through industrial injury and 154 million were lost as a result of sickness; in 1972 almost 24 million working days were lost through strikes, 16 million through industrial injury, and 156 million through sickness.

It is important to keep the impact of strike action in perspective because many people see the trade unions as organizations that are constantly holding the country to ransom rather than as organizations which assist industry to run smoothly by negotiating with employers, by preventing constant unofficial action by their more unruly members, and by helping their members by supplementing payments made under the national insurance scheme, for example, in the event of sickness, accident, or unemployment. However, strikes do damage the economy more than the actual number of lost days would appear to indicate because industry can compensate for days lost through illness by carrying a larger work force, while strike action will often mean the complete loss of all production for a period in a particular industry, or the complete lack of a socially vital service for a time.

Successive Governments have seen it as their responsibility to do what they could to prevent industrial disputes; the Conciliation Act (1896) and the Industrial Courts Act (1919) made it possible for the Government to help to settle disputes in industry by appointing someone to try to persuade the two opposing sides to reach a settlement. These Acts did not prove sufficient to prevent unrest and eventually, in 1971, the Government introduced the Industrial Relations Act 'for the

Industrial disputes

	Working days lost (thousands)					Civilian employment (millions)
	1967	1968	1969	1970	1971	1971
United Kingdom	2 787	4 690	6 846	10 980	13 551	24.3
Belgium	182	364	163	1 432	1 240	3.8
Denmark	10	34	56	102	21	2.3
France	4 204	—	2 224	1 742	4 388	20.5
Germany (Fed. Rep.)	390	25	249	93	4 484	26.7
Irish Republic	183	406	936	1 008	274	1.1
Italy	8 568	9 240	37 825	18 277	12 949	18.9
Netherlands	6	14	22	263	97	4.6
Canada	3 975	5 083	7 752	6 542	2 867	8.1
Japan	1 830	2 841	3 634	3 915	6 029	51.1
USA	42 100	49 000	42 869	66 414	47 417	79.1

Some minor differences in methods of compilation (e.g. some countries do not differentiate between strikes and lock-outs).

In the United Kingdom the approximate number of working days lost through industrial disputes in 1972, 1973, and 1974 were 24 million, 7 million, and 15 million respectively.

Source: Adapted from *Social Trends* **4**, HMSO 1973

1   *Which country has the worst record for working days lost through industrial disputes? How does the United Kingdom's record compare with that of other countries?.*

2   *There seems to be a world-wide tendency for the number of working days lost through industrial disputes to increase. Why do you think this is so?*

Sickness and industrial injury—males (Great Britain)

	Working days lost (millions)						
	1960–61	1965–66	1966–67	1967–68	1968–69	1969–70	1970–71
Days of certified incapacity							
Sickness (excluding absences of more than a year)	138	161	154	171	173	184	160
Industrial injury	17	21	20	21	20	20	17

Source: Adapted from *Social Trends* 3, HMSO 1972

purpose of promoting good industrial relations'.[1] The main provisions of the Industrial Relations Act were:

1. The right of anyone to join a union or not as they wish, unless an agreement has been made between a union and employer, or by two-thirds of the workers concerned voting by secret ballot, by which all workers in the appropriate category must join the union concerned. (With certain reservations if a worker refuses to join on the grounds of conscience.)
2. Written agreements are binding unless otherwise specified.
3. A new system of formal and informal Industrial Relations Courts to hear and settle complaints on unfair industrial practices
4. The right of the Government to apply to the National Industrial Relations Court to order a cooling-off period of up to sixty days when industrial action is threatened and to order a secret ballot of the workers involved if no settlement is reached within that period.
5. The Act also strengthened the Contract of Employment Act (1963) which specifies the minimum period of notice required to terminate a contract of employment and insists on every employee having a contract laying down holiday entitlement, etc. For example, a worker who has been employed for between ten and fifteen years should receive a minimum of six weeks' notice.

The trade unions saw the actual operation of the Act as infringing some of their rights and the TUC decided not to assist with the operation of the Act. In 1972 it voted to suspend the membership of any union which registered under the Act. In practice it was found impossible to operate the Industrial Relations Act, and in 1974 the newly installed Labour Government repealed most sections of the Act.

The unions exist to protect the workman's skill so that it can be hired only in exchange for proper rewards. This is a perfectly justifiable aim and in general the massive trade union machine works well. But although it may be that the Industrial Relations Act was not compatible with the voluntary arrangements preferred by the unions it is in the unions' own interests that some more efficient method than strike

action be found to settle industrial disputes. The strike weapon and the marginal issues such as the closed shop, the political levy, and the block vote lead to obvious injustices which make good copy for the media and bad publicity for the trade unions, so it is vital both for the individuals within the unions and for the unions themselves that issues of this kind can be settled with obvious justice for all concerned.

Up to now the power of the trade union movement has rested upon the number of manual workers among its members, but the number of manual workers in Britain is declining and the number of white-collar workers is increasing so rapidly that they will soon be in the majority.[2] If the trade union movement is to retain its power and continue to play a vital part in the administration of our industrial system it will have to recruit the white-collar workers. The latter are beginning to join unions in increasing numbers; one of the reasons for this may be that the wages of manual workers have increased at a faster rate than those of clerical workers who are now in a relatively worse position than they were before World War II. There may also be other reasons why the clerical worker can now feel that he can identify with a trade union. Civil servants were quickly recruited into the trade union movement because the standardization and grading of their work made the individual aware of his identity of interest with other civil servants.[3] Now large corporations are building up similar bureaucratic structures, in which the clerical workers can establish group identities. Opportunities for the clerical worker to rise to managerial level within his firm are decreasing as firms increasingly recruit graduate management trainees; there is therefore less reason for the routine white-collar worker to identify with the management rather than with manual workers receiving a similar salary to himself. However, white-collar recruitment to the trade union movement is not yet as fast as might be expected. One reason may be that employers try to ensure that staff do not begin to think of membership of a union as appropriate for them.[4]

At present the real power in industry lies with a self-perpetuating group of top managers and a relatively few large shareholders. It might be supposed that the trade unions would be eager to explore the possibilities of remedying this situation and would be the main group putting forward proposals to change the present system of industrial control by co-ownership and co-partnership schemes, the

Dockers march through London in 1972 to protest at the jailing of five of their members for contempt of the Industrial Relations Court. *Do you think there should be laws to control the activities of trade unions?* *Photograph:* Central Press underlying principle of both being that those who invest their labour in a firm have as much right to decide the firm's future as those who invest their money. However, the trade unions have not shown a great deal of interest in changes of this kind, possibly because the unions feel that if more power is given to the employees in a firm their position as organizations designed for the protection of the worker will be weakened. However in 1975 the Government set up the Bullock Committee to examine how industrial democracy could be extended in Britain; the report published in 1977 recommended that the Boards of British Companies with 2000 or more workers should have an equal number of shareholder directors and employee representatives—with a third group of co-opted directors chosen by agreement between the other two parties. The majority of the committee wanted the Trade Unions to be the vehicle for the selection of 'employee directors' and to retain a single board of directors (as happened when worker representation was introduced to Swedish Boards); the minority report however recommended that worker representatives should be selected directly by the workforce and not through the Trade Unions, they also favoured a two-board system on the West German model.

The system operating in West Germany provides a good example of worker–management cooperation. Companies have two boards, a part-time supervisory board which is responsible for basic policy decisions and a full-time management board which runs the day-to-day business of the company. Since 1951 there has been equal representation of shareholders and workers on all supervisory boards in the German coal and steel industries and the workers are also represented on the board of management by an elected 'Labour Director'. In 1975 the system operating in the coal and steel industries was extended to all firms with more than 2000 employees.

In addition to representation on the boards of companies German workers participate in the running of their companies through Works Councils. Under the Works Constitution Act of 1972 (which replaced the 1952 Act) a works council has to be elected in every establishment in private industry employing more than five people, with young employees under eighteen years of age electing their own youth delegation. The members of the works council enjoy protection from dismissal and special privileges; for example, in larger companies the chairman and some other members of the works council have to be free from normal work altogether, with the company paying all the expenses of the council and providing all the facilities for it. In personnel matters management can no longer act alone: hiring, firing, wages, promotion, working hours, and other related activities all require the advance consent of the works council.

This industrial partnership, the fact that there are only sixteen big industrial unions in Germany, and the independence of German trade unions from any political party would appear to be important factors accounting for the peace in German industry and may well be partially responsible for the booming German economy.

Although British trade unions are seen by many people as hotbeds of revolution and instigators of industrial unrest, other people see them as rather timid giants, suspicious of change and slow to seize opportunities to radically alter the power structure of British industry.

More discussion or written work

1 Should workers be compelled to join a trade union?
2 In what circumstances do you feel that strike action is justified? Are there any groups of workers, such as doctors, police, or teachers, who should not be permitted to strike?
3 Is the power of the British trade union movement excessive? Do you think trade unions should be associated with political parties?
4 'Many workers, frustrated, bored, and feeling antagonistic to employers, were just determined to do the best they could for themselves and their small group—I'm all right, Jack' (Dr Roger Tredgold). Is this a fair assessment of the current situation in British society?
5 'The shop steward is the most maligned and misunderstood of men ... he prevents far more crises than he causes. He is a father figure, fighter for justice, and a smoother of wounded feelings' (Dr Robert Murray, medical adviser to the TUC). Comment.

Research

1 Investigate a strike which has occurred in your locality. Try to find out the causes of the strike and say whether you think the strike action was justified. (The local newspaper may be able to help you; try to talk to the people involved in the strike.)
2 Find a country where trade unions are illegal or severely restricted and compare the living standards in that country with those in Great Britain or the United States. Say to what degree you feel that any differences are due to the existence, or lack, of trade unions.

Imagination

Imagine that you are a shop steward of a trade union. Members of your branch are to be made redundant because your firm is experiencing falling sales as a result of keen competition from other producers at home and abroad. There is a high unemployment rate in your area. Decide what action you consider appropriate and write notes for a speech to be given at a mass meeting of your fellow workers.

Reading suggestions

* L. Birch (ed.), *The History of the TUC 1868–1968*, TUC/Hamlyn
† H. Pelling, *A History of British Trade Unionism*, Penguin
† E. Wigham, *Trade Unions*, Oxford University Press
  G. Bain, *The Growth of White Collar Unionism*, Oxford University Press

Chapter 9

Leisure

Leisure may be regarded either as a time for idleness or as an opportunity afforded by unoccupied time. Most people tend towards one or other of these views, and the way people dispose of their leisure will be influenced by their education, their job-situation, their age, and many other factors. Television, for example, is the most obvious influence towards a passive attitude to leisure, while the car is the most obvious tool for a more active role. Yet television may well stimulate some people towards physical and mental activity while acting as a soporific to others; conversely the car may be used in a mindless way or as a vehicle to open up fresh horizons and opportunities. It is possible, however, that in thinking that we should use our leisure in a 'worthwhile' fashion we are merely continuing the puritan ethic which branded idleness as a grave sin, an attitude which took deep root in western thinking and is still with us. We do not usually think of the unemployed as being a leisured class; they may have free time, but it is not leisure.[1]

There may be a tendency to compare our preoccupation with television (an average of nineteen hours viewing per person per week in 1972) unfavourably with what we imagine to have been the more worthwhile leisure pursuits of our forefathers and J. H. Plumb's comments on life in Georgian England may be a useful corrective to this: *'What's My Line?, Coronation Street*, horror comics and glossies, bingo and the pools, are infinitely to be preferred to the mindless, drink-sodden, blood-splashed pastimes of our eighteenth-century forefathers, just as a suburb is better than a slum, health better than disease, a full belly better than an empty one ... and the greatest revolution in social living that has ever happened to man has not only given us bingo and the bomb but also brought to millions of men an appreciation of art, music, literature, and science that would never have been theirs. . . .'[2]

The way we spend our leisure will obviously have a profound effect upon us as individuals and upon the society to which we belong. The populations of the 'advanced' countries certainly have more leisure now than they had a few years ago, although the actual amount of this additional leisure may be disputed. The nominal weekly hours worked by men in manufacturing industries fell from forty-seven in 1938 to forty in 1968, but the fact that figures such as these may be misleading is illustrated by the fact that during this period overtime working increased to compensate almost exactly for the decline in basic working hours. The actual hours worked by men in the manufacturing industries were forty-eight in 1918, still forty-eight in 1938, and had dropped to forty-six in 1968—a drop of only two hours in fifty years! In addition, some five or six hours per week may be spent travelling to and from work (a survey in 1972 found a median journey time from home to work in Greater London of twenty-nine minutes, dropping to twelve minutes in East Anglia),[3] and the time spent in this way may well increase as more people move from inner city areas to new housing estates on the outskirts of the cities. The pressure for a reduction in the nominal working week has often been aimed at obtaining more overtime; in other words, a reduction in the working week has resulted in more pay for many people rather than an actual increase in their leisure.

Although the 'leisure boom' has not yet struck the manual workers of this country, the situation may now be changing rapidly, for between 1968 and 1971 the actual hours worked by men in manufacturing dropped from 45.8 to 43.6. A drop of two hours in three years, compared with two hours in the previous fifty. Up to now British trade unions have not been particularly militant about holidays, but have concentrated on wage claims. However, increased automation will result either in a large body of unemployed or a policy designed to share out the work available. The social and political implications of a large permanent body of unnecessary labour would surely make it essential to concentrate on work sharing, and consequently a change in emphasis from pay to leisure. A fear of inflation may also influence a change of policy from pay increase to other benefits, including holidays. In America sabbatical leave is becoming accepted, and some major companies give their manual workers additional leave of from four to six weeks at intervals of several years: US steel gives its workers thirteen weeks every seven years.

In Great Britain white-collar workers have been more successful than their blue-collar companions in obtaining a genuine reduction in working hours; most now enjoy a thirty-five hour week, do not work on Saturdays, and often have three or more weeks of paid holiday a year. But in Britain even white-collar workers have been lagging

Full house at the Theatre Royal, Margate—you are more likely to find bingo players than actors in theatres today.
Have we a moral obligation to use our leisure in a creative or useful way?
Photograph: The *Daily Telegraph*

behind the rest of Europe when it comes to the amount of time devoted to holidays. In Britain the average total of holidays a year per person in the mid-sixties was about 18 days; the French, however, got 35 days, the Italians 39, and even the Germans took 28 days.[4] However, the basic entitlement to annual holidays with pay has been increasing rapidly in Britain: in December 1969 50 per cent of all full-time workers had two weeks or less and 1 per cent had more than three weeks; by May 1973 the number entitled to two weeks or less had dropped to only 7 per cent while the number entitled to more than three weeks comprised 48 per cent of all full-time workers.[5] At least one commentator has seen the growth of holidays as encouraging democracy: 'in a bathing costume there are no longer bosses and workers'.

Although white-collar British workers may not enjoy the same leisure as their continental neighbours, they do have a privileged position compared with British blue-collar workers, and this alone will

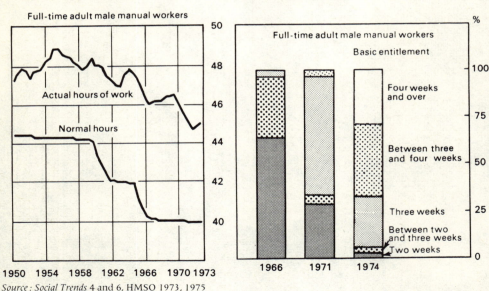

Weekly hours of work (United Kingdom)

Full-time adult male manual workers

Actual hours of work

Normal hours

1950   1954   1958   1962   1966   1970 1973

Annual paid holiday (United Kingdom)

Full-time adult male manual workers

Basic entitlement

Four weeks and over

Between three and four weeks

Three weeks

Between two and three weeks

Two weeks

1966   1971   1974

Source: Social Trends 4 and 6, HMSO 1973, 1975

1   *What evidence is there in the charts of increased leisure among adult male workers?*
2   *Compare the information given here with the hours of work and holiday entitlement of people known to you.*

lead to an expansion of leisure as the number of white-collar workers continues to rise relative to the number of blue. There is already one white-collar worker to every three blue-collar workers.

Apart from the rationing of leisure by employment there is also a rationing by age, for the young and the old have more leisure time than the middle-aged, and the proportion of young and old people in our population has been increasing. In Britain there are now 40 per cent more people aged over fifty-five than there were in 1951 and there are 30 per cent more people aged under twenty-five. These two age groups now make up more than half the total population. Even so, it has been suggested that the dramatically falling birth rate in Britain may lead to a dangerous shortage of young people in the future—and might even lead to an obligation on all women to have at least two children in order to maintain the population at a reasonable level![6]

The future expansion of leisure is likely to affect us all but will probably have its most profound effect initially on the elderly. The retired are already our largest class and the proportion is likely to increase. Since the passing of the 1946 National Insurance Act compulsory retirement at sixty-five has become normal for male workers; some companies now encourage retirement at sixty, and the age is likely to drop further still. Early retirement is one of the obvious ways of rationing a shrinking amount of available work, and where the work is largely physical the younger man is usually more able to cope with it; both the mining industry and the Dock Labour Board now give financial inducements to men who are prepared to retire early. In a situation where skills are changing rapidly it is also more economic to re-train younger rather than older men, and in the skilled trades and in some professions men are increasingly likely to be retired early. Men and women are also living longer: in 1910 the proportion of people in England and Wales aged over sixty-five was about 7 per cent; in 1960 it had risen to almost 12 per cent; and by 1980 is likely to be about 15 per cent. The retired are the people most likely to have time on their hands, but they are also likely to be those with the least money to spend during this enforced leisure.

A survey conducted by W. E. Beveridge in 1965 highlighted the situation.[7] The general feeling of those who took part in this survey might be summed up by one man who said: 'You're not wanted; you're on the scrap heap.' There seemed to be three main areas of loss to those who had retired. The first was social: 'You used to go in in the morning and it was, "Hi George" from your friends. You miss all that.' The second was financial, with consequent loss of status: 'It's better to stay at home if you can't pay your way.' The third loss was one of direction: 'It took six months to get used to having him around the house. You've got to be patient with him for it's a difficult life for him.'

Some thought is now being given to encouraging retired people to remain socially active and many educational establishments have introduced pre-retirement courses which serve as introductions to the many activities arranged in the field of adult education which are available to retired people (often free of charge), as well as giving them help in planning financially and otherwise for their retirement. There is, however, a natural reluctance to face up to the necessity of retirement and if these courses are to be successful they should really be attended some five or six years before retirement, so that people can be encouraged to build up new interests and plan for their retirement over a fairly long period. Young workers often receive day-release from their firms in order to help them to prepare for their careers, and those approaching retirement might also be given the same opportunity to prepare for the fourth quarter of their lives. A few enlightened firms have already adopted such a policy. However, in a society which has prepared people for work rather than for leisure it is obvious that many people cannot be suddenly trained to completely re-orientate their view of life. 'If your chief joy in life has been operating a capstan lathe, it is a little difficult to think of a similar satisfaction when economics and politics say you ought to stop. In practice, such men tend to spend their time talking about the past and waiting for each other to die.'[8]

Some firms have also opened a part-time department for retired workers. These departments are organized on very free and easy lines with the workers involved being paid for the hours they actually work. The retired person retains his sense of usefulness, a routine, the company of his or her old workmates, and some additional income. If the opportunities are made available, retirement need not be the end of active life but the beginning of a satisfying period of new interests and activities. One man known to the author spent all his working life in a shoe shop and now spends all his spare time oil-painting, something he has always wanted to do, but never had the time for.

The second largest leisured group is the young, and they are already catered for in their leisure much more than are the old. Schools and youth clubs are the main agencies caring for the under-sixteens and there is a host of commercial concerns waiting to welcome the new rich—the young worker who has not yet taken on family commitments.

Some people now claim that we are leaving the era in which leisure was a time to recuperate for work and approaching the era in which work is a time to earn money to spend in our leisure; leisure is certainly receiving more serious consideration from official agencies. But a survey by the North-West Sports Council carried out in 1972 suggests that the age of leisure has not yet fully dawned: the old have most leisure; the young marrieds least; with the middle-aged men bearing the heaviest work burden of forty-eight hours a week with 23 per cent

Chief leisure activities[1]

	Males %	Females %
Television	23	23
Reading	5	9
Crafts and hobbies[2]	4	17
Decorating and house/vehicle maintenance	8	1
Gardening	12	7
Social activities[3]	3	9
Drinking	3	1
Cinema and theatre	1	1
Non-physical games and miscellaneous club activities	5	4
Physical recreation:		
(i) as participant[4]	11	4
(ii) as spectator	3	1
Excursions	7	7
Park visits and walks	5	5
Anything else	7	7
No answer or 'don't know'	3	4

[1] Figures relate to the urban population of England and Wales, excluding Inner London, and are based on a sample of 2682 persons aged 15 and over.
[2] For women, mainly knitting.
[3] Visiting or entertaining friends and relatives.
[4] Includes dancing.

Source: Adapted from *Social Trends* 3, HMSO 1972

1   *Why do men and women spend their leisure time in different ways?*
2   *How far are the averages given in the table typical of the way that people you know spend their leisure?*

working at the weekend.[9] Although, curiously, some of those with least leisure time make intense use of it in time-consuming pursuits such as sailing and golf, the survey confirmed the conclusion of other studies that passive recreation dominates. Seventy-one per cent of the sample had taken at least one full 'day trip' in the previous twelve months, while only 37 per cent had participated in any form of sport. An earlier study in 1965 showed that although a typical evening at home was likely to be spent in front of the television there was a growing demand for cultural pastimes.[10] Book production and library loans had increased far faster than the population. Interest in the theatre, classical music, art, and creative hobbies had never been greater, and almost four million people seriously pursued 'do-it-yourself' hobbies, the annual turnover of the 'do-it-yourself' industry being estimated at £350 million. The 75 000 water skiing enthusiasts often competed with the 500 000 sailing enthusiasts for the same water, and in the ten years from 1955 to 1965 the number of underwater sportsmen had trebled. Membership of the Camping Club had risen from 18 000 in 1954 to 85 000 in 1965. The number of golfers had doubled between 1945 and 1965 to one million, and by 1965 there were 30 000 serious birdwatchers and 43 000 members of the Ramblers' Association. The survey found that even foxhunting had increased in popularity, with more packs in existence than there had been in 1939.

The same study concluded that free time in Britain was used more actively, more imaginatively, and was more organized. The reasons given for this change were more money (the big growth being in holidays and sophisticated leisure equipment), more education for more people (the better educated being more active), more working women (the rapid rise in married women in the labour force creates new leisure demands outside the home), more mobility (over 40 per cent of all families now own a car), more white-collar workers, more leisure time overall, more young and more old people.

A report called *Britain 2001 AD*, prepared for Post Office Telecommunications, shows that by the year 2001 one in every two people will have a car, there will be a four-and-a-half day working week, and seven weeks' holiday a year will be normal. Looking a little further ahead there may come a day when the alarm no longer rings for us on a grey November morning, or on any other day for that matter. Most of the routine work will be done by automated devices. Some see automation and mechanization as the means by which capitalists will throw workers on the scrap heap in order to reap the harvest of their unpaid mechanical slaves. One example to support this view may be seen in Harlan County in America's Appalachian mountains which is officially described as 'extremely poor' with rampant illiteracy and ill-health. Rich seams of coal run under the area, but the strip-mining which was introduced twenty years ago has reduced employment by 75 per cent— one machine, 'Big Muskie', lifts 325 tonnes of soil from the surface in one scoop.

Other people will claim that such a situation can only occur in isolation and that in the long term it would not benefit the capitalist, since unless everyone has adequate money to buy goods there is no purpose or profit in producing them. In fact, the non-consumer is as much an enemy of society as the non-producer, perhaps in the technological age a greater enemy! It would appear that arrangements will somehow be made to maintain a market, even if only for economic reasons, and that adequate funds will be made available to the 'non-producers'.[11] The pay cheques will arrive on the mat unearned. What then? Without exercise our minds do not develop, just as our legs would grow weak if we did not use them. Without work we might wilt, physically and mentally, perhaps finding an outlet for our energies in violence and aggression. On the other hand, automation and increased mechanization could mean that instead of being forced, by the need to earn a living, to do a job that we loathe, dislike, or are merely indifferent to, we could fulfil ourselves as human beings in art, sport, mechanics, gardening, or whatever branch of human achievement interests us most.

More discussion or written work

1 'The engineer of the future must develop a feeling of social responsibility, possibly take a Hippocratic oath, and make only those machines mankind actually wants.' What do you think?
2 Does the job we do have a great influence on how we spend our leisure time?
3 'With increasing affluence there may be a problem of preserving the countryside or the coast, a traffic congestion problem, a noise problem, a litter problem. But a leisure problem? No!' What do you think are the major problems connected with shorter working time?
4 With the inevitable expansion of leisure do you think it would be desirable to produce a society that is sport-orientated rather than work-orientated? Consider the implications of a society in which athletic prowess became the measure of status. Do you think there are other human activities upon which society could be based?
5 What effect would you expect increased leisure to have on educational expectation and provision?

Research

1 Try to discover the main leisure activities in your locality. As far as you can, relate these activities to the age and class of those engaged in them.
2 Discover how the pattern of leisure activities has changed during this century and account for these changes.

Imagination

Imagine that machines and computers have taken over most of the work previously done by human beings. Describe a typical day in the life of a non-employed man who was previously a semi-skilled worker.

Reading suggestions

Nels Anderson, *Work and Leisure*, Routledge & Kegan Paul
H. Bracey, *People and the Countryside*, Routledge & Kegan Paul
R. Glasser, *Leisure—Penalty or Prize?*, Macmillan
D. Thompson (ed.), *Discrimination and Popular Culture*, Penguin

Chapter 10

Pressure Groups

A 'pressure group' is any group of people who seek to influence events. The group may come together to fight for one specific issue and remain in existence for many years before this aim is realized: for example, the Abortion Law Reform Association was founded in 1936 with the object of legalizing abortion, but had to wait until 1967 before its aim was achieved. On the other hand, the pressure, or interest, group may exist only briefly in order to prevent some specific action that they feel threatens their locality, such as the building of an international airport or the holding of a pop festival: for example, the Save the Avon Gorge group that successfully resisted the building of a hotel which they felt would spoil the view of Brunel's suspension bridge spanning the River Avon.

The most potent of all pressure groups are the political parties but as these are dealt with under 'politics' we shall here only consider other groups which seek to change government policy or influence administrative decisions without themselves taking over executive power. The group may be a permanent organization representing the sectional interests of its members; groups in this category may be divided into those based on economic interests, and those representing non-economic sectional groups. They only become 'pressure groups' when they try to influence the Government or other public authority. The economic-interest groups can be subdivided into (*a*) the labour lobby, including all the trade unions which are members of the TUC, (*b*) the business lobby, including organizations such as the Confederation of British Industry, and (*c*) the professional lobby, including such groups as the British Medical Association. These groups have been so successful in persuading us that what they say should be heeded that it has become a constitutional convention for the Government to consult them before introducing legislation that might affect their interests. The non-economic-interest groups are such organizations as the churches, the RAC, Oxfam, the Ramblers' Association, and hundreds of other organizations whose prime functions are far removed from the exercise of political power but who will move into action in special circumstances.

Some people regard pressure groups as a danger to democracy.

Others feel that not only are they not dangerous to our political system but they are positively necessary for the proper functioning of that system. It is felt by some that under two-party government, with the ruling party safely in power for several years at a time, the gap in debate and opposition between elections must be filled by pressure groups, and that these groups form the link between government and governed, and enable the people to participate.

S. E. Finer in his study of pressure groups, or 'the Lobby' as he prefers to call them, had two main criticisms of these groups.[1] Professor Finer felt first that the Lobby was a very lumpy kind of self-government in which some associations carried much greater weight than others although without any intrinsic superiority. Secondly, he felt that the very process by which the group brought those they wished to influence into discussion would shut the general public out. However, Professor Finer found that, in general, pressure groups do perform a useful service in that they tell ministers and civil servants how people 'feel': 'Anger, contempt, or pleasure, expressed at first hand, are a valuable corrective to the bald facts of the case in an office file.'

With the exception of the trade unions and the Cooperative Societies, nearly all pressure groups declare that they are non-political. The Institute of Directors states, 'The Institute is far from being a political organization. It has no party ends to serve and no political allegiances.' It then goes on to declare: 'Any enemy of the free enterprise way of life, whatever his political views, is our opponent.' 'Non-political' in the sense used by pressure groups usually means merely that the organization is not affiliated to a political party. It is often clear that one or other of the political parties is likely to support the aims of the group, and most pressure groups try to get their own representatives into Parliament.

The measures used by pressure groups to put their views before the public form a seemingly endless list. They include the conventional ones—petitions, leaflets, films, television publicity, press coverage, posters, advertisements, sympathetic Members of Parliament, lobbying—and the less conventional (sometimes overflowing into the illegal), sit-downs, work-ins, barricades, occupations, and the like.

Petitions are still one of the favourite tools of those who wish to publicize the number of people who support a particular viewpoint. Sometimes a petition may rebound on the organizers if few signatures are collected, or if the signatures are found to be fraudulent. The most famous petition is probably the great petition presented in 1839 by the Chartists which reputedly contained over a million signatures; the Chartists' third monster petition of 1848, for which they claimed six million signatures, was found to contain only two million when counted, a great number of which were false (perhaps deliberately planted), and this helped the Government to discredit the Chartists and refuse their requests for reforms.

The most effective publicity now comes from television and newspaper coverage and although most newspapers have political connections many people feel that television has remained reasonably impartial in Britain, although there are complaints of political bias from time to time. It seems that in Britain an organization's wealth is now very much less important than its potential news value so far as publicity in the media is concerned.

However, publicity is not always the best way for pressure groups to achieve their ends and the big corporations in particular may find it more effective to work quietly in Whitehall, directly with the departments of government and the ministers whose cooperation they require. Pressure of this kind is difficult to illustrate as secrecy may be essential to its success, but one example may be the relationship between the Government and the National Farmers' Union which has been described as 'unique in its range and intensity'.[2] In 1971–72 government support to the industry was £339 million and this enormous sum of money is distributed in the form of grants and subsidies which are negotiated between the NFU and the Government annually. Usually the two sides reach an agreement, but if their negotiations do break down as in 1965 the farmers engage in more public methods of exerting pressure, such as tractor parades through London. In this particular case public money is involved and so the ultimate result of the pressure behind the scenes is public knowledge; however, where giant corporations gain government agreement for proposals which may earn the corporation great wealth but at no direct cost to the public purse it may be impossible for us to know anything of the way in which government policy has been influenced. Professor Finer comments on this sort of activity: through this secrecy 'the lobbies become—as far as the general public is concerned—faceless, voiceless, unidentifiable; in brief, anonymous'.[3]

One of the most successful pressure-group campaigns was waged by the British Medical Association, representing two-thirds of the country's doctors, against the Labour Government in 1945–46. The Labour Government wanted to introduce a salaried health service run by a Public Health Authority and the then Minister of Health, Aneurin Bevan, took up an attitude of 'non-negotiation', stating that the Government had been elected to rule and that it would decide the future of the British medical service. However, the doctors stated that they would not operate the service if it was introduced, and as a result the doctors have remained as independent operators, being paid on a formula by the number of patients registered with them rather than by a straight salary.

Another successful major campaign was waged by the advocates of commercial television who set up the Popular Television Association[4] in 1953 and waged a campaign which Lord Reith, the former Director General of the BBC, described as 'one of the most deplorable, subversive, and shocking actions in British history'. The opponents of commercial television saw it as an opportunity for a small number of people to make a great deal of money, and they foresaw a lowering of television standards. Those who supported commercial television saw it as an opportunity to break the monopoly of the BBC and to provide much higher quality, and a much greater variety of programmes, all at no cost to the public. A tremendous stream of feature articles by well-known people and letters to the press started a campaign which was eventually successful.

An even more contentious victory, the aftermath of which exists today, was the success of the Orange Lodges in the northern province of Ireland in preventing the inclusion of six of the nine counties of Ulster in a united Ireland, when the Home Rule Bill for Ireland was introduced in 1912. This is an example, rare in Britain, of a pressure group's campaign being backed by the threat of violence. Ultimately, the event culminated in the so-called Mutiny at the Curragh in which the majority of the officers at the big Curragh army camp said that they would resign their commissions if they were ordered to fight the Orangemen; the start of World War I prevented a showdown.[5]

Ultimately, the success of a pressure group will depend upon whether it can persuade Parliament to introduce or withdraw legislation, or whether it can persuade a local authority to adopt a particular course of action. Its success in gathering public support is only important in so far as public support may influence local councillors or Members of Parliament. Often, lobbying achieves nothing. One of the biggest ever attempts to influence MPs was in 1967 when great numbers of people wrote to their MPs protesting against the Bill designed to ban pirate radio stations; the lobbying was totally ineffective and the Bill became law. Propaganda from virtually every nation in the world is showered upon MPs—much of it remains unread!

Members of Parliament may themselves belong to pressure groups and their membership of these groups will usually be known before they are elected. Should an elector feel sufficiently strongly his feelings may override his usual political loyalties, but it is unlikely that a selection committee would allow a candidate to go forward who belonged to a group to which a large section of the electorate was hostile.

Most trade unions sponsor MPs, that is they pay a contribution towards the candidate's election expenses (not more than 80 per cent) and may continue to contribute to his constituency funds and help to pay the salary of his constituency agent. Some 130 of the Labour MPs

elected in 1970 were sponsored by trade unions. Although the sponsored MPs are expected to watch over the union's interests in the House of Commons the unions cannot dictate to MPs what they should do in Parliament. Some unions (such as the Post Office Engineering Union) do not have a sponsored Member of Parliament, and such a union may ask an MP to act as its political consultant in return for a contribution towards his parliamentary expenses. This practice of more directly paying an MP to represent the interests of a particular group has developed over a wider field during the last twenty years and many members are paid retainers of £500 a year or more to represent commercial or other interests. Just as trade unions are likely to be represented by Labour MPs the commercial interests are generally represented by Conservative MPs.

Since 1974, a Member of Parliament may receive up to £7000 a year (salary £4500, secretarial expenses £1750, overnight allowances up to £750), but the expenses of MPs are likely to be heavy. Although many MPs may have non-parliamentary incomes, particularly from legal practice, it is the genuine full-time member who is most likely to feel the need to accept 'retainers' from outside interests.

In July 1947 the House of Commons passed a resolution which declared: 'It is inconsistent with the dignity of the House, with the duty of a Member towards his constituents, and with the maintenance of the privilege of freedom of speech, for any Member of this House to enter into any contractual agreement with an outside body, controlling or limiting the Member's complete independence and freedom of action in Parliament, or stipulating that he shall act in any way as the representative of such outside body in regard to any matters to be transacted in Parliament, the duty of a Member being to his constituents and to the country as a whole, rather than any particular section thereof.' This view is reinforced by Erskine May's *Parliamentary Practice*, which is the main guide for MPs: this records a resolution of May 1695 which states that 'the offer of money or other advantage to any Member of Parliament for the promoting of any matter whatsoever, depending or to be transacted in Parliament, is a high crime and misdemeanour and tends to the subversion of the English Constitution.' It is unlikely that any MP offends against the letter of these resolutions, but it is possible that some may offend against the spirit. However, the limelight of publicity that shines on Parliament probably prevents any serious abuse by pressure groups and it may be that greater influence may be

Squatters occupy an empty house in London which is being let as offices.
In what ways can individuals influence authority in this country? How effective is this influence likely to be?
Photograph: Keystone

exerted on local authorities where the publicity is not so intense. This possibility has been highlighted by the 'Poulson Affair' in 1972–73 when a number of high-ranking local government members were found guilty of accepting bribes in return for awarding contracts to John Poulson's firm of architects.

Christopher Mayhew has expressed the view that 'no MP should be paid to represent any vested interest in Parliament',[6] but there may be nothing ethically wrong in being a parliamentary representative on a board of directors or a trade-union-sponsored MP. In fact such contact between the worlds of work and of Parliament may be a good thing. But it has been suggested that such arrangements should be public knowledge and that the American practice of registering lobbyists and of having an official register of the financial interests of Members of Parliament would make the activities of pressure groups less likely to provoke criticism. In 1967 the Liberal Party introduced a register which lists the financial interests of their Members of Parliament; and a Select Committee of the House of Commons was set up in 1969 to enquire into the advisability of such a register for all members. In June 1975 the final report of the select committee was debated by the House and it was decided to establish a compulsory register 'of any pecuniary interest, or other material benefit, which a Member may receive, which might be thought to affect his conduct as a Member, or influence his actions, speeches or vote in Parliament'. This 'Register of Members' Interests' was first published in November 1975.[7]

It would be quite wrong to suppose that pressure groups generally are small groups of people who seek to benefit at the expense of the majority. On the contrary, they may well provide the general public with their most effective means of making their views known to those in power, and often the people of a locality may successfully preserve their environment against the big battalions by joining together to exert pressure. It is a sad fact of life that people are likely to be ignored by the authorities until they make a nuisance of themselves!

More discussion or written work

1 'Money buys power.' How true is this statement?
2 Are there any circumstances in which a pressure group is justified in using violence or the threat of violence to achieve its end?
3 Should Members of Parliament represent business and other interests? If so, should they receive payment for doing so?
4 In what ways do you think that pressure groups could be dangerous to a democracy?
5 Pressure groups are merely safety valves which are tolerated by those who really control the country. How true is this statement?

Research

1   Discover a local pressure group that has operated in recent years in your community. Examine the methods used by this pressure group and try to explain why it was successful or unsuccessful.
2   Find out what sort of pressure groups exist in another country and assess how much influence they possess.

Imagination

Imagine that there is some specific local or national issue on which you feel strongly. Draw up a programme outlining the ways in which you would try to have your opinion accepted.

Reading suggestions

† S. Finer, *Anonymous Empire, Pall Mall Press*
  C. Hall, *How to run a Pressure Group*, Dent
  H. Wilson, *Pressure Group*, Secker & Warburg
  G. Roberts, *Political Parties and Pressure Groups in Britain*, Weidenfeld & Nicolson (Chapters 5–9)

Part Three
Power Over Us

Chapter 11

Government

Anarchists want to abolish all organized authority. They regard all government as evil and seek to establish a situation where individuals can live together without armed forces, courts, prisons, or written law. Tolstoy, for example, urged people to refuse to pay taxes, recognize the courts, or join the military forces—he thought that 'love could rule'. However, anarchism has never succeeded in establishing itself in any country and all countries now have a government of one sort or another. Governments can be broadly classified into three groups, autocracies, oligarchies, and democracies, although most governments have features from all three categories.

Autocracies are governments controlled by one man, either a dictator or an absolute monarch (who is effectively a hereditary dictator). Often a dictator is virtually worshipped and appears to have an almost magical ability to inspire awe—a quality which sociologists call charisma. People may often be prepared to accept one-man rule rather than what they believe to be the chaos of anarchy or weak government. Originally 'the dictator' was elected in ancient Rome when the State was in danger. He was given power of life and death with no appeal against his decisions—officially he was given power for six months and he usually resigned when the danger was past. Most modern dictators also come to power when the State appears to be in danger, but they rarely resign when the danger is over (General Franco became chief of the Spanish State (El Caudillo) in 1936). No dictator could rule without an inner ring of supporters, and so in all autocracies there will be an element of oligarchy (rule by a group).

An *oligarchy* is a group of people who control a government (this group is often part of the aristocracy and may sometimes be a group of priests called a theocracy). The longest lasting oligarchic government was the noble oligarchy of Venice. There is usually an element of oligarchy in every democracy.

Democracy is literally 'government by the people'. A direct democracy would be a country in which people decided everything concerned with the ruling of the country for themselves by public meetings or referendum, as in some of the city-states of ancient Greece. However, big modern states would find direct democracy impossible to operate and are forced to have an indirect democracy in which the people elect a parliament to represent their wishes.

In Britain and the West, democracy implies a parliament elected at regular intervals by free elections with an executive responsible to the elected parliament. We also expect to find other features in a democracy. For example, we expect to be charged with an offence if we are arrested, we expect freedom of speech and opinion, and we expect to be able to join any organization we like which is not obviously criminal. There are some non-democratic aspects to British government (some of which are mentioned elsewhere in this book), but in general people in Britain do have an opportunity to express their views and a chance of having these views implemented. Democracy in Britain does not mean that 'elites' do not exist but that these elites cannot do as they wish without being challenged. The western interpretation of democracy would not be accepted in Russia or other communist countries, where the private ownership of wealth would be regarded as undemocratic, as would the purchase of superior opportunities in health or education. Communist governments would claim that in their countries private interests are subordinated to the common good and because of this they would claim to be democratic; however, most people in Britain would regard these countries as oligarchies run by the caucus of a political party.

The sort of government a country has will depend largely upon its history. The more unified a country is in terms of history, language, territory, and culture the more stable that country is likely to be: the differing histories of the Catholics and Protestants in the north of Ireland has resulted in a lack of common identity; the difference in language between the Walloons and the Flemings in Belgium has contributed to unrest; the big physical gap between West and East Pakistan was a factor in the establishment of a separate state of Bangladesh; the differing cultures within the Federation of Nigeria led to the unsuccessful rebellion of Biafra. This rebellion in Nigeria illustrates the difficulties which have arisen in many former colonial territories which have gained independence as a unit, although their original formation by the colonizing power had been quite arbitrary, tribes with a distinct cultural identity often being divided under the jurisdiction of different European countries. When all parts of a nation have in common most of the unifying factors—history, language, territory, and culture—a single government will usually rule the whole country (a unitary system of government). When there are divisions of language, history, or culture, particularly where the territory is very large, a federal system of government is more usual. This means that the national government will retain control over those aspects of government, such as defence, which affect a nation as a whole; while

Military power in Greece—the colonels taking a salute in 1972.
Photograph: Camera Press

The two political systems reflected here could be called democracies.
What degree of autocracy and oligarchy are suggested in these photographs?
What advantages and disadvantages do you think an autocracy or oligarchy can have compared with a democracy?

Chinese airmen expressing Mao's thoughts.
Photograph: Central Press

the local 'State' governments will control more personal aspects of life such as education and law enforcement.

In Britain there is a unitary government with local authorities who have powers delegated to them by the central Government, but the central Government retains ultimate control over all services. In the United States, with its federal system of government, each State controls its own internal affairs; for example, one State can abolish capital punishment whereas another may retain it.

The legal head of the British State is the 'King or Queen in Parliament'. The monarch must sign all legislation before it is put into effect and normally does so as a matter of course. However, the monarch may be in a position to influence events. The power of the monarch has been called a 'reserve of power', because if he or she refused to sign a piece of legislation it is almost certain that a democratic Government would feel obliged to call for the monarch's abdication or to abolish the monarchy altogether. Such a move would provoke a major constitutional crisis, and it is probable that most Governments would bend their legislation a little to prevent such a situation arising. Additionally, most kings or queens reign while several Governments, often of differing political parties, come and go—they are in a position to advise Governments of past, often private, events which may not be known to the Civil Service. It is essential that the monarch does not present a political viewpoint. In this way he or she remains acceptable to whatever Government comes to power. By remaining above party politics some people believe that the monarchy becomes a unifying feature in British society and a focal point for national affection—fulfilling the same role in Britain as 'the Flag' does in America! It may be significant that so many countries with constitutional monarchies—Great Britain, Holland, Denmark, Norway, and Sweden—are among the most democratic. Monarchists also point out that if Britain became a republic it would still have to pay a president, keep the palaces in repair, and pay for the same sort of state banquets and garden parties. The cost per head of population for Britain's Head of State does, in fact, compare favourably with the cost of others in Europe. It is also suggested that if we ceased to pay the Queen's 'Civil List' we would have, in exchange, to return the Crown Estates handed over to the country by George III which now bring in revenue considerably in excess of the cost of the Civil List.

Not everyone would accept this view of the monarchy. Some would say that the hereditary principle is an anachronism in modern society and that the official acceptance of such a principle perpetuates the class structure of British society.

However, the main official power in the country is exercised through the *House of Commons*, from which the Prime Minister and most of his

Cabinet are drawn. Up to 1974 the House of Commons consisted of 630 MPs elected at intervals of not more than five years; constituency boundary changes have increased this number to 635. Within the five-year period the *Prime Minister*, who is also the leader of the governing party, can call a General Election at any time; he is most likely to do this when the feeling in the country is favourable to his party. There has been a constitutional convention that the Prime Minister would call an election if defeated on a major issue in Parliament. But if the Prime Minister feels he can attract majorities on other issues he is likely to retain office even when defeated, as happened in March 1976 in the Public Expenditure Debate.[1] However, the threat of dissolution is a useful weapon to hold over the heads of the governing party's more unruly backbenchers, many of whom will hold marginal seats which they may lose in a General Election. About one-third of all MPs in the governing party

Education and occupation of MPs, 1918–70

Figures are percentages	1918/35		1945		1951		1955		1959		1964		1966		1970	
	Con.	Lab.	Con.	Lab.	Con.	Lab.	Con.	Lab.	Con.	Lab.	Con.	Lab.	Con.	Lab.	Con.	Lab.
Education																
Elementary only	2.5	75.5	1.5	53.0	3.0	51.0	2.3	34.0	1.6	35.6	1.0	31.2	0.8	22.0	0.6	20.6
Grammar	19.0	15.5	13.5	24.0	14.5	26.5	22.1	43.7	26.3	46.1	23.7	51.1	18.6	60.0	24.5	57.8
Eton	27.5	1.5	29.0	2.0	25.0	1.5	5.8	0.3	5.5	0.0	5.6	0.0	5.5	0.0	4.2	0.7
Harrow	10.0	1.0	7.0	0.5	7.5	0.5	22.7	1.4	20.0	1.2	22.4	0.6	21.7	0.8	17.9	0.7
Other public schools	41.0	6.5	49.0	20.5	50.0	21.0	47.1	20.6	46.6	17.1	47.3	17.1	53.4	17.2	52.8	20.9
Occupation																
Employers/ managers/ non-employed	44.0	4.0	36.0	10.5	38.0	9.5	36.3	9.0	40.5	9.3	37.2	8.2	38.3	8.5	39.7	7.7
Professions	52.0	24.0	61.0	48.5	57.5	45.5	60.2	49.1	57.6	51.5	59.8	52.7	56.2	54.6	58.8	61.3
'Workers' (manual and white collar)	4.0	72.0	3.0	41.0	4.5	45.0	3.5	41.9	1.9	39.2	3.0	39.1	5.5	36.9	1.5	31.0

Notes
(a) Most Conservative 'professionals' listed are lawyers or doctors. Most Labour 'professionals' are teachers and lecturers.
(b) Many Labour MPs now send their children to private schools.
(c) In 1973, 20 miners were sitting as MPs, but 40 were sons of miners. (In 1955, 33 miners were MPs.)

Source: Figures published in W. L. Guttsman, *The British Political Elite*, MacGibbon & Kee 1968; and D. E. Butler *et al.*, *The British General Elections of 1955, 1959, 1965, 1966*, and *1970*, Macmillan 1955, 1960, 1965, 1966, and 1971

1   *Is there any evidence in the table to suggest that there is a growing similarity between the backgrounds from which MPs are drawn? If so can you suggest any reasons to account for such a tendency?*
2   *If the Labour Party representatives are, in the future, drawn less from working-class backgrounds than they have been in the past, what sort of impact do you think this might have on government in Britain?*·

will also hold an office in the Government and this further decreases the likelihood of a parliamentary revolt. Should the Government have a minority of votes in the Commons the threat of dissolution may also be useful in preventing other parties from defeating Government motions, at least until those parties feel that they could improve their own positions at a General Election. Between 1945 and 1974 one party always held an absolute majority in the House of Commons, and as legislation in Britain only requires a simple majority to become law the successful party in a General Election could regard itself as safely in office for up to five years. The pressure on the Government was, therefore, likely to come from outside Parliament.

It is suggested that the real power between elections now lies with the Prime Minister, who chooses his Cabinet (and the ministers of the various Departments of State who are not in the Cabinet) and who also controls the Cabinet secretariat, but this situation may change if minority Governments become the rule rather than the exception in British politics. This view of ministerial power was summarized during a debate in the House of Lords in 1950: 'The truth is that, under our present Constitution, when the Cabinet is once in power, there is no way of effectively controlling it. ...'[2] Winston Churchill's description of the role of an MP was similarly pessimistic: 'The earnest party man becomes a silent drudge, tramping at intervals through lobbies to record his vote, and wondering why he comes to Westminster at all.'[3]

On the other hand, in the last analysis a Government does depend for its power on the continued support of a majority of members of the House of Commons, a position expressed by Sir Ivor Jennings: 'A Government must perpetually look over its shoulder to see whether it is being followed.'[4] But it is rarely that an eminent member of the party in power will get up and exclaim to his leader 'in the name of God, go!' as Leo Amery did to Neville Chamberlain before the latter's resignation in 1940. However, the Prime Minister must always be careful not to go so far as to split his party—as Lloyd George did to the Liberal Party in 1916.

The *House of Lords* is not now a vital part of government machinery and some people feel that its hereditary component makes it unacceptable—they would either abolish or drastically reorganize it. However, it is the very anachronistic nature of the House of Lords which strengthens its position, as it cannot be regarded as a serious threat to the power of the House of Commons.

Although there are about 800 hereditary peers, more than half of these never attend the House of Lords and only about 100 attend more than half the sittings. In addition to the hereditary peers, the House of Lords also consists of the senior Bishops of the Church of England, a handful of Law Lords who are appointed by the Lord Chancellor (and three of whom must be present when the House is acting as the highest Court of Appeal in the country), and the life peers who have been appointed since 1958 and who are men and women who have performed distinguished service in many fields. The life peers in particular make the House of Lords a place where there are experts in most subjects, and, therefore, the House of Lords can be of use in revising Bills and discussing them more fully than is sometimes possible in the House of Commons. The Lords, not being subject to re-election, can afford to be impartial. They may hold up some Bills for a maximum of one year if there is strong public opposition (for example, the Immigration Bill of 1962 was held up in this way). On the other hand, 'money Bills' become law after one month even if they are opposed by the House of Lords.

Local government carries out certain functions and provides services which affect the lives of people most directly and which local people are most likely to be able to effectively direct. Public health, welfare, housing, refuse collection, police, education, and town and country planning are in part among these services. The powers and functions of local government are delegated by Parliament and are under the general supervision of the appropriate departments of the central government. Since 1974 local government services have been controlled by reorganized County Councils.

The Government makes decisions, but these have to be put into effect by the permanent organization which runs the various departments of government, the *Civil Service*. The establishment of the Welfare State and the expansion of government control in other spheres has meant an increase in the importance of the role of the Civil Service and a substantial increase in the number of civil servants. The number of non-industrial civil servants increased by 54 000 between 1964 and 1967 to a total of 470 000; this number had risen to over half-a-million in 1973.[5]

Theoretically, ministers are responsible for everything that their departments do, but they can obviously know only a fraction of what is done in their name—Morrison gave an example of the minister who insisted on seeing all letters going out in his name—he was absolutely swamped by them until he admitted defeat![6]

Britain appears to have a singularly uncorrupt and impartial Civil Service, but as the government minister is an amateur and does not stay long in his department he obviously depends heavily upon the advice of his civil servants. Sir William Harcourt summed up the situation: 'The value of the political heads of department is to tell the permanent officials, what the public will not stand.'[7] Harcourt made his estimate of the power of the civil servants (the permanent officials) in relation to the ministers (the political heads of department) in 1896;

since then the complexity and range of administration have increased enormously.

The senior British civil servant is non-political and may not engage in any public political activity, unlike his American counterpart who is often a political nominee and may be changed when a new administration is elected. This has the advantage that senior British civil servants have the opportunity to become very experienced but may as a result increase their relative potential power when dealing with their temporary superiors, whom they supply with information and advice. However, the higher civil servant himself is likely to be a pure administrator with no specialized training who is guided on technical projects by the experts on his staff; as the ideas he expresses are not his own, some people feel that, far from forcing his own views upon his minister, he is not likely to be sufficiently dynamic or enthusiastic.

Although the upper hierarchy of the Home Civil Service is not drawn mainly from the major public schools, the fact that a large proportion of the direct entrants to the Administrative Class (who are likely to occupy the senior posts in the service) are privately educated Oxbridge graduates may make them less attentive to social needs than they would be if they were recruited from a wider section of society.[8]

Public expenditure summary (United Kingdom)

	£ million		
	1951	1961	1971
Social services:			
Social security	689	1 628	4 307
Health and personal social services	587	1 088	2 754
Education	398	1 012	3 006
Housing and environmental services:			
Housing	404	555	1 268
Environmental services	189	379	1 157
Libraries, museums, and the arts	13	34	112
Justice and law	82	204	616
Roads and public lighting	99	276	836
Transport and communication	167	526	1 040
Commerce and industry	892	1 204	3 097
Defence and external relations	1 405	1 859	3 184
Other expenditure	206	285	619
Debt interest	688	1 257	2 244
Total public expenditure (including debt interest)	5 819	10 307	24 240

Public Expenditure in 1974 totalled £41 606 million.

Source: Adapted from *Social Trends* 3, HMSO 1972

1 *Which public services have shown the greatest percentage increase in expenditure during the twenty years shown?*

The concern that some people feel regarding the possibility of misuse of power by officials led to the establishment of a Parliamentary Commissioner for Administration (Ombudsman) in 1967 whose function it is to investigate complaints put to him by Members of Parliament on behalf of members of the public who feel that they have been unjustly treated by government departments. The Ombudsman is a valuable brake on uncontrolled bureaucratic power, but his existence is likely to have an impact mainly on the lower hierarchy of the Civil

Public expenditure, 1972

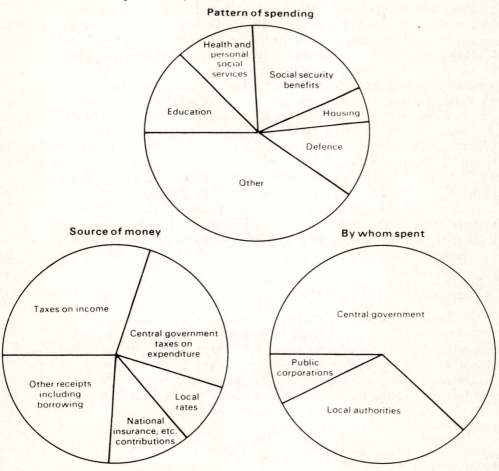

Source: Social Trends 4, HMSO 1973

2 *Do you think the way public money is spent is about right, or would you distribute it differently?*

125

Service, who are most likely to have direct dealings with the public. The potentially greater but less definable misuse of power by the faceless men at the top is both more difficult to detect and, if it exists, more difficult to control.

More discussion or written work

1   Do you agree with John Grigg's view of the British political system: 'Our system can now best be described as autocracy tempered by public opinion polls'?

2   How much importance has the formal and informal hereditary system in the British system of government? Do you think a hereditary system has any advantages or disadvantages?

3   How much power has a backbench Member of Parliament?

4   How are rates assessed? Who imposes and collects them? What are they used for? Are rates the best method of raising local taxation?

5   If Britain had to have a dictator, whom would you choose and why? (Some time ago a *Daily Telegraph* Gallup Poll produced a list in this order: 1. The Duke of Edinburgh; 2. Enoch Powell; 3. Harold Wilson; 4. David Frost; 5. Barbara Castle; 6. Frank Cousins; 7. Edward Heath; 8. The Queen.)

6   'The mass of men require symbols, and nobility is the symbol of mind. The order also prevents the rule of wealth . . . the reverence for rank is not so base as the reverence for money, or the still worse idolatry of office' (W. Bagehot, *The English Constitution*, 1867). Do you think there are any reasons for maintaining or increasing the power of the House of Lords?

Research

1   Find an example of each of the following types of government either from the past or the present: (*a*) an autocracy, (*b*) an oligarchy, (*c*) a democracy. Outline the main features of the governments that you choose and say which system of government you prefer—and why.

2   Discover someone from your locality who has become a life peer, and by investigating their past behaviour and the posts that they have occupied say why you think they were chosen as a life peer, and how effective you think they are or will be.

Imagination

Imagine that you could make any changes that you wished in the British system of government and list these changes in what you would regard as their order of importance.

Reading suggestions

† A. Hanson, *Governing Britain*, Collins (Fontana)
† I. Jennings, *The Queen's Government*, Penguin
† E. Taylor, *The House of Commons at Work*, Penguin
  L. Mair, *Primitive Government*, Penguin

Chapter 12

Supranational Authority

A *supra*national authority is an organization that rises above the old concepts of nationalism and whose authority is accepted, if only in theory, by the governments of member sovereign states.

There have of course been many empires in the past, but these have not been groupings of equally important states—one state has always dominated the others. Some of the empires of the past have had pretensions at various times to internationalism. For example, Roman citizenship was ultimately extended to all the subjects of the Empire and 'foreigners' often became Emperor; but the temptation of the founding power to benefit at the expense of the subordinate territories has always proved too great for a genuine supranational authority to emerge. For example, the constituent parts of the Portuguese 'Empire' were all regarded as part of Portugal: since 1961 all the inhabitants of the 'overseas territories' had been full Portuguese citizens and the National Assembly was composed of Deputies from all Portuguese territories—but the increasing opposition to the retention of these overseas territories was the main reason for the overthrow of the Portuguese Government in 1974.

The Roman Catholic Church in the Middle Ages might be regarded as a genuine supranational authority in that the countries of Europe acknowledged the temporal as well as the spiritual supremacy of the Pope (even if only in theory); the clergy spoke an international language, Latin, and formed an international civil service—often serving different countries.

Many of the countries included in the British Empire chose to join the Commonwealth when they achieved independence. The Commonwealth is now composed of thirty-two sovereign independent states, mostly parliamentary democracies, and has an estimated population of 900 000 000. The British monarch is regarded as the symbolic Head of the Commonwealth by all the member nations, although not regarded as Head of State by all of them. The Commonwealth is defined by the Statute of Westminster (1931) as 'autonomous communities within the British Empire, equal in status, in no way subordinate one to another'. Many of the member states of the Commonwealth are openly antagonistic towards each other and some people believe that the Commonwealth is now outdated and will gradually break up as the economic advantages of membership decrease. Other people feel that the consultations between the Governments and ministers of the Commonwealth are invaluable and believe that the policies of individual Governments are often influenced by these consultations.

Some people might also see the Communist Bloc as a body of independent nations under the influence of a supranational authority— the Communist Party. Others regard this group of countries as merely an old-fashioned empire under the domination of Russia, the central founding power.

There are many supranational organizations within which nations cooperate for their own economic benefit. Among these organizations are: the World Bank (established in 1945) which provides loans to member countries (for example, the Bank provided loans of 497 million dollars for post-war reconstruction in Western Europe); the International Monetary Fund (also set up in 1945) which assists in obtaining international cooperation in economic affairs (for example, the rescue of the pound sterling in 1976); and the General Agreement on Tariffs and Trade (GATT—established in 1948) which tries to encourage international trade by reducing tariff barriers and helps to promote economic development. Other trading alliances with political power are the Council for Mutual Economic Assistance (COMECON) which links most communist countries, and the Organization of Petroleum Exporting Countries (OPEC).

There are also military alliances with central organizations such as the North Atlantic Treaty Organization (NATO) composed of thirteen non-communist European countries plus the United States and Canada; the Central Treaty Organization (CENTO) which consists of Britain, Turkey, Iran, Pakistan and the USA; (SEATO is being phased out following communist successes); and the Warsaw Pact which consists of Albania, Bulgaria, Czechoslovakia, East Germany, Hungary, Poland, Rumania and Russia. These military alliances are, however, similar to other military alliances of the past and may even retard the development of internationalism rather than contributing to it.

Similarly, the European Economic Community (the Common Market), which Britain joined in 1973, is sometimes regarded as inward looking and against the concept of internationalism. Others consider it the foundation of a United States of Europe and a necessary counter to the military and economic might of America, China, and Russia. It is, however, a supranational authority in that all the member states are bound by treaty to accept Council decisions. The nine states of the EEC are controlled by, first, a Commission which draws up the proposals which are the basis of the Council decisions, and secondly, the Council itself which can make decisions on finance, trade, or agriculture, and although each state has a right to vote, these decisions do not have to be ratified by the independent parliaments of the member countries. Thirdly, there is the European Parliament which will develop into an elected legislative assembly.

The first faltering step towards a world government was taken when the destruction resulting from World War I prompted the victorious nations to establish the League of Nations as part of the Versailles Treaty of 1920. The League was intended to be an organization within which countries could resolve their differences by negotiation rather than by violence. The League's Covenant bound members not to employ force to settle a dispute until they had first submitted it to the League or to arbitrators; even if a settlement was not achieved within six months the countries concerned bound themselves to wait for a further three months before declaring war. The League was a failure: the United States retreated into isolationism and refused to join; Russia was ostracized by other members; France and Britain were only luke-warm in support; and Germany, Italy, and Japan simply ignored their pledges.

During World War II, at the Moscow Conference on 1 November 1943, the representatives of China, Britain, the USA, and Russia recognized 'the necessity of establishing at the earliest practicable date a general international organization, based on the principle of the sovereign equality of all peace-loving states, and open to membership by all such states, large or small, for the maintenance of international peace and security'. The United Nations came into formal existence on 24 October 1945 with fifty member states; by 1973 the number of member states had risen to 131 and included most of the countries in the world, with the People's Republic of China replacing Nationalist China (Taiwan) in 1971.

The United Nations has had many failures in trying to maintain peace among its members who have 'not been united in the pursuit of the purposes of the Charter' (U Thant, Secretary General of the United Nations, 1967). The Charter should perhaps be regarded as a document pointing to the ideals towards which to strive rather than as an actual working agreement.

The governing body of the United Nations is the General Assembly, which is composed of all the member states, having only one vote each, and needing a two-thirds majority for all important decisions. The

During the Congo crisis in 1962, the Irish commander of a UN contingent reviews his Ethiopian troops.
Should the United Nations have a permanent army?
Can an organization made up of varying nationalities ever operate effectively?
Photograph: United Nations

Security Council has the primary responsibility for the maintenance of peace and consists of fifteen member countries, each of which has one vote: there are five permanent members (Britain, China, France, Russia, and the United States) and ten temporary members elected for a two-year term. Although in theory the General Assembly can recommend that its members take appropriate action if the Security Council fails to maintain international peace, in practice each of the five permanent members has the right to veto any decisions. This right of veto is necessary at the moment because, if a serious dispute arose, the defeated super-power would almost certainly leave the United Nations, thus destroying the organization; and the United Nations seems, on balance, to be well worth preserving. For example, the many resolutions taken

by the United Nations over South Africa might appear futile; yet they do indicate world opinion and may be helpful in preparing for gradual changes in South Africa's policy of apartheid. The United Nations has also had some limited success with its peace-keeping forces in countries such as Cyprus, and some people would like to see a permanent 'army' of this kind attached to the United Nations, rather than just raising troops from member countries as the need arises.

The main political advantage of the United Nations may be summed up in the words of the Ethiopian delegate in 1967: 'Despite many frustrations and disappointments my faith in the United Nations is as strong as when I came to this job. It is a spiritual force that helps to keep the major Powers on speaking terms.'

Despite the importance of the United Nations' political activities, more than three-quarters of its work is in the economic, social, and humanitarian fields through its many allied organizations and specialized agencies. Some of these have already been mentioned; others deal with such matters as the peaceful use of atomic energy, the raising of living standards and the improvement of labour conditions, the production and distribution of the world's food supplies, and the improvement of health standards throughout the world. The United Nations Educational, Scientific, and Cultural Organization (UNESCO) is particularly important since it encourages peaceful cooperation between the member states in the fields of education, science, culture, and communications. It is financed by the UN and had a budget of 60 million dollars in 1972. The United Nations Children's Fund (UNICEF), on the other hand, depends upon voluntary contributions from governments and private individuals and this sense of identity with individuals is something which most international organizations lack.

Many of these organizations pre-date the United Nations and are examples of much earlier international agreements. The World Meteorological Organization, which exists to exchange data on the weather and to establish a world-wide network of weather stations, developed from the International Meteorological Organization which was set up in 1873; while the Universal Postal Union was founded in 1874 and the International Telecommunication Union was established in 1865.

The increase in the number and power of nuclear weapons, escalating military expenditure, and the development of deadly bacteria (for example it is claimed that one pound of botulinum toxin Type A would kill everyone in the World) has led the 'Super Powers' to realize that, despite their enmity on some issues, they have certain interests in common, not only to limit their own armaments but to prevent their acquisition by other nations. For example the Nuclear Non-Proliferation Treaty in 1968 aimed to prevent the spread of nuclear weapons.

Supranational organizations

(On 24.9.75 it was decided to phase out SEATO over a two-year period)

SEATO
(USA, UK, France, Australia, New Zealand, Pakistan, Phillipines, Thailand)

Commonwealth

NATO
(Canada, USA, 'Western Europe' including Turkey) – fifteen countries

EEC

United Nations

International Court of Justice

General

Secretariat

Security Council

Secretary General

Trusteeship Council

Assembly

Economic and Social Council (agencies)

Warsaw Pact
(USSR, 'Eastern Europe') – eight countries

CENTO
(USA, UK, Iran, Pakistan, Turkey)

OAU

1   *Do you think that the world would be a safer or a more dangerous place if military alliances such as NATO did not exist?*
2   *Do you think that the United Nations is an effective organization?*

Many people believe in world government as an ideal even though they regard it as impossible to achieve. However, it is interesting to note that Auguste Comte, who is generally regarded as the founder of modern sociology, did not regard the development of huge national or international institutions of this kind as desirable.

Comte (1798–1853) believed that there are three normal forms of human association—the family, the State, and humanity.[1] He saw this association as most intense in the case of the family and most general in the case of humanity; the State was the connecting link between the two, appealing to man's sympathy in a wider sense than just the interests of the narrow family group and so helping to raise him to a consciousness of his duty to humanity. Comte believed that as the principal States in the world became more and more enormous they would become too large to inspire genuine affection, and he regarded it as desirable that they should ultimately break down into a pattern of small city-states about the size of Belgium.

More discussion or written work

1 (*a*) Do you think the British Empire did more good than harm or vice versa? (*b*) Do you think that the Commonwealth has a role to play in the world?
2 How effective do you think the United Nations is? Suggest some ways in which it could improve its effectiveness.
3 Do you think that a United States of Europe is a possibility? Is such a development desirable?
4 Nationalism and Patriotism—how desirable are these concepts?
5 Do you take a pessimistic or an optimistic view of the future of the world? What do you think will be the major developments in the world in the future? Why?

Research

1 Find out as much as you can about the work of any international organization not mentioned in this chapter.
2 Find out *either* (*a*) how the peace-keeping forces of the United Nations are raised and used, *or* (*b*) as much information as you can about the work of ONE of the economic, social, or humanitarian agencies of the United Nations.

Imagination

Design a government for the world—say how it would be organized, who would elect or appoint it, where its headquarters would be situated, and what powers it would have.

Reading suggestions

* K. Savage, *The Story of the United Nations*, Bodley Head
† S. Bailey, *The United Nations*, Pall Mall Press
 J. Burros (ed.), *The United Nations, Past, Present and Future*, The Free Press
 J. Fawcett, *The Law of Nations*, Penguin

Chapter 13

The Welfare State

Nearly every society has had to make some provision for those unable to care for themselves. In mediaeval Europe most ordinary people served a feudal lord and, although their condition of life was grim, at least the lord was under some sort of obligation to look after them when they were old or ill. In fourteenth-century England the lords began to enclose the land, turning it to less labour-intensive but more profitable sheep rearing, and began to free their serfs. But although some people enjoyed a better life as free men, those who were unfortunate enough to be unemployed, or too old, ill, or young to look after themselves, had lost the little security they would have enjoyed during the earlier period. Early attempts to reduce vagrancy from the fourteenth century onwards usually took the form of punishing the unemployed by branding and whipping, although some attempt was made to ensure that the 'helpless poor' were looked after by the parish in which they were born.

Just as the serfs had been cared for after a fashion by the feudal lords so too the craftsmen who congregated in towns had grouped themselves into Guilds which cared for those of their members who became ill or unemployed. But the Guilds declined under attack from the Government, which was afraid of their growing power, and as cottage and factory industry increased.

The monasteries also helped to care for the poor until their dissolution began in the sixteenth century. In 1536 an Act was passed which for the first time established machinery for the collection and distribution of funds for the relief of the poor; this was enlarged by subsequent statutes. In 1601 a Poor Law Act was passed involving the building of poorhouses and the raising of a tax for the purpose. This Act remained the basis of pauper legislation until this century. Most legislation was aimed at giving some relief to those who could not possibly be blamed for being poor (although they were often treated as though they were responsible), while forcing the able-bodied to find work (even if there was none) by threatening them with branding, slavery, whipping, or even execution.

Workhouses were first introduced in 1722 but became generally established by the Poor Law Amendment Act of 1834, the aim of which was 'subjecting the applicant to the discipline of a workhouse and other restraints, in order that the condition of a pauper, living upon the parish fund, should be depressed in point of comfort below that of the ordinary labourer'. This was part of the start of major state involvement in social welfare, albeit a grudging involvement.

Until the nineteenth century it was generally accepted that the function of the State was to provide a general framework of rules within which people could behave more or less as they chose. However, the movement of people from the country to the towns as a result of the Industrial Revolution, the increasing population (from nine million to thirty-two million during the century), and increasing unemployment as specialization and foreign competition grew, resulted in large sections of the population being degraded to subhuman levels. As conditions worsened the State was forced to deal with working conditions and wages, to protect public health, and to introduce compulsory education.

The first Factory Act of 1802 (the Health and Morals of Apprentices Act) laid down rules about hours and the conditions under which child apprentices were permitted to work. The Act was ineffective and was succeeded by another in 1819 which limited the work of all children in cotton mills to twelve hours a day, this time with rather more effective penalties. Eventually, in 1833, a third Factory Act prohibited the employment of children under nine in textile factories, and nightwork for all persons under eighteen. It also limited maximum working hours for children under thirteen to forty-eight per week and for other young persons to sixty-nine, provided for six days' holiday a year, and appointed inspectors to make sure the law was obeyed. In 1844 the working hours of children under thirteen were reduced to six-and-a-half a day and adult women received the same protection as young people. A succession of Acts followed which helped to improve working conditions in the factories and by 1883 no child under ten could legally be employed in any factory and up to the age of fourteen they could only work half-time unless they had passed an examination in reading, writing, and arithmetic.

The Education Acts of 1870 and 1876 introduced compulsory education for the first time, but owing to a shortage of schools many exemptions were still allowed: for instance, children living more than two miles from a school were allowed to work. But the Act of 1880 compelled all children between the ages of five and ten to attend school.

In 1872 and 1875 Public Health Acts established sanitary authorities under medical officers who were responsible for sewerage, water supply, refuse disposal, and the prevention of the spread of infectious diseases. In 1875 the Artisans' Dwellings Act empowered local authorities to demolish slums (and resulted in the destruction of the London 'Rookeries'), although they were only permitted to build houses if no commercial undertaking was interested in doing so; this Act was re-inforced by the Housing Act of 1890 which stimulated the building of council houses. These are only a few of the major Acts of Parliament concerning health. During the latter part of the nineteenth century there were many more, such as the Baths and Washhouses Act of 1847, the Common Lodging House Acts of 1851 and 1853, the Bakehouse Regulation Act of 1863, the Sale of Food and Drugs Act of 1875, and the Pollution of Rivers Act of 1876. The major epidemics of killer diseases such as cholera disappeared and the death rate began to fall.

Many people still believed in the *laissez-faire* doctrine that the State should not interfere with the rights of individual people, even the rights of parents to send their small children out to work, or the right of women—on all fours and almost naked—to pull trucks through coal-mines.[1] These rights of course included the right to starve: in the 'good' year of 1849, 28 per cent of all families in Northampton had an income below subsistence level; in South Shields 23 per cent and in Oldham 15 per cent of all families were also surviving on an income which theoretically could not sustain life. In the slump year of 1847, 41 per cent of all families in Oldham were in this category.[2] While up to the end of the nineteenth century there was still considerable con-cern that in 'improving the physical condition of the working classes, special care be taken not to damage their moral independence'.[3] How-ever, a more humane approach began to be adopted at the beginning of the twentieth century with the election of the Liberal Government of 1906, and the social stigma of poverty began to fade. In 1908 Old Age Pensions were introduced, in 1909 Labour Exchanges were established, and in 1911 the Insurance Act provided compulsory insurance against illness and, in certain trades, against unemployment.

World War I gave an added stimulus to the extension of public control as it became necessary to organize every activity that would improve the chance of victory: manpower, industrial production, food supplies, and shipping were brought under government control. This process was intensified during World War II, and the Labour Party, which came to power immediately afterwards, was more fully com-mitted to state intervention than any other party. The Labour Party did not see state control as merely a temporary expedient but as something essential to the remodelling of society. As much of the neces-sary administrative machinery was already in existence as a result of war-time regulations—guided by the controls and powered by the sense of unity the war had fostered—the establishment of a comprehensive scheme of welfare was generally acceptable. The old Unemployment Assistance Board had been converted into the National Assistance Board in 1940 and the hated 'means test' formally abolished in 1941.

The foundation of the Welfare State, then, had already been laid before 1945, and the structure was built up from the recommendations of Sir William Beveridge. Beveridge had been Lloyd George's principal assistant in executing the social reforms of the 1906 Liberal Government, and in 1942 was Chairman of the Committee on Social Insurance and Allied Services. This Committee reported to the Coalition Government and nearly all its recommendations for a greatly improved system of social security were accepted.

The Beveridge Report firmly established the desirability of a society free from want and from fear of unemployment, in which benefits were to be allowed on the basis of need, and would be a right rather than charity. The Welfare State was to be financed jointly by employees, employers, and the Government.

The Family Allowance Act was passed in 1945 and the National Insurance Act followed in 1946 (with a separate Act dealing with industrial injuries). A free National Health Service was established by the Act of 1946, and despite some alteration to the original concept of a salaried public service because of the opposition of the British Medical Association, it has become one of the cornerstones of the Welfare State which included, by 1950, 95 per cent of the country's general practitioners. The food subsidies, originally introduced in 1940, were expanded, and by 1948 were costing £485 million a year: the malnutrition of the pre-war years became a thing of the past—its disappearance hastened by subsidized welfare foods for children and expectant mothers, and free milk for school children. The National Assistance Act was passed in 1948, and Acts on Housing, Prisons, Child Care, and Legal Aid followed. The Housing Act of 1949 which extended the policy of subsidized council housing was symbolic in that, for the first time in a Housing Act, the phrase 'working class' was omitted.

Some of the benefits now available are Unemployment Benefit, Sickness Benefit, Invalidity Benefit, Widow's Benefits, Retirement Pensions (the latter three related to earnings from 1978), Death Grant, Industrial Injuries Benefit, Supplementary Benefits (replacing National Assistance), and Family Allowances. Family Income Supplements were introduced in 1970 to help families (and single people) with small incomes where the wage-earner was in full-time work and there were one or more dependent children; in 1973 about 70 000 households containing about 300 000 children benefited under this

Some people have largely escaped the attentions of social workers and the benefits of the Welfare State.
Has a person a right to opt out of the Welfare State?
Why do you think people become tramps?
Photograph: Pip Payne, Somerset College of Art

scheme. Some people feel that no-one in full-time employment should
be in a position to need help given in this way and have suggested
that a national minimum wage, coupled with a negative income tax
scheme, would ensure an adequate income without any feeling of
obligation on the part of the recipient.

The Welfare State has brought about a very great improvement in
the health and well-being of the community. Many people feel that
when basic needs are satisfied, basic fears defeated, and a good standard
of comfort and leisure established, a community should be able to
achieve its highest cultural potential. Just as the point at which a
society moves away from a purely subsistence economy and can maintain non-producers from the surplus will also be the point at which
civilization starts, so it might be argued that civilization can reach its
highest point when everyone can enjoy comfort, leisure, and freedom
from fear.

Critics of the Welfare State fall into two categories: those who feel
that the growing power of the State will sap human endeavour, impose
a drab uniformity, create a despotism of civil officials, and even increase
crime;[4] and those who feel that the Welfare State has still not been

Taxes and social security contributions as percentage of national output, 1969

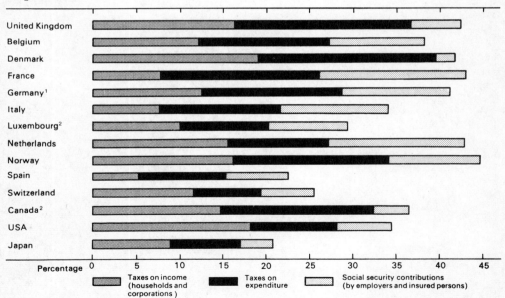

1 Federal Republic of Germany and West Berlin
2 1968 data

Source: Social Trends 3, HMSO 1972

developed sufficiently and still fails to reach those who most need its benefits.

The first school of thought believes that the Welfare State puts too much power in the hands of Government; for example, the Governments of Britain, France, Germany, Sweden, and Norway now control two-fifths or more of the national product. In 1841 Alexis de Tocqueville, a French political philosopher, thought that the State should exercise its authority like a good parent in preparing its subjects for eventual manhood, but felt that if the aim of the State was to keep its subjects in perpetual childhood by providing security, foreseeing all their necessities, assisting in their pleasures, and directing their industry, then it might as well spare them all the care of thinking and all the trouble of living.[5] In de Tocqueville's time many other people saw state control as something that might be necessary as a purely temporary expedient; Nassau Senior thought that by the latter part of

Standards of living

	Population per			Average number of persons per household	Percentage		
	Doctor	Nurse	Dentist		Piped water	W.C.	Owner-occupiers
United Kingdom	820	320	3 790	2.9	98.7	98.2	47.8
Belgium	640	—	5 230	3.0	76.9	99.9	49.7
Denmark	690	180	1 480	2.8	96.7	90.9	44.4
France	770	380	2 520	3.1	90.8	54.8	43.3
Germany (Fed. Rep.)	590	360	1 940	2.9	99.0	86.5	34.3
Irish Republic	960	—	4 810	4.0	51.0	64.9	59.8
Italy	560	530	—	3.6	62.3	89.5	45.8
Luxembourg	980	430	3 150	3.3	98.4	99.5	54.7
Netherlands	820	220	4 020	3.6	89.8	99.9	25.7
Canada	710	160	3 040	3.7	95.2	93.5	65.4
Japan	900	380	2 810	4.3	88.5	100.0	80.6
USA	650	200	1 990	3.2	97.5	96.0	62.9
USSR	430	240	2 760	—	—	—	—
Brazil	1 950	3 300	3 470	4.8	32.8	60.2	60.4
India	5 420	8 800	76 710	5.2	—	—	85.2
Philippines	10 220	7 820	88 480	6.1	34.4	66.4	89.4

Some of these figures are based on samples or estimates and are only a guide. Health Service figures are for 1969 except for the Irish Republic (1966).
Housing figures are from 1960 to 1970 (UK 1966).

Source: Adapted from *Social Trends* 4, HMSO 1973

Is there a connection between the level of taxation and the standard of living in the countries for which figures are given?·

the twentieth century such assistance would no longer be necessary.[6]

We ourselves are now in the 'latter part of the twentieth century', and some people say that it is time to stop national schemes for education, health, housing, and pensions: time to make people fend for themselves—with the State perhaps supplying cash only to people with low incomes to enable them to pay fees for education, rents for housing, and insurance for medical care. Other people, however, feel that, far from decreasing national provision, it is necessary to improve welfare services still further. In 1965, a report by Brian Abel-Smith and Peter Townsend showed that the proportion of the population with an income of not more than 40 per cent above the National Assistance scale rates increased between 1954 and 1960, and that in 1960 more than 600 000 children came from homes with incomes below subsistence level.[7] In 1973 it was found that 30 per cent of a Bethnal Green sample lived at or below the official poverty line, while it was also found that the stated attempt of the incomes policy to improve the relative position of the low paid had failed to do so.[8] The Crowther Report[9] and the Robbins Report[10] both demonstrated the handicaps which children from large families still labour under in the field of education. Some authorities have claimed that poverty is actually increasing.[11]

Housing is still an area where there is considerable hardship, particularly when the family concerned is a large one. Family allowances and retirement pensions now compare unfavourably with those in Europe. The areas with the greatest social needs are often those where the welfare services are most likely to be stretched. Many older people are still reluctant to use services which they regard, quite wrongly, as 'charitable'.

State aid is, of course, not charity as it has been raised by rates and taxes to which old people in their time have also contributed; but there is nothing wrong with the real charities, which provide an opportunity for individuals to demonstrate their real compassion for those less fortunate than themselves. Charitable organizations plug many of the gaps in the fabric of the Welfare State and often work in conjunction with official agencies; much research work is sponsored by charities, as are many valuable services which would probably not be acceptable if they were thought to be 'official'.

The Charity Commission was established by an Act of Parliament in 1853 and reconstituted under the Charities Act of 1900 with a duty of ensuring that charitable income is used effectively, and to keep a register of charities. Since 1960 the Charity Commissioners have been compiling a register of charitable trusts, and they have received more than 70 000 applications for inclusion.

Charities include organizations like the Samaritans, Shelter, Oxfam, the Women's Royal Voluntary Services, the Royal National Institute for the Blind, and the NSPCC. What constitutes a charity has, however, nothing to do with virtue, but is merely a matter of law: a charitable object is whatever a Court of Chancery says it is. A registered charity is not liable to income tax, surtax, corporation tax, or capital gains tax, and can therefore benefit from Deeds of Covenant. One of the richest charitable foundations in Britain is the Wolfson Foundation with an annual income of over two million pounds. It provides money for scientific and medical research, preserves old cathedrals and churches, buys works of art for the nation, founded a University College (Wolfson, Oxford), and gave the Royal College of Physicians its new premises. Another large charity of this kind is the Nuffield Foundation, which has financed research, among other things, into the effects of television on the young and into race relations. The Guinness Trust specializes in supplying cheap housing to those whose earnings are below the national average.

In America, where gifts to charity are tax-deductible, the amount given each year to charity is about 2 per cent of the gross national product. It is not so large in Britain, but here too the loss of charitable income would seriously affect many fields of welfare. The Wells Fund Raising Group estimated in 1973 that the total amount given to United Kingdom charities in 1971 amounted to £250 million, the average individual giving £2.27 per year, compared with £30.69 in the United States. The existence of charities also provides people who feel strongly about a particular situation with an opportunity to do something personally about it: perhaps by helping to provide hostels for ex-prisoners, funds for cancer research, help for spastics, or money to prevent famine abroad.

Some charities, such as Shelter, while helping to alleviate a particular social problem, concentrate mainly on trying to involve the Government in plans to reduce it.

The Welfare State has provided a better standard of living for the bulk of Britain's population although at the expense of additional government interference. It has not, however, completely solved any problem. There are still homeless families, still alcoholic derelicts, still battered babies, still old people dying of hunger and cold, and still men in full employment who are dependent on welfare benefits to maintain their families. Some, indeed, claim that certain social problems have actually become more acute in recent years.[12]

More discussion or written work

1 'A State which dwarfs its men, in order that they may be more docile instruments in its hands—even for beneficial purposes—will find

that with small men no great thing can really be accomplished' (John Stuart Mill). Do you think that this statement could be applied to the Welfare State?

2   How has the development of the Welfare State influenced family life?

3   How well do you think the Welfare State actually provides for our welfare? What improvements would you like to make to existing services?

4   Is there still a place for voluntary organizations within a Welfare State?

5   In what ways can the individual still provide for his own welfare, e.g. medical provision? Do you think it is fair that people should be able to buy a superior standard of welfare?

Research

1   Find a local voluntary organization which is engaged in some sort of welfare work. Discover how it is financed, and the sort of people who run it. Assess the effectiveness of its function in the local community.

2   Find out what services are provided by the Welfare State in your locality, and assess the effectiveness of the organization of this provision. For example, is the child welfare clinic easily accessible to mothers with prams? Is the Employment Exchange sited in a convenient place? How long do you have to wait for attention at your local doctor's surgery? Do people feel that they are well received when they apply for supplementary benefits?

Imagination

Imagine that you are in a position to create a Welfare State. What additional services would you provide and what existing services would you abolish? How would you finance your system of welfare?

Reading suggestions

* A. Fried and R. Elman (eds.), *Charles Booth's London*, Penguin
* I. Martin, *From Workhouse to Welfare*, Penguin
* P. Willmott, *Consumer's Guide to the British Social Services*, Penguin
† M. Hall, *The Social Services of Modern England*, Routledge & Kegan Paul
† D. Marsh, *The Welfare State*, Longman
  J. Kincaid, *Poverty and Equality in Britain*, Penguin

Chapter 14

The Law

Some anthropologists such as Radcliffe-Brown would limit the term 'Law' to socially expected behaviour which is 'sanctioned' by some sort of court;[1] whereas others, like Malinowski, would include all the customs which are binding on the members of a society.[2]

Written law is certainly only one form of control over our behaviour. There is what most people would loosely term 'good manners'—the conventions which rule our behaviour towards each other and which aim at making our relationships rather less abrasive than they might otherwise be—although breach of the code would not institute a threat to the society at large. Good manners will naturally vary from society to society and will even differ among groups within the society: they might include such things as avoiding unpleasant personal remarks, or shouting at each other, or eating noisily. At their most socially valuable, good manners may involve a sensitive consideration for other people's feelings and a wish to help. But often what are called good manners are the accepted modes of behaviour in the middle and upper classes in a society, especially when laid down in formal rules of etiquette, and they may fulfil no social function other than that of maintaining the class distinctions within the society. The sanctions which can be invoked to ensure that people obey rules of good manners will vary from exclusion from a particular social group to exclusion from certain job opportunities. These good manners are part of our customary behaviour and help to establish the pattern of behaviour which we call our role. Sociologists describe these expected patterns of social behaviour as 'folkways' and these folkways may not only help us to establish our role but also to reconcile our behaviour when we are playing 'multiple roles'.

'Mores' are the rather more important customary rules governing our relationships within the society. These rules include, for example, professional ethics, and there may be powerful sanctions to invoke against those who transgress these codes; for example, a doctor may be struck off the Medical Register and have his career ruined if he has a sexual relationship with a patient, although he is breaking no official law. Just as folkways help us to establish our role, so mores help us to operate within our 'role-set'.[3] Our role-set consists of the roles which we play in relating to the roles of other individuals or groups of individuals; for example, a nurse will have to relate to several 'role-others', that is, enact her role in relation to her matron, her ward-sister, her fellow nurses, and her patients. Mores will help her to operate within this area of potential conflict. Malinowski would accept folkways and mores as law but Radcliffe-Brown would not: 'the obligations imposed on individuals and societies where there are no legal sanctions will be regarded as matters of custom and convention but not of law; in this sense simple societies have no law, although all have customs which are supported by sanctions'.[4]

For the remainder of this chapter we shall regard 'the Law' in the sense favoured by Radcliffe-Brown as being those rules of conduct which have been officially announced essential in a particular society, and which are officially enforced. The 'legal system' is the process by which these laws are administered and enforced. Apart from anarchists, most people would accept that the law in this context is the foundation of all complex societies: if there were no law, life for the majority of people would be what Thomas Hobbes in the seventeenth century described as 'nasty, brutish and short'. In this context the law derives from the customs or social norms of the society; but unlike mere custom it is sanctioned by the use, or threat, of physical force. The apparent sanction may be a fine, but it is understood that refusal to pay the fine may ultimately lead to the use of force, in imprisonment.

Unless a law is acceptable to the majority of people in a society it will be widely evaded and will bring the law as an institution into contempt: it may even provoke the very violence in the society that it is the ultimate aim of the law to prevent. For example, the prohibition of alcoholic drinks in America during the 1920s and 1930s was not acceptable to the mass of the people, who sought to evade the law—thus increasing the power of gangsters in Chicago and the other major American cities. It was not until the Prohibition Act was repealed in 1933 that the law was able to bring under control the widespread violence and general contempt for the law.

Most people in a society must look to the law for protection and must generally obey it (including individual laws that they may disagree with); otherwise the law becomes impossible to operate. For example, in Sicily in the fifteenth century historical circumstances made the official law unacceptable to the majority of people, who therefore formed their own law-enforcement agency, the Mafia, which has now become a major force opposed to the law in other countries.

As the law derives from the customs of a society, it will be constantly changing as those customs alter; and as the law follows after custom it will often appear to be a bit old-fashioned in some respects. Sometimes the law may move so slowly behind public opinion that the ordinary people involved in its process may force change; for example, a jury in the eighteenth century found the death penalty as punishment for theft over the value of forty shillings unacceptable and brought in a verdict of 'guilty—to stealing a ten pound note to the value of thirty-nine shillings'.

It is suggested by some people that the law in Britain tends to be based upon middle-class values and that it is the resulting middle-class customs that are embodied in our legal system. There does appear to be a general pattern in societies for the law of the higher classes in the society to become the law for all: for example, until 1969 the legal age of majority was twenty-one—perhaps a hang-over from the eleventh and twelfth centuries, a time when a knight's son came of age at twenty-one, a 'socman's' heir at fifteen, and a burgess's son was of age when he could 'count pence, measure cloth, and conduct his father's business'. Gradually the rule for the knight became the rule for all, until its partial reversal in our day.

In England and Wales there are three sources of law: *common law* which is based on custom and on recorded precedents which have been built up in the course of thousands of trials since the thirteenth century; *equity* which takes precedence over common law and is the results of appeals to the King and Lord Chancellor since the fifteenth century; and *statute law* which follows from legislation by Parliament and 'orders in Council' passed at the request of government departments.

In order that the legal system shall be acceptable to the majority of people it must be seen to be fair in operation: law-abiding people have to feel reasonably certain that they will not be mistakenly found guilty of a crime or unnecessarily harassed by the law-enforcement agencies. Such security from injustice and harassment has been laid down in a series of measures.

First of all, the Habeas Corpus Acts of 1676, 1816, and 1862 make it illegal for anyone to be detained without a charge being brought, or to be sent out of the jurisdiction of the British courts, although in an emergency this right may be waived—for example, by the Special Powers Act in Northern Ireland. Should an unjust arrest be made, damages may be claimed for 'wrongful arrest'.

In all serious criminal cases, which are tried in the 'Crown Courts' established in 1971, everyone has the right to trial by jury—the jury consisting of twelve ordinary men and women over the age of eighteen, picked at random from those qualified on the voters' lists. Since 1974, when the 1825 property qualification ceased to apply under the Criminal Justice Act 1972, virtually everyone resident for at least five years in the United Kingdom and aged eighteen to sixty-five is eligible for jury service—the exceptions include those sentenced to five years or more imprisonment, those suffering from mental illness, the clergy, and the judges. MPs, medical workers, and members of the forces can claim 'exclusion as of right'; and those who have been imprisoned for three months or more are disqualified for up to ten years. Until 1967 the verdict of the jury had to be unanimous, but in 1967 evidence was produced in Parliament that some criminals were managing to corrupt one or two jurors in some trials; hence, majority verdicts were introduced, which means that up to two jurors can disagree with the actual verdict which is brought. (It is interesting to note that until 1870 juries were kept without food, drink, or light until they had returned their verdict!) The accused person may also object to having people on the jury whom he thinks may be biased against him.

In less serious cases the matter may be dealt with by unqualified justices of the peace (or qualified magistrates in the larger towns) without a jury, at the Petty Sessions (Courts of Summary Jurisdiction). These courts dispose of 98 per cent of all criminal cases and also conduct preliminary enquiries in more serious cases to see if there is sufficient evidence to justify the accused being tried by a higher court. In all cases the accused person must either be brought before a magistrate within twenty-four hours or released on bail. He must be presumed innocent until proved guilty 'beyond all reasonable doubt'. If he has been found 'not guilty' he cannot be tried again for the same offence (unless magistrates have made a legal mistake at the Petty Sessions). No mention of any previous convictions may be made unless or until he is found guilty, and it is an offence to publish anything which might result in a biased trial. There is a right of appeal against the decisions of the courts, and if the defendant cannot afford representation he may claim 'legal aid' to cover part or all of the cost of the necessary solicitor or barrister under the Legal Aid Acts of 1949 and 1960. Free or subsidized legal advice has also been available for some time in the United Kingdom, and under the Legal Aid and Assistance Act (1972) solicitors and counsel are able to give advice and assistance (short of actually appearing in court) up to the value of £25 to anyone who would normally be eligible for legal aid. Everyone is, at least theoretically, 'equal before the law'.

To prevent the Government controlling the decisions of the judges they cannot be dismissed or have their salaries reduced except by Parliament, and then only for gross misconduct.

Some people have said that the British system of justice makes too many concessions to ensure fairness, and that this results in too many criminals being found not guilty. Others feel that the system, particularly the Petty Sessions, leads to a bias against the working-class sector of the population, and that the gross inequality of sentencing in some instances brings the law into disrepute.

Where the matter under dispute is more a matter of concern to the

Motoring offences, 1971 (England and Wales)

	Total offences and alleged offences (thousands)	Charges of which offenders were found guilty (thousands)
Manslaughter or causing death by dangerous driving	0.8	0.6
Dangerous driving	10.7	7.9
Driving or in charge of vehicle while unfit through drink or drugs	46.0	42.3
Careless driving	139.4	121.3
Speed limit offences	272.1	249.3
Unauthorized taking or theft of motor vehicles	52.6	44.0
Neglect of traffic directions	86.9	64.1
Neglect of zebra crossing regulations	33.0	27.0
Obstruction, waiting, or parking	201.3	151.8
Lighting offences	117.8	69.3
Vehicle in dangerous or defective condition	208.4	180.1
Noise offences	16.4	13.3
Vehicle testing offences	106.9	81.5
Driving licence offences	211.0	176.4
Accident offences	30.9	23.8
Vehicle insurance offences	146.5	119.5
Vehicle registration or licensing (excise) offences	66.8	45.1
Other motoring offences	81.2	62.9
Total motoring offences	1 828.7	1 480.3

Total motoring offences in 1974 had risen to 2 223 400.

Source: Adapted from *Social Trends* 3, HMSO 1972

1   *It has been suggested that judges and magistrates are more inclined to be lenient with motoring cases than other offences. Why do you think that this might be so?*

2   *Which motoring offences would you regard as the most serious?*

parties involved than to the society at large, it is settled in a 'Civil Court' which has powers to order compensation to be paid for such 'torts' (legal wrongs) as trespass, slander, 'nuisance', or breach of contract. As some torts may also be crimes, proceedings may also be taken in the Criminal Courts; for example, libel, which is defamation of character in writing or on radio or television, may be a crime; whereas 'slander', which is defamation of character by speech or gestures, is only a tort. The Civil Courts consist of the County Courts where cases involving less than £750 (1970) are tried (although in 1971, 83 per cent of all proceedings were for amounts of £100 or less

Civil justice (England and Wales)

	1951	1961	1971
Total number of proceedings commenced			
Courts of First Instance			
High Court of Justice	159 781	173 208	303 728
County Courts	535 374	1 683 582	1 538 874
Other	21 403	25 497	31 277
Total proceedings	716 558	1 882 287	1 873 879
Courts of Appeal			
Judicial Committee of the Privy Council	56	54	33
House of Lords	35	59	50
Court of Appeal	711	690	922
High Court of Justice	507	455	784
Total proceedings	1 309	1 258	1 789

Total proceedings 1972 = 1 986 156

Legal aid available: in County Courts from 1956
                     in House of Lords from 1960
                     in Magistrates' Courts from 1961

Source: Adapted from *Social Trends* 3, HMSO 1972

1 *What sort of factors might account for the increase in the number of cases coming before the civil courts between 1951 and 1961?*
2 *Would you say most people are reasonably happy with the results of cases coming before these courts?*

and usually settled without a trial); the Queen's Bench Division which tries the more serious civil cases (as well as supervising the Petty Sessions); the Family Division which deals with divorce, adoption, and related family matters; and the Chancery Division which deals with cases involving wills, company disputes, taxation, and land.

There are also Tribunals which provide cheap, quick decisions on matters such as sickness and unemployment benefits or rents; nearly 130 000 such cases were handled by tribunals in 1971.

The main agency for the enforcement of law in advanced societies is the police force. In the early periods of British history law-enforcement

Much of a policeman's time is taken up with activities unconnected with crime prevention.
What 'community' roles do you think the police should have?
In what ways might the various roles of the police clash?
It has been suggested that the function of the police be split into separate organizations as in some other countries, dealing with, for instance, traffic, crime, political matters, community matters, and riots. *Would this be a sensible solution?*
In what sort of situations would you say the police are justified in using force? How much force?
Photographs: upper, Press Association; *lower*, Keystone

was based on the principle that every member of the community was bound to support the law when required, and might be called upon by the magistrates to protect life and property. But gradually some towns began to pay watchmen or constables; and as the movement to the towns made the old system unworkable, a number of private law-enforcement organizations grew up which were a potential threat to the security of the State. To replace these, the present police force was established by Robert Peel in 1829.

Just as the law requires the approval of the majority of people if it is to remain workable, so the police force requires general approval if it is to maintain the law effectively. Generally the police in Britain seem to be well regarded, although occasional charges of corruption or malicious prosecution do inevitably occur. Some common criticisms of the police are that, in maintaining close contact with the criminal elements in society, they may themselves become corrupted; that they are unfair to particular classes or ethnic groups within the community; or that they use 'unfair' methods to secure arrests. It has also been suggested that good relations between the police and the public are endangered by the mounting number of motoring offences, for whereas previously a law-abiding citizen was unlikely to come into conflict with the police, now motoring offences are committed from 'the palace' downwards! It has been suggested that a separate motoring police should be established both to maintain the reputation and spare the time of the main police organization.

Ultimately, responsibility for enforcing the law of the State rests with the armed forces, for if the law is disregarded to the extent of near or actual rebellion, as in Northern Ireland in recent years, the law can only be enforced by calling upon the military for assistance.

The need for a state to maintain armed forces to suppress internal as well as external threats is a constant danger to that state itself, since the armed forces may use their power to overthrow the established order. There have been many examples of this, such as Greece in 1967 and Chile in 1973. But even a successful military coup can prove abortive if it is resisted by the majority of the population; for example, the 'Generals' Revolt' in Algeria in 1961 was overcome in a matter of days by civilian non-cooperation. However, armies do, indeed, seize control—in the later years of the Roman Empire the army decided who was to be Emperor, just as the army has seized control in recent years of several countries throughout the world. Usually this happens in undeveloped or developing countries, but people like C. Wright Mills have suggested that even in America the military elite in the Pentagon have a strong influence on government policy.[5] In Britain the armed forces have remained loyal to the State for centuries (the last time the army seized control was under the leadership of Cromwell), and serving servicemen cannot be involved in politics; but even in Britain there is a latent danger of military control.

The officer class in an army is often drawn exclusively from one sector of the population, and if the interests of this sector appeared to be seriously threatened by a government representing the interests of a different sector, it might be difficult to maintain the impartiality of the armed forces. The nearest Britain has approached to this situation was the so-called Mutiny at the Curragh just before World War I (see Chapter 10). It might be advisable, if one wished to ensure a State's stability, to draw the officer group from as varied a background as possible; and there does seem to be some evidence that the officer class in Britain is being recruited from a rather wider section of the population than was previously the case. For example, the proportion of officer cadets at the Royal Military Academy, Sandhurst, who had been educated at public schools decreased from 58.9 per cent in 1961–63 to 48.6 per cent in 1971–73 (see table).

Intake 31 September 1961 to August 1963 (before amalgamation with Mons Officer Cadet School)		Percentage of British total
Officer cadets from HMC schools	156	58.9%
Officer cadets from other schools	109	41.1%
Total British officer cadets	265	
Overseas cadets	32	
Total intake	297	

Intake 31 September 1971 to March 1973 (after amalgamation with Mons)		Percentage of British total
Officer cadets from HMC schools	73	48.6%
Officer cadets from other schools	77	51.4%
Total British officer cadets	150	
Overseas cadets	27	
Total intake	177	

Source: Royal Military Academy, Sandhurst

HMC = Headmasters' Conference schools. These schools are generally known as public schools and in 1972 included 218 schools in the British Isles, 202 of which require payment of fees; the remaining 16 are mainly old-established grammar schools, although one comprehensive (Banbury) was included until 1973. (About 2 per cent of the child population is educated at these schools.) There are also 53 overseas members of the HMC.

More discussion or written work

1 Contrast the social roles of the judge and the jury.

2 Do you think that the general public is sufficiently protected from mistaken arrest and imprisonment by the British legal system? Do our rules to safeguard the rights of the individual make the task of the police unnecessarily difficult?

3 The police are sometimes accused of being antagonistic towards some sections of the community. Do you think there is any truth in this view, and if so, why? If you do not, why do some people think there is?

4 Do you think our laws are biased against the working class?

5 What sort of 'mores' and 'folkways' are there in our society which are not legal rules? What sanctions are invoked to ensure that these 'mores' and 'folkways' are adhered to?

Research

1 Find an example of a demonstration, march, or protest meeting held in your area at which there was some violence or disorder. Why do you think this violence or disorder occurred? How effective do you think the control measures were? (Choose another area if there has been no violence or disorder in these circumstances within your own.)

2 Some people have suggested that the existing legal-aid schemes give the poor a second-class service. Find out about the existing schemes for legal aid and try to assess their adequacy.

Imagination

Imagine that you are in a position to alter our legal system in any way that you wish. State what laws you would abolish and what laws you would introduce—and why.

Reading suggestions

* N. Lewis, *The Honoured Society: The Mafia*, Penguin
* B. Whitaker, *The Police*, Eyre & Spottiswoode
† A. Harding, *A Social History of English Law*, Penguin
† R. Jackson, *Enforcing the Law*, Penguin
  V. Aubert (ed.), *Sociology of Law*, Penguin

Chapter 15

The Economy

The economic structure of a society is the base on which all the other relationships within it are founded, and it will be economic forces, including changes in population and technology, which will be the main triggers of social change. During the Industrial Revolution dramatic changes in technology and great increases in population interacted with urbanization and other social change such as the movement of political power from the landowner to the industrial capitalist and the creation of an organized industrial working class.

The population is both the reason for the existence of an economic structure and the raw material of that structure. Population increase in a primitive society may result in starvation; in a modern industrial society it will result in more young people and consequently an increasing pressure on educational and welfare services. It may also cause pressure for further advances in technology and will ultimately result in demands for more housing and employment.

In both primitive and advanced societies population increase may lead to migration, which will in turn affect the social structure; for example, the migrants may be mainly male, and the lack of young adult males in the society for long periods will drastically alter the family structure. Population increase may also lead to war. The structure of the population will influence social patterns: the proportion of young people to old people, the proportion of males to females, the distribution of the population, will all affect personal relationships within the society. The social structure may also be influenced by changes in the geographical structure of the society; increasing industrialization during the nineteenth century attracted large numbers of people from the countryside to the towns, so that by the end of the century three-quarters of the British population were living in towns. Now one-third of the population live in seven huge conurbations, the areas in and around London, Birmingham, Liverpool, Leeds, Manchester, Newcastle, and Glasgow; in fact, four-fifths of the population now live in half the area of the country.

This urbanization has caused great social problems and it may be some consolation for us to know that most of them are not new. Traffic congestion became intolerable in ancient Rome, and, immediately he gained power, Julius Caesar banned all wheeled traffic from Rome during the day; despite a marvellous sewage system, pollution was also a chronic problem in Rome with piles of ordure and offal rotting in open pits. The Romans, too, had a housing problem with the great mass of the Roman proletariat living in tenement slums, each containing an average of two hundred people. And just as we see problems of leisure looming so did the Romans: by the year AD 354 there were 200 public holidays and 175 of these were devoted to the Games— 'attendance at public spectacles became the principal occupation of their existence ... Just as today 'real' life, for the millions, exists only on the television screen.'[1]

The systematic study of population (demography) really started with the publication of Malthus's *Essay on Population* in 1798. In this essay Malthus stated his 'law of population': that the human species, 'when unchecked, goes on doubling itself every twenty-five years, or increases in a geometrical ratio', while 'the means of subsistence, under circum-

Population of England and Wales

Date	Total population	
1600	4 812 000	
1700	6 045 000	
1750	6 517 000	

Census enumerated		Increase over ten years
1801	8 893 000	
1811	10 165 000	1 272 000
1821	12 000 000	1 835 000
1831	13 897 000	1 897 000
1841	15 914 000	2 017 000
1851	17 928 000	2 014 000
1861	20 066 000	2 138 000
1871	22 712 000	2 646 000
1881	25 974 000	3 262 000
1901	32 528 000	
1961	46 072 000	
1971	48 594 000	

1 *Why do you think the population of England and Wales increased so dramatically in the nineteenth century?*

2 *What sort of effects did the eighteenth-century growth have on social conditions?*

3 *Has the population growth had any marked effect on social conditions during this century?*

stances the most favourable to human industry, could not possibly be made to increase faster than in an arithmetical ratio'. Man 'would increase as the numbers 1. 2. 4. 8. 16. 32. 64. 128. 256 and subsistence as 1. 2. 3. 4. 5. 6. 7. 8. 9'. Malthus believed that any improvements in economic conditions could only be temporary as they would result in a rapid increase in population, until this was again restrained by 'vice and misery'. One by-product of Malthus's theory was an excuse for the upper classes not to better the conditions of the poor, since such betterment would merely cause them to have more children, until conditions were again reduced to their previous level. This argument is still occasionally put forward today; for example, by opponents of family allowances.

In 1882 Behm and Wagner estimated the population of the Earth as 1434 million, and in 1972 the estimated population was 3706 million. Yet there is no evidence that proportionately more people are suffering from starvation than a hundred years ago. This may be because of improved communications and aid for famine areas. Overall, indeed, there may be a higher standard of living. But some people claim that in the long term rich nations are getting richer and poor nations are getting poorer.

In 1974 the United Nations declared a World Population Year and stated 'every second there are two additional mouths to feed. Every day there are 200 000 more births than deaths, six million more every month. . . .' As infant mortality is reduced and the average length of life extended, a new population greater than that of Britain is created every year, partly because many people in the world still believe that they must have many children so that a few may survive. It may be that the world is approaching crisis-point as four babies continue to be born every second, but ever since the times of Malthus impending doom has consistently been prophesied—and, consistently, food supplies have expanded. Even Japan, where it is estimated that only 10 per cent of the land area is under cultivation, supports a population of 653 per square mile as compared with the United Kingdom's 558 and Brazil's 20. Vast areas of land still remain unused, and little attempt has yet been made to farm the oceans systematically. However, even assuming that all the world's resources were exploited to the full and distributed satisfactorily, there is a theoretical point at which no further expansion of population would be possible. What then?

If the negative theory of population control put forward by Malthus was the only possibility, then we could look forward only to eventual widespread starvation until the population was reduced to a subsistence level. Population can, however, be socially controlled. As people become aware of the pressure of population and the economic disadvantages of a large family in an industrial society, the values of the

World population increase

Figures in millions	Actual			Projected		
	1950	1960	1970	1980	1990	2000
Africa	217	270	344	457	616	818
North America	166	199	228	261	299	333
Latin America	162	213	283	377	500	652
East Asia	657	780	930	1 095	1 265	1 424
South Asia	698	865	1 126	1 486	1 912	2 354
Europe	392	425	462	497	533	568
Oceania	12	16	19	24	30	35
USSR	180	214	243	271	302	330
Total	2 486	2 982	3 632	4 457	5 438	6 494

Source: Adapted from *Social Trends* 3, HMSO 1972

1   *Which areas on this table are now experiencing a 'population explosion'? What do you think may be the causes and the results of these increases in population?*

2   *What sort of social and economic measures might be used to restrain a 'population explosion'? What sort of religious and cultural objections may there be to such measures?*

society may change, and, for example, contraception and abortion, previously regarded as immoral, become acceptable. In Britain there has been a steady decline in the birth rate since 1965, and in nearly all the major European countries birth rates have declined since the forties and fifties. J. A. Banks has made the point that family limitation in England appears to have started among the middle class in the depression of the 1870s and spread to the lower classes later.[2] It is suggested that the standard of living of the middle class first rose substantially in the second half of the nineteenth century, and that they did not wish to lose the comfort, security, and status which they had experienced during this period when economic circumstances worsened; an obvious way to retain their standard of living was to reduce the size of their families.

Apart from these social controls on population levels, the study of animal behaviour (ethology) has also suggested that animals often seem to have their numbers limited according to the available food supply before starvation level is reached, by becoming less fertile. For instance, when myxomatosis drastically reduced the rabbit population in England in 1954 the buzzard, which depended upon the rabbit as its principal prey, did not breed at all in some cases while in others abnormally small clutches of eggs (many addled) were laid; this reduced level of fertility continued until the buzzard population shrank to about half the level it had been before myxomatosis.[3] It has been suggested that people living in modern industrial communities may similarly adjust to a physically lower level of fertility.[4] It may be that as the underdeveloped countries become industrialized there will be a slowing down of population increase—either because fertility is decreased or because technological development means that insurance policies and pensions replace children as guarantees for old age—and thus an apocalyptic collapse of the world's population will be avoided.

The size and distribution of population is a vital factor in determining the economic structure of a society. If the number exceeds or merely matches the available food resources, there can be no move away from a purely subsistence economy; but once a consistent surplus of food is achieved some non-primary producers can be supported, and some of these may discover and invent things which will in turn increase the economic surplus and allow more non-primary producers to be maintained. Some of the non-primary producers may become priests, courtiers, teachers, architects, or engineers, but the surplus may also support a vast army of labourers who can be used to build temples, palaces, cities, or huge monuments.[5] For example, the Great Pyramid of Egypt was built before the invention of the wheel and was only possible because some hundred thousand labourers, engineers, and architects were not concerned with producing their own food. The economic surplus made possible by the rich soils of the Nile, Euphrates, and Tigris resulted in the appearance of the first cities in the Middle and Near East about 6000 years ago; and although Lagash in Sumaria with a population of 36 000 people may not appear large by modern standards (Shanghai has a population of 10 820 000), the economic system needed to maintain a non-primary producing population of this size must have been quite sophisticated.

Having achieved the required economic surplus, the next problem is what to do with it. The size of the surplus will, of course, partially settle the number of non-primary producers that can be maintained. However, the non-primary producers may be kept to a minimum, as in the feudal system in which most of the economic surplus was distributed to a few rich men who dominated the others; or the primary producers may be kept to a minimum and the non-primary producers may become more numerous, as in our modern urban societies. These secondary producers may in turn produce the major economic surplus.

In the modern situation two economic systems have become dominant—'capitalism' and 'socialism'. In a capitalist system the means of production, distribution, and exchange are in private hands. This private enterprise system depends upon the profit motive to stimulate some people to exert themselves to produce a surplus—and thus, in turn, to stimulate other people to produce a surplus for them and for their profit. Under capitalism the 'profit mechanism' will determine what is made and how and where it is made. In a socialist system the means of production, distribution, and exchange are controlled by the State, and the public good is supposed to provide the motivation to produce the surplus, which would not of course be distributed into private hands. In this case, the 'public good' would determine what is made and how and where it is made.

The capitalist will see the socialist system as failing to provide a proper motivation for hard work, and will believe that socialism means dull mediocrity. The socialist will see the capitalist system as one whereby the worker is robbed of the surplus he has produced, and will believe that capitalism results in unfairness, hardship, and conflict. Most modern industrial societies are neither fully capitalist nor fully socialist, but will have a tendency towards one or other of these systems.

Once a society produces an economic surplus, this surplus can be carried about, used as a means of exchange, or disposed of publicly to demonstrate social superiority. But soon this method becomes too cumbersome, and tokens are substituted for the surplus article. This 'money' can then, again, be disposed of publicly to demonstrate social superiority, used to buy other surplus articles, or be given to others who perform jobs for the giver, thereby perhaps producing a still greater

United Kingdom population increase

	Census enumerated				Mid-year estimates				Projections			
	1901	1911	1921	1931	1941	1951	1961	1971	1981	1991	2001	2011
Total population (millions)												
By sex:												
Males	18.5	20.4	21.0	22.1	23.3	24.4	25.7	27.1	28.2	29.5	31.0	32.7
Females	19.7	21.7	23.0	24.0	24.9	26.1	27.3	28.6	29.6	30.7	32.0	33.6
All persons	38.2	42.1	44.0	46.0	48.2	50.6	53.0	55.7	57.7	60.3	63.1	66.3
Percentage of population												
By age group:												
School age or under (0–14)	32.5	30.8	28.0	24.3	21.0	22.5	23.3	24.2	23.2	23.6	23.5	22.8
Working ages (15–64/59)	61.3	62.3	64.2	66.1	67.2	63.9	62.1	59.8	60.0	60.1	61.5	62.0
Retirement ages (65/60 and over)	6.2	6.8	7.9	9.6	11.8	13.6	14.6	16.0	16.8	16.3	15.0	15.2

Note: by 1975 the projections of population growth given above had been cut substantially, the figure for 2001 dropping from 63.1 million to 59.9 million.

Source: Adapted from *Social Trends* 3, HMSO 1972

How has the changing ratio of males to females helped to change behaviour in the UK during the present century? What factors do you think will influence the population changes envisaged on this population growth map?

Projected population growth by regions, 1969–2001

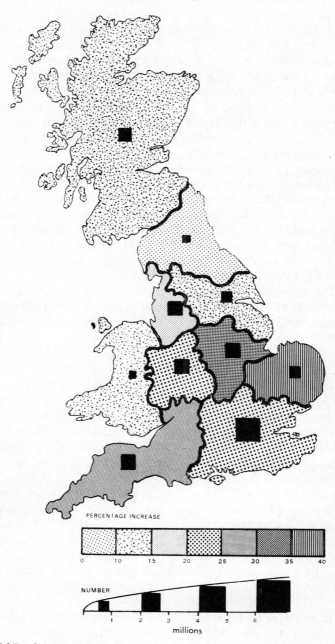

PERCENTAGE INCREASE

0   10   15   20   25   30   35   40

NUMBER

1   2   3   4   5   6

millions

Source: Social Trends 3, HMSO 1972

161

surplus. The owner of the surplus may, however, have no immediate use for the money he has acquired, and may wish to lend it to other people who have more use for it; if these other people need the use of his money badly enough, they may be prepared to pay back considerably more than was originally lent. Ultimately, the owner of the money may be able to stop producing anything: he can live off the surplus produced by his surplus money. When the first man became a financier in this way, capitalism was born.

The growth of an economy based on the ownership of capital was slow in Europe. Usury (the lending of money at a profit) was regarded as unfruitful and a mortal sin. In 1139 the Second Lateran Council stated 'We condemn the disgraceful and detestable rapacity of usurers', and ruled that they should be refused Christian burial. But as a new kind of borrower appeared, who was not poor but wished to borrow money because he thought he could pay back both capital and interest and still make a profit, the rules against usury were relaxed. For example, a lender was entitled to charge interest if he could show that he suffered a loss in parting with his money, and wealthy banking families like the Medicis of Florence achieved great political power as bankers. Capitalism had come of age.

With the development of overseas trade in the sixteenth century it became increasingly difficult for individuals to finance trading ventures on a long-term basis to the more distant markets, and Joint Stock Companies began to develop. These companies made it possible for people to pool their resources to finance single expeditions, recovering their contributions and their shares of any profits at the end of each voyage. Gradually capital came to be invested on a permanent basis and by 1660 the East India Company was fully financed by this means. This method of accumulating capital allowed the large industrial undertakings of the nineteenth century to be financed, although all the shareholders in the company were liable personally for all the debts of the company should it run into difficulties, and someone who had taken only a small shareholding in the company could be faced with complete ruin, his possessions being seized to pay the company's debts. People were sometimes reluctant to take risks to finance commercial expansion on these terms and in 1855 a Limited Liability Act (reinforced by the Companies Act of 1862) made it possible to form a Limited Liability Company in which a person was only liable to lose the shares he had actually bought in the company should that company go bankrupt. Capitalism could now develop with less risk for the capitalist.

Capitalism increased in power with increasing urbanization and mechanization, and the obvious evils that resulted from it led to attacks upon the system. In the middle of the nineteenth century the opposi-

Dependent age groups (United Kingdom)

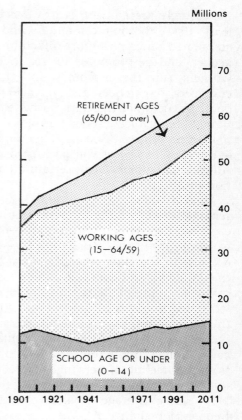

Millions

RETIREMENT AGES
(65/60 and over)

WORKING AGES
(15–64/59)

SCHOOL AGE OR UNDER
(0–14)

70
60
50
40
30
20
10
0

1901 1921 1941 1971 1991 2011

1 If the projected population in the United Kingdom for the year 2011 is correct, how will the number of people under school-leaving age and over retirement age compare with the number now?

2 What changes would you expect in the school-leaving age and retirement age by then?

3 Overall, what changes would you expect to result in our society?

Source: Social Trends 3, HMSO 1972

tion found its most famous spokesman in Karl Marx. Marx believed that industrial society was destined to transform itself speedily into a society completely polarized: a tiny handful of huge exploiters at one pole, and an overwhelming mass of miserable, dehumanized, and outraged proletarians at the other. All other classes would be crushed and disappear into the proletariat. Eventually the outraged and the injured, having lost their last stake in society and their last semblance of humanity, would rise in righteous anger and expropriate the handful of expropriators; they would burst existing society asunder and humanize all mankind.[6] Marx died in 1883 but his friend Engels, when he died in 1895, still gave the old order only 'until the end of the century'.

Although the cataclysmic collapse of capitalism as forecast by Marx has not transpired, the 'alienation' of the worker which he saw in the Industrial Revolution has continued to increase. Automation and increased mechanization are gradually removing the middle band of jobs which allowed the worker a visible road to the top.[7] In the

163

increasingly mechanized factory it is becoming more and more rare to learn a skill, become a foreman, and progress to management; in the automated office it is more difficult to start as a clerk, become a book-keeper, and be promoted to treasurer. In the factory the semi-skilled workers run the machines and the trained and highly educated engineers, researchers, and management enter industry by a different door. In the office the clerk pushes the buttons and feeds the tape that writes the invoices, sends out bills, and orders replacements, but the management are increasingly recruited direct as management trainees —the kind of school you go to and your success or failure within the educational system fairly certainly puts a limit on your future promotion prospects.

Marx thought that increasing mechanization would assist in the final removal of class differences; in fact it, and automation, seem to be increasing the worker's alienation—his feeling of powerlessness and isolation from the work process—without as yet any sign of the collapse of the class structure. As at the end of the nineteenth century the employee still does not usually own the tools with which he works or have a share of the capital employed in the production process (he is 'alienated from the means of production'). So, too, he is separated from the product of his work: he produces not for himself but for a market; increasingly he produces only a small part of a finished product or carries out a simple routine operation which removes him still further from any feeling of personal involvement with his job. It may be that not only boredom at work but also this feeling that he lacks all power helps to encourage strikes, absenteeism, accidents, lateness, and frequent job changes.[8]

Our economic system exerts an immense power over us. It will govern who does what and on what terms, and this in turn will affect our attitudes to society as a whole. Young people today are increasingly working in jobs that require adult skills; they are working with adults

Contrasts in industry: in the upper photograph barrels are being made by hand by skilled craftsmen; in the lower photograph one man commands the control room at the great Europoort oil refinery in Rotterdam from which all processes and movements are automatically remotely controlled.

'Automation is the name given to industrial processes which use machinery and computers not only to make goods but also to control, by "feed-back" mechanisms, the rate of production, the input of raw materials and the co-ordination of separate processes. In automated factories less manpower is needed, but workers have to understand the whole process and their responsibility is much greater.' (AEB O-level paper, June 1973.)

Why are sociologists interested in automation?

Photographs: upper, Syndication International; *lower,* BP

as equals and earn wages approaching adult levels. As a result, they are not prepared to accept a subservient role in the adult community. Women have also found new economic power by entering industry and the professions, transforming their social role within a period of sixty years. All of us still wait to see whether automation and increasing mechanization are leading us towards a bright new future or towards the total collapse of our society.

More discussion or written work

1   Marx thought that economic power was all-important. Do you?
2   In their ceremonial feasts (Potlatches) the Indians of North-West America gained prestige by destroying or giving away as much of their accumulated wealth as they could. What similar ways of achieving status are there in our own society?
3   Some parts of Britain have high rates of unemployment (for example, the North-East) while other areas have jobs available. Why do you think the population does not quickly redistribute itself?
4   If the population of Britain rose dramatically, what differences would you expect in the sort of life we live?
5   'To be a human being means the possession of a feeling of inferiority that is constantly pressing on towards its own conquest' (A. Adler). Do you agree? If true, what effect would this have on economic systems?

Research

1   Find out what controls exist to prevent the creation of monopolies in Britain. How effective do you think this control is?
2   Find out how the earnings of young people in your area compare with the earnings of older people. Account if you can for the pattern.

Imagination

Imagine that it has become necessary to restrict population. Draft a scheme of population control (for example, licences to have children) stating how you will operate your proposals.

Reading suggestions

* W. Clarke, *The City in the World Economy*, Penguin
* D. Hay, *Human Populations*, Penguin
* V. Packard, *The Waste Makers*, Penguin
† L. Rainwater, *And the Poor get Children*, Quadrangle
  S. Brittan, *Steering the Economy*, Penguin
  E. Wrigley, *Population and History*, Hutchinson–World

Part Four
Our Attitudes

Chapter 16

Communications

All societies are based on their communications, for without some form of communication men could not come together to form societies. The more complex the forms of communication, the more complex the society is likely to be where these communications exist.

The presence or absence of physical barriers to communication helps to decide the basic form of the society, since natural boundaries prevent the mixing of peoples and encourage the development of separate languages, social customs, and forms of government. The boundary may be a river, like the Rhine between Germany and France; a mountain range, such as the Pyrenees between Spain and France; a sea, as between England and France; or it may be sheer distance, as between the scattered Indian tribes of North America, among whom hundreds of separate languages developed.

The development of sophisticated devices for bridging natural boundaries will allow the development of a common culture: the Roman Empire would have been impossible without the scientific development of road-construction, and a postal service; the Industrial Revolution would have been impossible without the development of canals and railways.

Obviously physical communications have played an important part in the development of the present structure of society and in assisting social patterns to change by increasing mobility, but they are subordinate to the ability of human beings to engage in the personal interchange of ideas, information, and opinion. Our ability to communicate as individuals has an obvious impact on our personal relationships and position within our society. But as the size of human societies increases, and technology advances, group communications become increasingly important, notably by means of books from the sixteenth century onwards, newspapers and magazines from the time of the Licensing Act (1695), and in the twentieth century, by radio and television. These methods of mass communication, or 'the media' as they have come to be called, reach into every home in a way that individuals could not, and obviously have a great potential for influencing our opinions and behaviour; yet the degree to which they do influence us is very far from certain.

We know that our attitudes and values tend to be formed in the first few years of life and that later we receive information through a shield of preconceived opinions; but it is equally true that millions of pounds would not be spent on advertising if there were no possibility of our being influenced by the media.

Now that 94 per cent of the population have easy access to a television set, and watch it on average for fifteen hours a week,[1] television is potentially the most potent form of mass communication, and there is a tendency to assume that it is likely to have a drastic effect on our attitudes and actions. Together with other branches of the media, television is condemned by some people as causing crime, immorality, violence, and escapism (although the undesirability of escapism is a matter of opinion), while others see it as socially and educationally useful. However, there is evidence that the media tend to reinforce existing views and behaviour rather than changing them, and are likely to have the greatest effect when we are unaware that anyone is trying to influence us, or when they create opinions on matters about which individuals are unlikely to have pre-existing opinions. The section of the population most likely to be without preconceived opinions on most subjects and to be unaware of being 'got at' are children, and so it has naturally been the effect of television on children that has caused most concern.

In 1962 the Pilkington Committee reported on the effect of broadcasting and confirmed that the information available was very incomplete, but the committee did state that: 'Dr Hilde Himmelweit told us that all the evidence so far provided by detailed researches suggested that values were acquired, that a view of life was picked up, by children watching television. Professor Eysenck told us that there were good theoretical grounds for supposing that moral standards could be affected by television and that these grounds were largely supported by experimental and clinical evidence.'[2] In a study for the Nuffield Foundation, Dr Himmelweit also reached a number of interesting conclusions on the effect of television on children. She found that television makes an impact if it touches on the ideas and values for which the child is emotionally ready; that the children most likely to be affected are those who are least critical, in particular the less intelligent thirteen to fourteen year old; and that the world of television drama tends to be upper middle class, and shows the world of the majority of children, that of manual work in an urban society, as being uninteresting and perhaps worthy of rejection. In a later study the same investigator found her earlier findings confirmed, in particular that the more able the child the less television he viewed, the brighter children reaching saturation point and turning to other interests earlier than the less intelligent children. More hopefully, Dr Himmelweit found that children with access to only one channel were likely to watch programmes in which they did not expect to be very interested, but in fact they often were, and as a result their tastes developed.[3] However, the introduction of choice, with more than one channel available, has resulted in the partial loss of this advantage.[4]

The possible effects of violence when shown on television are also much debated. In one experiment a group of children were frustrated so as to develop a high degree of aggression and then compared with a normal control group.[5] Both groups were then shown a television recording containing a great deal of aggressive behaviour, and the behaviour of the children in the two groups after viewing the recording were compared. The control group seemed uninfluenced by the violence they had seen, but the frustrated group had not had their tension released by the screen violence (as is sometimes supposed); on the contrary, there was evidence that they found that by copying actions shown on the television recording they were able to release their aggression. There does seem to be evidence that children with aggressive tendencies are attracted to violent programmes on television and there is little evidence to support the view that television reduces the likelihood of real-life violence; television may, on the other hand, give hints to the frustrated children on how they can release their aggression in real-life situations. However, Himmelweit in her study found no evidence to support the view that children become more aggressive as a result of television, and a psychiatrist has stated that young children 'spontaneously ... create for themselves the same images of horror and terror without ever having heard a fairy story, much less seen TV violence or read horror comics'.[6]

It may be that heavy exposure to television is not the main factor in causing delinquent acts, but there does appear to be evidence that a heavy dosage of violence heightens the probability that a viewer, perhaps with an existing predisposition towards violent conduct, will behave aggressively in a later situation. It has also been suggested that isolated programmes do not make the major impact: it is the 'drip effect' of constant repetition that influences the child, perhaps to a view that violence is necessary and normal.

In 1961 a sociologist, Dr Bryan Wilson, reporting in the *Criminal Law Review*, stated that the mass media exaggerate the amount of crime, provide ideas and technical knowledge of criminal activity for those criminally disposed, transmit criminal ideas from one society to another, have created a greater tolerance of deviant behaviour, and create a delinquent hero-type. In this way, while not actually causing crime, they do create confusion, particularly among young people, about standards of behaviour, and in a subtle and gradual way alter our attitude to crime.[7]

If the media do have a major influence on changing our attitudes and behaviour it would appear that it is a slow and subtle influence. A study by J. Trenaman of two Leeds constituencies in the 1959 General Election found that 'no part of the political campaign ..., either on television or through other media, was found to have any direct bearing on the way in which people decided to vote or even on their attitudes towards the parties'.[8] On the other hand, before 1959 the Conservative Party discovered by market research that their party was associated in the public mind with the more privileged sections of the community and so concentrated their national advertising campaign on showing working-class people voting Conservative. After the campaign more market research showed a drop of 7–8 per cent in the association of the Conservative Party with privilege. It may be that indirect persuasion has some effect in changing prejudgements originating from background and environment, provided people are unaware that an attempt is being made to influence them. People can screen themselves from direct persuasion in the short term, but we do not know whether persuasion by the media over a period of time can change attitudes.

Although it is difficult to measure the impact of television content upon our attitudes and resulting behaviour, it is easier to see the way that the physical presence of television has altered behaviour patterns— for example, in declining cinema audiences in the 1950s (21 million a week in 1956 declining to 8 million in 1964). However, even in this area there is room for debate: it has been suggested that the main alteration television has made in our way of life has been in the home, with the family staying together at home more and a better home atmosphere with less opportunity for friction through boredom. It is said that not only is television a great educator, widening cultural horizons, but it stimulates conversation in the home by presenting differing viewpoints. The opposing view is that, although the family may be in the home together more, television has disrupted family life, reduced discussion on family affairs, and reduced normal exchanges between parent and child, children being dumped in front of a television set rather than encouraged in creative play.[9]

The accuracy of the information which we receive from television has also been criticized. It has been suggested that the very presence of television cameramen creates news because people act in a way they would not otherwise do. Television as a medium needs to dramatize

A scene from a children's television serial—'The Pathfinder'.
Such scenes may not seem very relevant to everyday life in Britain, but do you think they can influence children's attitudes to violence?
Is too much violence shown on television?
Photograph: BBC

in order to make an impact and there will be a tendency to select dramatic news even although it may not properly represent actual events. Some people have even accused television reporting teams of acting as 'agents provocateurs', for example, encouraging clashes between gangs of youths. It was suggested at the time of the Investiture of the Prince of Wales that the BBC deliberately sought out hostile views where few existed. One Welshman wrote to a local newspaper after an incident: 'How can we be sure that people are dying in Biafra and Vietnam? The BBC tells us so, but is it true?'

It is probable that most of the attacks on television are exaggerated, and it may well be that we have a television service as well controlled as it is possible to have. But the very nature of television makes it necessary for individuals to select and produce the information that is to appear, and it would seem impossible to prevent those individuals' unconscious prejudices and preconceptions from influencing the information we receive.

The same sort of bias is also likely to appear in the other branches of the media, and newspapers in particular, with an estimated daily circulation of about eight million, are potentially powerful communicators of slanted or misleading information. Michael Schofield has illustrated the way in which newspapers may influence opinion by a selective presentation of the facts: 'But the newspapers are still run by adults and still reflect the views of the adults who respond to the new economic power of the teenagers with a strange mixture of bewilderment, scorn, and envy. So teenagers are news, but only certain kinds of teenagers—those who are in trouble, those who are defying convention, those who are good copy.'[10]

Starting with the same facts we might all quite conscientiously arrive at different decisions or opinions, and the same applies to those who control the media. However, opinions presented by the organs of communication, often being accepted as facts, may have a considerable effect on the actions of individuals and groups and thus on the structure of society. In 1972 the National Child Development Study reported on 16 000 children born in one week of 1958, and showed that the average gap in reading attainment between children from unskilled working-class families and those from professional families was well over two years at the age of seven. On 3 June 1972 the *Daily Telegraph* commented: 'Attainment in reading and arithmetic of seven-year-olds in private schools was also checked. They were found to be well ahead of their State school contemporaries. Even when State school children of similar home and family background were compared, the private school children were ahead.' On 4 June the *Observer* wrote of the same report: 'At the other extreme are the well-off parents who send their children to independent schools. But the study concludes that the benefits of this, when all other relevant factors are taken into account, are marginal in both reading and arithmetic.'

The implication is obvious—so far as skill in reading and arithmetic is concerned the *Daily Telegraph* reporter feels that private education is beneficial, while the *Observer* commentator is dubious of its value: but note that both reports give the impression that their view is the one accepted by the National Child Development Study. Most newspapers frankly admit their political alignments so we can, if we wish, bear these in mind when reading opinions expressed in them. But the selection of news is a more subtle way of opinion-forming; and as, obviously, no newspaper can report everything that happens, it will emphasize some facts and consign others to the inside pages—or even omit them altogether!

As most of the national newspapers and a large number of provincial ones are owned by a handful of proprietors, these owners have very considerable power to influence the opinions of the public although this power will be modified by the fact that people will anyway tend to buy a newspaper which reflects their own attitudes and therefore reinforces their own prejudices rather than altering them.

Since 1900 the readership of newspapers in Britain has been steadily increasing, from one daily paper for every two adults in 1920 to more than one copy for every adult in 1947. However, the number of different newspapers has been decreasing: out of nine evening papers in the London area in the nineteenth century only two remain; five daily or Sunday papers with a combined readership of about six and a half million were closed in the decade from 1960. At the same time, ownership of newspapers has become increasingly concentrated: by 1967 seven out of eight copies of all national morning papers were controlled by the three major newspaper groups. This modern trend towards limited ownership has attracted the comment that the 'cultural conditions of democracy are in fact being denied'.[11]

To counteract the dangers of such concentration it has been suggested that newspapers be put into the hands of the active contributors who would run the organizations under the control of intermediate bodies subject to public control. This proposal is similar to the one which removed broadcasting from private ownership in 1927. There are already stipulations in the Television Act (1963) and the Sound Broadcasting Act (1972) that prevent the existing newspaper proprietors from taking control of Independent Television and local radio stations. In addition, the Monopolies and Mergers Act (1965) gave the Department of Trade and Industry power to control the transfer of newspapers to other newspaper proprietors.

Despite the power of newspaper proprietors, they must themselves pay some regard to the wishes of the large advertisers who provide the

National newspapers—circulation and ownership 1975

Daily newspapers	Year of origin	Circulation (to nearest thousand)	Owner
Daily Mirror	1903	4 018 000	International Publishing Corporation
Daily Express	1900	2 894 000	Beaverbrook Newspapers
Sun	1969 (succeeded *Daily Herald*)	3 435 000	News of the World Organization
Daily Mail	1896 (merged with *Sketch* 1971)	1 730 000	Associated Newspapers
Daily Telegraph	1855	1 353 000	Daily Telegraph Ltd
The Times	1785	327 000	Thomson Organization
Guardian	1821	336 000	Guardian Newspapers Ltd
Financial Times	1888	186 000	Financial Times Ltd
Morning Star	1966 (succeeded *Daily Worker*)	49 000 (1972)	People's Press Printing Society
Sunday newspapers			
News of the World	1843	5 646 000	News of the World Organization
Sunday People	1881	4 219 000	International Publishing Corporation
Sunday Mirror	1963	4 284 000	International Publishing Corporation
Sunday Express	1918	3 786 000	Beaverbrook Newspapers
Sunday Times	1822	1 396 000	Thomson Organization
Observer	1791	761 000	The Observer Trust
Sunday Telegraph	1961	757 000	Daily Telegraph Ltd

Note on regional newspapers. In 1973 there were 86 morning, evening, and Sunday regional newspapers and 750 newspapers appearing once or twice a week. The total circulation of regional morning and evening papers is about 8 million. Three morning papers—the *Liverpool Daily Post*, the *Yorkshire Post*, and the *Northern Echo*—have circulations of over 100 000. The two London evening papers—the *Evening News* (founded 1881) and the *Evening Standard* (1827)—had circulations of 650 000 and 485 000 respectively in 1975 (the *Evening News* is owned by Associated Newspapers and the *Evening Standard* by Beaverbrook Newspapers).

Some of the papers with lower circulations are viable because the social and economic status of their readership attracts a higher proportion of advertisers.

1 From the information given in this table assess which publishers are in a position to influence most people.
2 Obtain a copy of each of the newspapers listed and examine the political views expressed in them. Do any of the newspapers appear to be biased?

bulk of their revenue. In the case of the 'heavies', such as *The Times* or the *Guardian*, the advertising revenue will represent about 75 per cent of the newspaper's total income; among the 'tabloids', such as the *Daily Mirror* or the *Sun*, the advertising income will be some 40 per cent of the total. In most cases advertising space is allocated first and the paper is built up around the advertisements.

It is, of course, impossible to gauge the exact effect of advertising moguls' and 'press lords' on the news we read; but it is important to be aware of their presence and potential.

Advertising itself is obviously biased: it would be unreasonable for us to expect the advertiser to present information in a disinterested way. Without advertising it would be almost impossible for our 'advanced' society to operate—it brings new products to our attention and helps to boost demand and hence production. Advertising also conveys official information—on welfare benefits, cutting down accidents, preventing diseases; it provides information on political matters, cultural events, and entertainment. Advertising is a valuable means of communication, but some people feel that, despite certain restrictions on some of the more blatant forms of deception, it can still be used to make extravagant and misleading claims, and it tends to use sex, vanity, fear, snobbery, and envy to sell its products and thus increases the emphasis on these factors in society. One view of advertising is that although it helps to raise standards of living it also raises people's expectations beyond the point at which they have any hope of realizing them by normal means so that ultimately 'the whole thing is going to explode'.[12]

A further criticism of advertising is that it involves the expenditure of vast sums of money in boosting the claims of identical products— needless expense for which the consumer must ultimately pay. It might be argued, on the contrary, that if large subsidies were not paid indirectly to newspapers and magazines by advertisers it would be necessary to increase their cost very considerably. Television advertising, which of course combines the spoken word with the picture, is likely to be most effective, as it reaches us when we are at our most relaxed and least likely to be putting up a conscious defence against it. It is because of its possible potency as an influencer of opinion that rigid regulations have been imposed on its use for advertising. Cigarettes, birth control devices, and political opinion cannot be sold through television advertising in Britain, and the actual techniques used are also controlled: for instance, 'subliminal' advertising is prohibited. The object of subliminal advertising is to imprint information on our subconscious without our normal reasoned defence against propaganda coming into play. This imprinting might be done either by flashing the message on a screen for a split second or by reducing its intensity to a level below that at which it can be consciously perceived. The effectiveness of subliminal advertising is disputed, but in any case it cannot insinuate an idea into an unreceptive mind any more than hypnotism can.[13]

All advertising is at its most effective when it is reinforcing attitudes and desires and is least effective when trying to run contrary to such preconceived ideas. It is pointless to try to sell a car by illustrating its mechanical excellence if the prospective customer really wants a symbol of virility; it is equally pointless to emphasize the hygienic qualities of a toothpaste if people really want a nice taste first thing in the morning. That is why advertisers spend millions of pounds on market research to ensure that they are aiming at the market which is likely to desire products of the kind that they have to sell!

Equally, communicators will try to use words that already convey an appropriate image to those whose approval they wish to attract, and the use of 'emotive language' is an important aspect of all communications. The words we use will have an influence on others: if we say that a man is 'tolerant', people will regard him in a different light than if we used the word 'soft'. Advertisers are very well aware of the power of particular words: additions to a piece of equipment are 'refinements'; salesmen are instructed to use the powerful adjective 'tough' rather than the less emotive 'strong'; politicians have always spoken of 'advances', 'improvements', 'justice', and 'freedom', although like all emotive words, these are meaningless without additional information.

'Freedom' for example, is meaningless unless we are told freedom from what; yet it is undoubtedly a 'hurrah' word, signifying approval, since we use 'free from' only of something we are glad to be without. For instance, we say a 'trouble-free job' but not a 'money-free job'; and though some terms such as 'free-love' or 'free-thought' are used by people who oppose these concepts, they were probably coined by supporters of the concepts. Freedom, like all emotive words, is only fully meaningful if we are given more information. For example, in the American Civil War when both sides said they were fighting for freedom, neither side was lying; they were just making incomplete pronouncements—the South could claim that it was fighting for the freedom of State governments from federal interference, while the North could claim that it was fighting to free the South from slavery.

'Democracy' is another word which must be interpreted with caution, and which emphasizes the importance of care in the use and understanding of emotive words. In Germany the Nazis, while allowing the word to keep its conventional meaning, changed it into a 'boo', an insulting word. In Eastern Europe the Communists have altered the term 'democracy' to refer to their own totalitarian style of government, but have allowed it to keep its laudatory meaning.

Not only do the same words mean different things to different people, but our ability to communicate and receive communication will be influenced by what we wish to hear and see and what we have learnt to hear and see. Obviously a blind man will have a different view of his environment from someone who can see but is deaf; these are extreme examples, but all of us depend upon different senses to varying degrees. The world is full of stimuli, and we cannot pay attention to all of them; we therefore select those that we have learned to pay most attention to—hence the fallacy that sailors have particularly good eyesight, for in fact they see things at sea before the passengers do because they have learned to pay attention to certain stimuli. We also see most quickly and readily the things we want to see; one experiment showed that people who disliked negroes exaggerated the negroid features when asked to assess photographs of negroes.

Not only do we select what we wish to see or hear, we also interpret what we perceive within the context of our own norms and values, which are often the norms and values of the group we are in: a rich man will often consider something cheap that a poor man would regard as expensive. People in the same group will often give similar opinions. In one experiment a pin-point of light was shown in a completely dark room, and, although static, this light appeared to move. At first the audience gave different accounts of the movements of the light, but gradually all members of the group came to see the light moving in the same direction as those who had spoken before them—individuals were accepting the opinion of the group. This collective consciousness is most marked in crowds where the members of the crowd may become more emotional, more suggestible, less self-critical, less intellectual, and less responsible, but will gain a feeling of anonymity and increased power. The fact that a member of a crowd will only be susceptible to attitudes and ideas that appeal to him may not reduce our concern when we consider the attitudes and desires that some people may have, even if only at a subconscious level, a facet of communications that has been used to advantage by many people, from religious evangelists to Adolf Hitler.[14]

There are certainly limits to the influence which communications can have, but their potential power as stimulators and strengtheners of preconceived attitudes and opinions should be sufficient to ensure that a close watch is kept on the control and use of the media.

More discussion or written work

1 Does the showing of disasters such as wars, famines, and floods on television increase people's sense of responsibility or does it create emotional numbness?

2 Should there be some form of public accountability by 'those new and powerful personalities' the political interviewers and commentators?

3 Overall, do you think television is a good or a bad invention?

4 Do you think there is a case for greater censorship of the media, for example, in the fields of politics, sex, or violence?

5   To what extent do you think that opinions and attitudes are influenced by the popular press?

Research

1   Find out to what extent censorship exists in Britain today, and discover what censorship regulations were in force in Britain during World War II.
2   Collect examples of advertisements which you think are trying to sell products by appealing to (*a*) vanity, (*b*) fear, (*c*) sexual appetite, (*d*) envy, either overtly or by implication.

Imagination

Imagine that you have seized power in Britain and you are now Dictator. Outline the sort of Britain you wish to create (this manifesto can be completely fictitious!). Then draw up a list of edicts directed at the organs of communication—these edicts should aim at creating the right climate of public opinion for the establishment of your 'new Britain'.

Reading suggestions

* R. Hoggart, *The Uses of Literacy*, Penguin
† V. Packard, *The Hidden Persuaders*, Penguin
† R. Williams, *Communications*, Penguin
  J. Brown, *Techniques of Persuasion*, Penguin
  H. Himmelweit, *Television and the Child*, Oxford University Press
  M. McLuhan, *Understanding Media*, Sphere

Chapter 17

Class

Although most people talk glibly of belonging to the 'upper', 'middle', or 'working' class and have a pretty good idea of what they mean by these terms, we find on closer examination that the concept of 'class' is a rather vague one, and that different people mean different things when they use the term. Class can be used simply as a term to define the occupational category which someone occupies. This is the method used by the Registrar General in the census returns where five classes are recognized. The first includes big employers and upper professional and higher managerial workers (2.9 per cent of the population); the second, lower professional and managerial workers, upper clerical workers, some self-employed workers, and very small employers (14.6 per cent of the population); the third category includes skilled manual and routine non-manual workers (49.1 per cent of the population); the fourth, semi-skilled workers (22.3 per cent of the population); and the fifth group is made up of the unskilled workers (8 per cent of the population).[1]

Although this method of division has practical advantages, many people when they refer to a class are thinking primarily of income. Others are thinking of education, of a particular life style, or of property ownership, and this has led sociologists to devise differing schemes (such as the Hall-Jones scale) for assigning people to classes for comparative examination—for example, an index based on occupation, education, and area of residence.[2] However, some people merely base their assessment of a person's social class on an automatic and unconscious study of their behaviour.

For example, it is claimed that only the working class handle their cigarettes by cupping the lighted end in their palm, perhaps originating from the need to conceal the lighted end from the foreman in the factory or the corporal in the army. The middle and working classes insist on putting the milk in the cup before the tea, while the upper class put the tea in first—perhaps the upper class did not have to clean tannin stains off their cups themselves in the past or perhaps the fact that the upper class had their cups warmed for them made it unlikely that hot tea would crack the cup. The working class tend to dress 'up' when they go out to the pub, while the middle class tend to dress 'down'—both probably reactions to how they have to dress at work. It is said that working-class men roll their shirt-sleeves up higher and tighter than middle-class men. The way you cut your bread, the names you call your meals, the clothes you wear, your accent, and the food you eat may all label you in many people's minds as belonging to a particular 'class'.

The existence of social classes with common interests because of their ownership or non-ownership of wealth had been recognized by people such as Adam Ferguson before Marx began to develop his theory of social class in the middle of the nineteenth century. However, Marx did not see classes merely as groups of rich or poor people, but as groups of individuals with a common identity of interest in relation to the means of production, people who either owned or did not own capital. Marx saw that human society could not exist without production and that this production could only be effective in producing the surplus which is necessary for the development of complex societies if men cooperated with each other. This cooperation inevitably led to a division of labour and private ownership of the means of production, and this private ownership influenced the social relationship between those who owned the means of production and those who did not and led to the development of classes.

Marx saw society as being fundamentally composed of two classes, the bourgeoisie and the proletariat—the owners and the dispossessed. He accepted that these could be subdivided into more classes but saw these intermediate classes as being temporary, and believed that—as capitalist society developed—it would polarize until everyone would belong to either one or the other of his fundamental classes. As ownership of property is basic to this Marxist view of class, the amount of income which people have is not the main factor in determining their position in the class structure (a teacher, a skilled mechanic, and the owner of a small factory may have the same income but would not occupy the same class position). The Marxist would see the struggle between the classes as the main agent of social change, with the disappearance of private property as a necessary part of that change, but would hold that this could not happen unless people were aware of belonging to a particular class and conscious of the fact that they could only improve their own positions at the expense of another class. Marx believed that the development of large-scale industry and the consequent concentration of labourers in large units would lead these labourers to realize that they had class interests in common, so that they would come together as effective political units and produce the revolution which would lead to a communist society where private property, and therefore social classes, would be eliminated.

It is interesting to note that some modern liberals take the essentially Marxist view that the ownership of property is fundamental to the organization of society, but that—seeing the capitalist ethic generally accepted—they hope to change the structure of society by redistributing ownership on a more or less equal basis, so that every man becomes a capitalist, and a 'pan-capitalist' rather than a 'communist' society develops.

Max Weber followed Marx as the main observer of class, but while accepting that the ownership of property was basic to the class structure, he considered that the more important aspect of class was a person's ability to gain access to goods and services ('life chances').[3] Weber saw four main classes rather than the basic two of Marx: the property owners; the professionals; the petty bourgeoisie; and the manual working class. Weber saw that divisions would exist within the classes themselves and that, in addition, society was further divided on the basis of status and power. Very often individuals within a class would also share status and power in more or less the same proportion, but this was not necessarily so (for example, a labourer may become a cabinet minister having low class but a high degree of power, or a rich and aristocratic man may commit a repulsive crime and end up in prison, having high class but low status).

More recently sociologists, while still accepting that the ownership of the means of production is fundamental to the class system of an advanced society, have concentrated on the large majority of people who are not property owners and among whom the division of labour is the main means by which they gain access to life chances.

Normally the highly trained person can command a higher return for his services than can the unskilled. The higher the education and training, the greater the skill, and therefore—usually—the rewards. It is possible that our society would disappear under a deluge of refuse quicker than it would from a lack of lawsuits, so one cannot necessarily claim that a lawyer is more indispensable, and therefore more important, than a dustman. But the unskilled are usually in greater supply than the skilled and cannot compete on equal terms for scarce resources.

Market forces may not be the only factor in allowing particular occupational groups to possess goods and acquire income, and some trade unions or professional organizations may be successful in creating a monopoly situation in which their members are in a more favourable position than are other people of similar skill; but it is doubtful whether they have had any influence on altering the class background of their members, although the unions' activities may influence the status which is accorded to their members within a particular class. This may work in reverse, however: for example, some people would regard the militant approach adopted by some teachers' unions as reducing the status of teachers by identifying them with manual workers rather than with other professional groups.

A status system results from the judgements which people make of the worthiness of other individuals or groups to command respect. Status systems will be much more diffuse than class, for the concept of class is only useful in so far as it identifies a small number of groups containing many members with common life-styles and interests, but within each class there will be many thousands of status rankings. Usually a higher class will also imply a higher status, but sometimes a successful businessman may have to acquire the social skills or material attributes (for example, a country mansion) expected by the elite status group before he is accepted by it. Sometimes his background will result in him remaining unaccepted by the high status group and he will have to use his newly acquired wealth to buy the 'correct' education, accent, and manners for his children so that they will become 'acceptable'.

Sometimes there will be a clear difference between class and status because of cultural and historical factors. This may be based on religion

Accents

One hundred and seventy-seven pupils at comprehensive schools in South-West England and South Wales were asked to give their opinions on accents. Their views are listed below. As most pupils found BBC English the most 'intelligible' it is listed first, ranging down to number 13 (a German accent) which was found to be the most difficult to understand. (Bristol University psychologist Howard Giles at British Psychological Society Conference.)

Pleasant sound	Intelligibility	Status
1 BBC English	1 BBC English	1 BBC English
2 French	2 North American	2 Affected English
3 Irish	3 French	3 North American
4 South Welsh	4 Irish	French
5 Northern England	5 South Welsh	5 German
6 Indian	6 Northern England	6 South Welsh
Italian	Somerset	7 Irish
Somerset	8 Cockney	8 Italian
9 North American	Italian	9 Northern England
10 Cockney	10 Indian	10 Somerset
11 Affected English	11 Affected English	11 Indian
German	Birmingham	Cockney
13 Birmingham	13 German	13 Birmingham

Source: The Daily Telegraph

1   List the accents given according to your opinion of their sound, intelligibility, and status.
2   Why do you think some accents have a higher status than others?
3   In what ways can a dialect be a drawback?
4   What effect can living in a town or in the country have on a person's speech?

as in Ulster, or race as in the United States. Many black Americans have low status because of their colour and because of the jobs they do; but the professional or executive negro may still have low status because of his colour—the poor white may claim superiority over the richer black. In this sort of situation the group that does not have the status of its members recognized by society generally is likely to develop a status structure of its own.

C. Wright Mills called status 'prestige' and described it as 'the shadow of money and power'.[4] He felt that people justified the positions that they occupied in the society by adopting visible symbols appropriate to their rank; in this way they showed their cultural and moral superiority over those who did not behave in the appropriate way. Status affects the way that most people behave, it enters into their choice of friends and choice of husband or wife, what organizations they join, how they dress, how they behave—sometimes consciously but more often subconsciously. Status is related to class but may not be the same!

There is nothing magical about labelling people as belonging to one class or another. Class only exists if people accept its existence; it only exists if one group of people in a society exercise more power than another group, can afford to buy more goods and services than another group, dress differently, behave differently, and live and enjoy themselves differently.

It would appear that classes do exist in Britain and do adopt different modes of behaviour which in turn help to identify them and reinforce their solidarity. Obviously a higher income enables a particular style of behaviour to be indulged in, but this is only part of the reason why there are obvious class differences (a working-class man would regard many middle-class men dressed for leisure as being scruffily dressed). Different educational opportunities also may encourage different leisure activities; but whereas football is often regarded as a working-class sport it is no less intellectual than golf which is still often regarded as a middle-class pastime. One does not require a superior education to watch polo-ponies rather than greyhounds.

It has been suggested that education and income are less important in influencing behaviour than is the work-situation itself. David Lockwood claims that, in the workplace, social relationships between various grades of employees (and customers) determine feelings of class.[5] If the clerk works with executives and is physically separated from the blue-collar workers, he will identify with the middle class rather than the working class and adopt middle-class norms of behaviour.

No doubt the work-situation does reinforce class divisions in the way that Lockwood suggests, but in any case the modern equality of

Television viewing (United Kingdom)

	February 1968	1975
Average weekly hours viewed		
Age groups:		
5–14	19.4	24.0
15–19	15.6	17.3
20–29	15.6	18.2
30–49	17.4	18.4
50 and over	17.5	19.6
Social class of adults (15 and over):		
A	13.9	14.0
B	15.9	16.6
C	17.9	20.0
Overall average weekly hours viewed		
by all persons aged 5 and over	17.6	19.7
Television broadcast licences current		
at 31 March (millions):		
Monochrome	15.1	10.1
Colour	—	7.6

Social class (BBC definition)

Class A. Five per cent of population: including such people as doctors, professors, clergymen, lawyers, architects, directors, senior civil servants and senior executives (and their families).

Class B. Twenty-five per cent of population: including such people as bank clerks, teachers, senior clerical and supervisory workers (and their families).

Class C. The remaining 70 per cent of the population.

Source: Adapted from *Social Trends* 4 and 6, HMSO 1973, 1975

1   *What sort of reasons might account for the differences in the amount of television viewing by different age groups?*
2   *How does social class influence the amount of television watched?*

earnings between some manual and non-manual workers may indicate an identity of interest that is more apparent than real. In the work-situation the non-manual worker is more likely than the manual to be a member of a private pension scheme and to be on an income scale that will increase with service and experience; he will have greater security of employment (unemployment has always been lower among non-manual than manual workers); and he is likely to be working shorter hours than a manual worker who earns the same salary. The manual worker sometimes has fringe benefits in the form of subsidized

The people at Ascot and the men in the betting shop are all concerned with the winner of the 2.30 but in widely differing environments.
Is this a reflection of class differences or are other factors more important?
Does Britain really have a divisive class system?
Photographs: Camera Press

canteens and travel, but is unlikely to have the more substantial fringe benefits of company cars, houses, and entertainment allowances.[6]

These differences between manual and non-manual workers are emphasized when one examines the amount of capital that the two groups are likely to possess.[7] Although most capital is still owned by relatively few people (see pages 189, 190), even the lower grades of non-manual workers (for example, clerical and sales) are likely to be

Wealth of individuals (Great Britain)

Distribution of wealth by groups of owners	1961	1971
Percentage of wealth owned by:		
Most wealthy 1 per cent	28.4	20.4
,, ,, 2 ,, ,,	37.1	27.7
,, ,, 3 ,, ,,	42.7	32.8
,, ,, 4 ,, ,,	47.0	36.8
,, ,, 5 ,, ,,	50.6	40.1
,, ,, 10 ,, ,,	62.5	51.6
,, ,, 25 ,, ,,	79.2	72.1
,, ,, 50 ,, ,,	92.5	90.2
All owners	100.0	100.0
Total wealth (£ thousand million)	54.9	112.7

Source: Adapted from *Social Trends* 3 and 4, HMSO 1972, 1973

Notes

Estimates of wealth distribution vary widely depending upon the factors taken into consideration and upon whether the wealth is measured among families or individuals, among the whole population, or only among those above a certain age. If based on taxes on income they are biased by tax avoidance, which should result in an under-estimation of the concentration of wealth in the hands of the most wealthy; if on estate duty they may also be biased for the same reason—but this may be counterbalanced to some extent by the omission of small amounts of assets which can be transferred on death without formality.

If all state and occupational pension schemes are included the inequality of wealth distribution is reduced considerably. But if house ownership, which represents about half the total wealth of those in the bottom 95 per cent of the population, is not considered then the inequality of wealth redistribution increases substantially and the apparent increase in equality over the years is largely nullified; some would take the view that housing and many consumer durables are necessities and do not increase the 'power' of the person possessing them in the way that shareholdings and other easily realizable assets may do. (For example, in 1973 a survey (*Business Observer*, 20 Jan. 1974) showed that the portion of the population over twenty-four with a total net wealth each of £10 000 would have been in the 10 per cent of the population immediately below the richest 10 per cent. But if household goods, houses, and insurance policies were deducted they would have been left with £1250 each. Those in the top 0.1 per cent of the population had a total net wealth of £300 000 each; when household goods, houses and insurance policies were deducted they were left with £259 000 each.)

The Gini 'coefficient of wealth' was 87 in 1960 and 84 in 1971; these measurements of the distribution of wealth represent a slight trend towards greater equality.

In 1974 the Government announced that a capital transfer tax would replace existing death duties; this tax would obviate tax avoidance by gift.

1   *Is Britain a 'property owning democracy'?*
2   *Is there any evidence in the table to suggest that the poor are getting richer and the rich poorer?*

better off in terms of capital ownership than the skilled manual worker; and this implies a greater degree of security and a greater vested interest in the *status quo* by non-manual workers.

The narrowing of the income gap between manual and non-manual workers has probably not removed the conception of class differences between the groups themselves ('self-assigned class').[8] One survey in 1962 showed that 61 per cent of non-manual workers described themselves as middle class, while 19 per cent said they were working class; 29 per cent of manual workers described themselves as middle class and 52 per cent described themselves as working class. It has even been suggested that as the manual workers approach the same standards of income as the non-manual workers they feel 'relatively more deprived' than before.[9] For example, when working-class children were not expected to receive a secondary education, the school was not a reference group; now that more children stay on at school to a later age those that do not are likely to feel deprived of the status and job expectations that go with extended education.

Melvin Kohn in America has tried to prove a link between manual and non-manual work-situations, and the way working and middle-class parents bring up their children.[10] He claims that the white-collar emphasis on abstract ideas and manipulation of personal relationships within the job-situation leads white-collar parents to lay emphasis on the importance of a child making his own decisions; while the blue-collar worker—following a set pattern of work activity, externally controlled—will tend to make his child conform and be obedient and respectful.

Some societies have a completely rigid system of social stratification ranging through slavery, caste, and feudalism to our modern class system of comparative mobility. How mobile a person can be in the British class system is open to argument. Some, such as Professor MacRae of the London School of Economics, wonder if it is even a system;[11] others would claim that it is still the most immobile system of all among those of the industrialized nations. Sometimes, particularly among the young, it would appear that class differences are disappearing. During the 'Flower Power' period of the middle 1960s young people of all classes were brought together by an apparently similar philosophy of life, code of behaviour, and dress style. But by the early 1970s the 'skinhead' or 'bovver' gangs had emerged, gangs almost exclusively working class in origin.

In Britain wealth is much more unequally shared than earnings. A top manager may earn fifty times as much as an average worker, but a top 'wealth owner' may hold more than a thousand times more wealth than the average person. Inheritance is still the major means by which wealth is distributed in Britain. C. D. Harbury showed that in

1956–57 two-thirds of those leaving more than £100 000 upon their deaths had fathers who had themselves left large fortunes.[12] A comparison of these results with earlier ones of 1924–26 shows that there has been little decline in the importance of inherited wealth in the course of this century.[13]

It used to be possible to think of the British class structure as a pyramid, with a large base of unskilled workers narrowing upwards through the skilled to the managerial and professional, and narrowing still further to the apex of the top-managerial, administrative, and upper professional occupational group. Today, however, the shape of the class structure is more like a haystack, narrower at the base than in the middle, though still with a sharply tapering peak. At the one extreme are the 5 per cent of the population who, it has been claimed, own about 75 per cent of all personal wealth;[14] at the other are the four million or so people who live in poverty. The great movement has been to the skilled manual and clerical groups, which are much closer today in economic terms than are the skilled workers to those at the bottom of the class structure.

The line between manual and non-manual occupations is now no barrier, for a third of the sons of manual workers are likely to enter non-manual jobs, whereas nearly as high a proportion of boys from non-manual families will move to manual employment.[15] This mobility is, however, limited: the children of skilled workers may quite often become clerks, draughtsmen, salesmen, or teachers; but the sons of labourers rarely reach the higher professional or executive roles. Despite increasing educational opportunities over the last thirty years the proportion of people who rise from families at the bottom of the occupational hierarchy to occupy a position at the top is low. A failure to succeed academically increasingly means the end of any prospect of upward mobility as the opportunities to work one's way up from a job entered at the age of sixteen decrease.

Occupational mobility, of course, is not the same as cultural mobility. Getting to the top does not always mean being accepted by 'top people'. 'Top people' may not even be the richest: just as the rich Indian leatherworker could not rise from his position at the bottom of the caste system, so the rich scrap-metal tycoon may not find many invitations to dine with the aristocracy. One council estate in an industrial town may seem to an outside observer exactly the same as another, but one may be regarded locally as a 'cut above the other'. Even gypsies regard themselves as superior to Irish tinkers.

Marx predicted that the completion of automation and the consequent abolition of the division of labour would lead to the disappearance of class differences, but as we saw on page 164 automation may merely widen the gap between the skilled and non-skilled worker. Marx believed that with the elimination of the bourgeois class a truly classless society would emerge. After more than thirty years of communist government in Russia one researcher in 1950 was able to claim that Russia had evolved a ten-class social system, 'from the ruling elite (officials, scientists, top artists and writers) down through managers, bureaucrats, and three classes of workers and two classes of peasants, to the slave labourers'. Even in the collective farms of Israel it is claimed 'an aristocracy of old-timers emerged'.[16]

A classless society may be very desirable—but is it possible?

More discussion or written work

1 'It takes three generations to make a gentleman.' How true is this old axiom today?
2 In England today 'there are always Top Dogs and there are always Under Dogs. Strung out between the two poles is the rest of the population, going up, coming down, or coasting in neutral.' How do you see the British class system?
3 'Managers, not Owners, control industry and commerce today.' Is this true?
4 'America is Middle Class'—how true is this famous headline? To what extent could the same headline apply to Britain?
5 'The middle-class virtues that are sneered at today—thrift, hard work, independence, and the postponement of immediate gratification for future benefit—are the very foundations of civilization.' What do you think of this statement?

Research

1 Using as many facts as you can discover, write an account of a day in the life of a shop-assistant 100 years ago.
2 Try to find examples of different types of group behaviour, language, and dress in your own locality and assess to what degree these differences are the result of class.

Imagination

Imagine that you live in a totally classless society. List the differences that you would expect to be apparent in this society as compared with contemporary Britain.

Reading suggestions

† B. Jackson, *Working Class Community*, Penguin

† V. Packard, *The Status Seekers*, Penguin

† W. Runciman, *Relative Deprivation and Social Justice*, Penguin

A. Betéille (ed.), *Social Inequality*, Penguin

The Changing Social Structure of England and Wales 1871–1961, Routledge & Kegan Paul

Chapter 18

Race

Biologists usually divide mankind into three racial divisions based on physical differences, particularly the structure of the hair. These physical differences between the races are relatively minor: indeed, there is a much greater measurable difference between the Tutsi negroes from Ruanda (the tallest people in the world) and the Bambuti pygmies from the Congo (among the smallest) than there is between other negroes and Englishmen.

The largest racial group, the Mongoloid, has straight hair, noses of medium width, and yellow or brown skin; it includes such peoples as the Malays, American Indians, Eskimos, Chinese, and Japanese. The second group, the Caucasoid, has wavy hair and narrow noses with pink or brown skin; it comprises such peoples as the Arabs, Europeans, and Indians. The smallest group, the Negroid, has wiry tightly curled hair and broad noses with dark brown or yellowish skin pigmentation; it includes the bulk of the people of Africa south of the Sahara and the peoples of Melanesia.

The Australian Aborigines do not fall into any of these categories, having caucasoid hair but negroid noses. Some authorities regard the native Australians as a distinct race which has undergone a separate evolutionary development, having been separated from the bulk of mankind for almost as long as modern man has existed. It is even suggested that these people may most closely resemble the ancestors from which modern man has developed. However, some anthropologists consider that the Australian form may have developed from a mixture of two or more of the three main racial groups.

In order to differentiate further between the physical characteristics of the various human groups, the three main races are sometimes sub-divided into about thirty sub-groups; for example, the three main European types are Mediterranean, Alpine, and Nordic. But just as there has been considerable admixture between the races there is even more mixing between the sub-groups, so that even in Sweden only about 10 per cent of the population would approximate to the Nordic type.

Racial classification is not merely based on superficial appearance: for example, the composition of the blood and the form of the skull are also taken into account. Some experts have not restricted themselves to three main races: in 1974 John Baker distinguished six races—the 'Europid', the 'Negrid', the 'Mongolid', the 'Indianid', the 'Australasid', and the 'Khoisanid'.[1] The main differences here compared with the easier three-race classification is that the American Indians, the Australian Aborigines, and the Bushmen and Hottentots (Khoisanid) are being distinguished as separate races.

Sometimes people describe one race as being more 'primitive' than another, by which they usually mean more closely resembling an ape—although there is no reason for supposing that a gorilla, which has also undergone evolutionary change, closely resembles our common ancestor. It is interesting to note that although negroes may be more ape-like in that they have wide noses, the more obvious characteristic of the ape, hairiness, is most clearly defined in the caucasoid: the Ainu of Japan (a 'primitive' caucasoid people among their more 'advanced' mongoloid neighbours) are reputed to be the hairiest people on earth.

Some theorists, to justify their view that some races are superior to others, have put forward a theory that human beings did not all originate from a common group of ancestors (polygenesis).[2] This view was propounded in the middle of the last century by de Gobineau but is now generally discredited; the contrary opinion, that man had his origin in one place (monogenesis), is much more likely to be accurate. One piece of evidence in support of the latter view is that in order to mate successfully creatures must be very closely related. In nature creatures do not reproduce outside their own species; even the black-backed gull will not mate with the herring gull in England. A donkey and a horse are sufficiently related to be able to produce young—but only the infertile mule; however, there is not the slightest difficulty, from a biological point of view, in the successful mating of different human races, although there may be social problems. It has even been suggested that the mating of diverse human types is desirable from a genetic viewpoint.

The most obvious of the superficial differences between human types is the colour of the skin caused by a black pigment 'melanin' found in all people (except albinos). It is believed that melanin protects the sweat glands from damage in hot climates; people vary in their ability to produce melanin (that is why some of us 'tan' quicker than others in summer), and the natural process of selection which ensures the survival of the fittest has meant that those with the greatest amount of melanin have survived in those areas where this quality has survival value—the hottest parts of the world. Over the millions of years of human evolution the capacity to form melanin has meant the fairly regular distribution over the world of people with this quality in appropriate degrees.[3] Of course, the migration of peoples has affected the exact distribution of dark- and light-skinned people; for example, the dark-skinned Bantu arrived in South Africa, a country with a fairly temperate climate, at about the same time as the first whites, and obviously there has not been time in the ensuing 300 years or so for natural selection to change the colour pigmentation on either side! Hair colour is also governed by melanin. Other superficial physical differences also seem to reflect climate. The pigment of the iris of the eye protects it from sunlight, and so people with light-coloured eyes would not tend to develop in countries with strong sunlight. It has also been suggested that long narrow noses allow the air to be warmed before entering the lungs, and so are an advantage in cold countries. The process of natural selection has not affected all the physical characteristics in all racial types: for example, Eskimos have flat noses although they live in a very cold climate; while relatively recent migration (of less than 10 000 years ago) has resulted in American Indians of similar colour from the far north to the southern tip of the continent.

However, in general, the physical differences between racial groups are governed by the same process of natural adaptation to the environment as has allowed some groups of men to develop height while others remain small—depending on whether they live in mountainous or flat country or whether food supplies are scarce or plentiful. There is no more reason to assume that men with different physical characteristics have differing mental abilities than there is to assume that cows of different colour vary in intelligence. Racist writers such as Houston Stuart Chamberlain[4] in England have declared that races vary in intelligence, in order to justify racial discrimination. In 1972 Arthur Jensen claimed that intelligence is mainly the result of genetic factors and that black Americans suffer from a hereditary handicap in intelligence compared with white Americans.[5] Views of this kind have also been expressed by other authorities, such as A. Shuey[6] and H. Eysenck, and because of their controversial nature these views tend to attract a good deal of publicity. However, even if there are genetic differences in intelligence the majority of experts seem to feel that the effects of environmental differences are likely to be considerably greater.[7] In the United States intelligence tests given to army recruits have shown that in each state the negroes scored lower than the whites, but the negroes from the northern states had a higher average score than the whites from the southern states.[8] The fact that the southern states are economically and socially more 'backward' than the northern probably accounts for the low average score recorded there; while negroes throughout the United States suffer from economic and social inferiority.

All the methods used to measure intelligence are open to criticism: the first problem is to find a test that does not represent a culture, for example by using written words; the second, to find one that measures a person's potential intelligence rather than their existing accomplishment; the third is to find a testing situation that is not influenced by outside factors, such as distrust of the tester, a cultural inability to appreciate that the time taken to do the test is important, or sheer unwillingness to compete. (Australian Aborigines would not attempt to compete against each other.) Attempts to compare racial groups are obviously much more susceptible to criticism on all these points than are attempts to compare individuals within a group of similar individuals.

At one time it was believed that it was possible to gauge intelligence by measuring the size of the brain—an article on 'Negroes' written in 1882 states: 'The average cranial capacity of the negro is considerably less than that of the average European, the weight of the negro brain being about 35 ounces, 15 ounces above that of the highest gorilla, but about 10 ounces below that of the average European . . . With respect to intellectual capacity, the inferiority of the negro race to the white is beyond question.'[9] Some people at that time went considerably further and believed that one could gauge intelligence by examining the contours of the head, and the 'science' of phrenology had a considerable vogue. We now know that methods of judging intelligence by the measurement of brain size have no validity; the largest brain measurements have been found among Eskimos, but no-one has suggested that Eskimos are basically more intelligent than other groups.

Physical differences make it easy to recognize other groups, and if these physical differences are reinforced by cultural differences of language, religion, dress, and customs it makes the 'out group' an even easier target for those who want to exploit or oppress it. When differences of culture coincide with physical differences they are called 'ethnic' differences.

All races have practised discrimination against members of other races at some time; until recently the Chinese regarded other races as inferior; in Uganda the African General Amin was guilty of blatant racism against the Indian community in 1972; but racism does seem to have taken its most extreme form among Northern Europeans. It has been suggested that this prejudice against other races is the historical result of the fact that Northern Europeans were in the past less likely than most other peoples to come into contact with coloured people, and thus regarded their own civilization and themselves as superior in the absence of any evidence to the contrary—something difficult for the illiterate Spanish peasant to do when confronted with his cultured Moorish overlord.[10] A rather more far-fetched explanation is the psychological one that the Anglo-Saxon attitude to other races is the result of the 'long North European winter nights of blackness and fear ... Darkness and the colour black came to be associated with evil and death. Black devils were conjured up by black-robed witches ... it is a natural act to try to enslave that which we secretly fear.'

Much of what is loosely called racial conflict is not confined to the biological divisions of 'race'; for example, the Cubans are closely related physically to the Americans. Although Judaism is a religion including people of many nationalities and racial types, the Jews in Germany were easy scapegoats for Germany's pre-war economic problems because as a group they still contained some physical features reminiscent of their Mediterranean origin and tended to live in identifiable Jewish communities.[11] Conflict between countries is mainly political, although racial prejudice may be used as a propaganda weapon when required. Conflict within a country being mainly economic, racial conflict will also take an economic form.

When the British Empire was at its peak in 1900 and depended on its colonies for cheap raw materials and ready markets for its factory produce it is not surprising that some Englishmen tried to rationalize this economic position: 'God has not been preparing the English-speaking and Teutonic peoples for a thousand years for nothing but vain and idle self-contemplation and self-admiration. No! He has made us the master organizers of the world to establish system where chaos reigns ... He has made us adept in government that we may administer government among savage and servile peoples.'[12]

It is no accident that the Afrikaans-speaking South African white is more likely to be strongly racialist than the English-speaking white. The Afrikaner was historically the rural settler, and still owns 80 per cent of the country's farms, while the English-speaking settler was essentially urban and initially controlled the industry of the country. The Afrikaner 'watched as English capitalists gave jobs they sought to black men. The blacks may have spoken English better than the Afrikaner or have been willing to work more cheaply. But for a white man to employ them when other whites needed work was incomprehensible to the Afrikaner. ...'[13]

Racism usually arrives when a vested interest is at stake, the vested interest being often that of the underprivileged. They are the most likely group to feel threatened, because their position is only marginally better than that of the group which seems to threaten them. A feeling prevails that there is only a fixed quantity of money, work, and social benefits to be shared out, and that if these benefits are extended to members of the 'out group' there will be even less for others at the bottom of the economic pile.

Marx saw the Irish migration to England as undesirable because it divided the working class: 'English proletarians and Irish proletarians. The ordinary English worker hates the Irishman as a competitor who lowers his standard of life. In relation to the Irish worker he feels himself a member of the ruling nation and so turns himself into a tool of the aristocrats and capitalists of his country against Ireland, thus strengthening their dominion over himself.'[14]

In Britain the first wave of coloured immigrants arrived in the early 1950s from the Caribbean, India, and Pakistan, and like the Irish before them they had one objective—to find work. They generally went to cities where unskilled work was to be found—the West Midlands, Nottingham, Bradford, Leeds, Huddersfield, Leicester, Peterborough, and London—crowded areas where the pressures on housing and education were already great but where there was a demand for workers, particularly on unattractive night shifts, in transport, in hospitals, and other essential but often dirty or badly paid jobs. Between 1951 and 1961 in England and Wales the number of Indian immigrants increased from 30 800 to 81 400, of Pakistanis from 5000 to 24 900, and of West Indians from 15 300 to 171 800. In the same period the number of immigrants from the Irish Republic increased from 472 100 to 644 400. The greater 'visibility' of the coloured immigrants, however, meant that prejudices previously directed at the Irish were now directed at the Commonwealth immigrants, and with increased vigour. The flow of immigrants was halted by the Commonwealth Immigrants

People in Great Britain born overseas

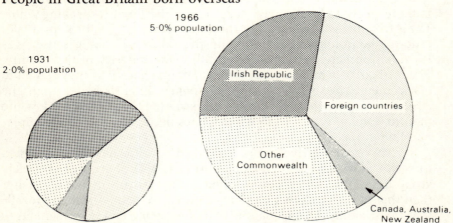

1966
5·0% population

1931
2·0% population

Irish Republic

Foreign countries

Other Commonwealth

Canada, Australia, New Zealand

Source: Social Trends 3, HMSO 1972

Note—comparative figures for 1971. Immigrants total 5.5 per cent of population divided as follows: foreign countries 1.8 per cent; Canada, Australia and New Zealand 0.3 per cent; other Commonwealth 2.1 per cent; Irish Republic 1.3 per cent.

Act of 1962 by which immigration was restricted to dependants joining the heads of families and a trickle of skilled and professional men. By 1966 there were 595 100 coloured immigrants in Britain, and though they represented only some 1 per cent of the total population they were concentrated in a few areas where they were highly noticeable. As with the Jews at the end of the nineteenth century and the Irish for the first half of the present century, they were accused of being dirty, of spreading disease and criminality, of being a burden on the rates and taxes, of changing the character of towns, and of taking jobs away from British workers.

In any large group of people, particularly of adult males separated

Selected categories of people born overseas resident in particular areas of Great Britain, 1971

	India/ Pakistan/ Bangladesh	West Indies	Total 'New' Common- wealth	Irish Republic	'Old' Common- wealth and foreign
Thousands resident in:					
Greater London	137	169	476	241	352
Outer Metropolitan area	48	19	105	75	146
Outer South-East area	25	9	68	43	118
West Midlands conurbation	68	39	120	56	27
West Yorkshire conurbation	38	10	55	20	30
SE Lancashire conurbation	25	11	47	51	39
Scotland	13	2	30	33	65
Other Great Britain	109	46	250	190	347
Total Great Britain	462	304	1 151	709	1 123
Percentage of population:					
Greater London	1.8	2.3	6.4	3.3	4.7
Outer Metropolitan area	0.9	0.4	2.0	1.4	2.8
Outer South-East area	0.5	0.2	1.5	1.0	2.6
West Midlands conurbation	2.9	1.6	5.0	2.4	1.1
West Yorkshire conurbation	2.2	0.6	3.2	1.1	1.7
SE Lancashire conurbation	1.0	0.4	1.9	2.1	1.6
Scotland	0.2	—	0.6	0.6	1.3
Other Great Britain	0.4	0.2	1.0	0.8	1.4
Total Great Britain	0.9	0.6	2.1	1.3	2.1

Figures based on 1971 census.

Source: Adapted from *Social Trends* 4, HMSO 1973

1 *What changes have there been in the numbers and origins of people resident in Great Britain who were born overseas during the forty years from 1931 to 1971?*

2 *From the figures in the table, which areas of Great Britain are most likely to have been affected by immigration? What are the effects likely to be?*

from their families, there will be some who break the legal or social codes. Antisocial behaviour by a member of a majority is accepted as not being typical of all its members; but if this antisocial behaviour is carried out by the members of a group easily recognized by accent, colour, dress, or religious affiliations, then the behaviour can easily be accepted as representing how that group as a whole behaves.

The Race Relations Board was established in 1966, under the Race Relations Act (1965), to deal with complaints of racial discrimination in public places. The Act did not, however, cover racial discrimination in employment, housing, and services such as insurance. In 1966 a carefully controlled survey was undertaken to discover the extent of discrimination in the fields not covered by the 1965 Act, and substantial evidence of discrimination was produced.[15]

Discrimination in employment had been personally experienced by 36 per cent of all immigrant respondents (ranging from 45 per cent of West Indians to 6 per cent of Cypriots). In the subsequent tests there was usually a bias by both employers and employment bureaux against coloured applicants with the same qualifications and experience as the white control group; the West Indian group received the most rebuffs, being discriminated against by employment bureaux on 11 out of 15 occasions (for example, being told that vacancies, which were later offered to the white tester, were filled).

Discrimination by landlords had been personally experienced by 26 per cent of all immigrant respondents (ranging from 39 per cent of West Indians to 8 per cent of Cypriots). In the tests, 120 groups of telephone applications for accommodation resulted in 74 cases of discrimination. The West Indian was told that the accommodation had already been taken on 63 occasions (but the Englishman was later told in each case that it was still available); on 5 occasions the West Indian was asked for a higher rent than the other applicant; and on 6 occasions he was asked for a month's rent in advance while the other applicant was not. This pattern of discrimination was also apparent in tests involving accommodation bureaux and estate agents.

Discrimination against coloured members of the community was also experienced, and validated by tests, in the spheres of hire purchase, motor insurance, hotel accommodation, holiday accommodation, hairdressing, and entertainment (Indians being the most discriminated against in the last four of these fields). In the field of motor insurance 61 per cent of West Indians had personally experienced discrimination,

This photograph was taken in England some years ago.
This could not happen now—or could it?
How can people be discriminated against in housing, leisure, and job opportunities without any law being broken?
Photograph: Keystone

and in the later tests the rates quoted were usually higher for West Indians than for the English control group of similar background; for example, a West Indian was quoted £88 for a comprehensive insurance policy, while the same firm quoted a rate of £50 for the Englishman.

The number of immigrants with personal experience of discrimination in all fields would probably have been higher but for the fact that

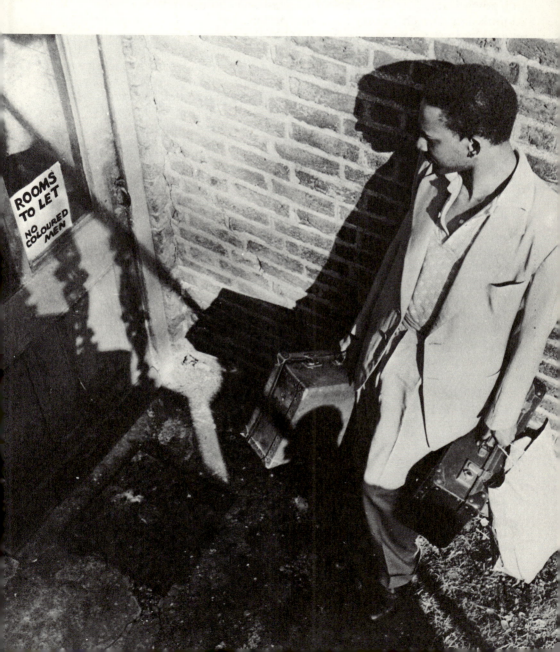

immigrants may have avoided situations where they knew that they were likely to be humiliated or rejected.

The results of this survey helped to establish the need which culminated in the Race Relations Act of 1968. This Act extended the scope of the 1965 Act by making discrimination unlawful in the provision of goods, facilities, and services, and in employment, housing, and advertising. The Act also established the Community Relations Commission, which coordinates the activities of local community relations councils (seventy-eight in 1972) that employ full-time community relations officers.

By mid-1970 there were almost 1.5 million coloured Commonwealth immigrants and their families in Britain (about 2.5 per cent of the population), and about 60 per cent of these had settled in Greater London and the West Midlands.[16] It is to be hoped that the attempts to integrate these immigrants amicably into their host communities will be successful. However, as long as there is a shortage of housing, jobs, and educational opportunity, there is a likelihood of bitterness between those who feel that they are being discriminated against for racial reasons on the one hand, and those who feel that they are losing what is 'rightfully theirs' on the other.

Although there may be a period of uneasy coexistence with minority groups in Britain it is probable that in time the most recent waves of immigrants will be assimilated into the fabric of society as previous waves of immigrants have been—and like those immigrants will help to enrich the quality and variety of our lives, without necessarily losing their own group identities.

Nations are not static institutions: the Japanese quietly ignored the outside world for 2000 years but became a major military nation in the nineteenth century, fighting five overseas wars in less than 150 years; the neutral Scandinavians were once the Vikings! Five hundred years ago a traveller from outer space might have chosen India, China, Japan, or the Islamic Empire as the most civilized part of Earth—he would certainly not have chosen the rough squalor of England or the vast emptiness of North America!

More discussion or written work

1   What are the causes and results of colour prejudice?

2   Cross-breeding (miscegenation) is often socially taboo or even illegal, and 'cross-breeds' are sometimes criticized as being morally inferior. Why do you think that these prohibitions and criticisms are so prevalent?

3   How effective can legislation be in curbing racial prejudice?

4   Attempts have been made in both Britain and America to disperse

coloured children into schools outside their own neighbourhoods ('bussing'). Why do you think such a policy was thought to be necessary? How effective do you think it is likely to be?

5   Give examples of how you think immigrant groups have, or could, enrich the society of their host countries.

Research

1   Find and describe some examples of ethnic or racial prejudice which are not white versus black.

2   Find out how other countries (for example, Holland) have reacted to immigration and say how effective you think these immigration measures have been.

OR

If you have an immigrant community in your locality, or are a member of such a community, compare the standard of living, occupations, and behaviour of the immigrant group or groups with that of the native-born section of the community.

Imagination

Imagine that you are an immigrant arriving in a country where the people have a different colour, customs, and religion to yourself (language barriers optional!). Write an account of the difficulties you encounter and describe your reactions.

Reading suggestions

* D. Humphry and G. John, *Because They're Black*, Penguin

† W. Daniel, *Racial Discrimination in England*, Penguin

   M. Banton, *Race Relations*, Social Science Paperback

   E. Krausz, *Ethnic Minorities in Britain*, Paladin

   E. Rose *et al.*, *Colour and Citizenship*, Oxford University Press

† K. Richardson and D. Spears (Ed.), *Race, Culture and Intelligence*, Penguin

Chapter 19

Crime and Punishment

Every society has certain values which the majority of people in that society accept. These values require a certain kind of behaviour if they are to be maintained, and this behaviour is the normal behaviour, the 'norm', of most people in that society. In order to ensure that most people behave in the expected way, the society will make rules. These rules may be unwritten and maintained by social disapproval; for example, we do not expect people to spit on the floor when they come into our homes—if they did we should not invite them again! Behaviour constituting a more serious threat to the society's stability will be officially prohibited, and the breaking of these rules will constitute a crime and be punished by the State.

It is important to remember that the concept of what constitutes a crime is constantly being adapted to meet the particular needs of any society. There may be some constant concepts in all societies, such as respect for property, life, and sexual rights; but the actual nature of the act which constitutes a crime will vary.

Obviously most people are capable of committing a crime in sudden anger, drunkenness, or as a result of stress, and there may be little that we can do to prevent isolated acts by individuals. But if we can ascertain that certain groups or certain individuals are more likely than others to commit crimes, then we may be able to reduce the amount of crime by removing the factors which predispose these individuals or groups towards criminal acts.

First, there are the physiological and psychological explanations, for some people consider that crime is a personal rather than a social problem. This approach will vary from those who believe that some people are innately wicked to those who think there is a genetic cause for criminality connected with the endocrine glands. In 1876 an Italian criminologist, Lombroso, came to believe that criminality was inborn when he examined the skull of a notorious bandit and found characteristics which he believed to be the result of a 'throw back' to an earlier evolutionary type. He believed that there was a criminal physical type which resulted in 'insensibility to pain, extremely acute sight, tattooing, excessive idleness, love of orgies, and the irresistible craving for evil for its own sake'.[1] No expert now accepts the existence of such a criminal type, but there is still some support for the view that there may be an inherited element in criminality; for example, in 1972 Dr David Rosenthal suggested a possible genetic link with crime, quoting studies of twins made in three continents over a period of forty years, in which he claimed that identical twins shared crime traits at a rate more than double that of non-identical twins.[2] From this biological approach, we move to the psychological—to those who have found a connection between criminality and the way in which a child is treated by his parents: the child who is rejected or has conflicting demands made upon him may grow up to be a criminal as a result.[3] Equally, a child is a young animal that seeks gratification of his powerful biological needs with little regard for the needs or wishes of other people. We accept this behaviour as normal in young infants, but if the child is not socialized to moderate his egotistical attitude before he becomes adult his attitude is then regarded as abnormal and he is likely to become a criminal.

Secondly, there is the sociological explanation of crime. The so-called 'culture transmission theory' views crime as the end-product of a process of social learning. As early as 1886 Gabriel Tarde suggested that criminal behaviour is learned in the family and the community in areas where this behaviour is the 'norm'.[4] This view has had a great deal of support from sociologists throughout this century, for obviously, if fathers and elder brothers have been in prison, the young child will identify with them. Hence he will grow up to regard the police merely as a hazard to be circumvented while he goes about his perfectly reasonable, family business of stealing, receiving, or procuring! In such a deviant sub-culture there will of course be rules: for example, it might be considered beyond the pale to steal from a blind man; and sexual offenders against children are abhorred by professional criminals.

Another essentially sociological theory of crime is that propounded by Robert Merton, the American sociologist, who found that people could be divided into five main groups based on their adjustment to the norms of society.[5] First there are the Conformists who accept the goals of their society and set about achieving these goals in the most generally acceptable way. Secondly, there are the Innovators who do not entirely accept either the goals or the means of achieving them, but keep within the bounds of acceptable behaviour—the Innovator may be regarded as an eccentric, but he may also be instrumental in changing goals or the methods of achieving them. Thirdly, there are the Ritualists who do not believe in the goals of the society but behave in the accepted way because most other people do. Fourthly, there are the Retreatists who avoid a decision on either the goals or the methods of achieving them, and who therefore withdraw from society as much as they can. Fifthly, there are the Rebels who may reject either the goals of the society or the acceptable means of achieving them, or both. Although all these modes of behaviour except Conformity are deviant, that is they do not follow the norms and rules of the society, it is 'Rebellion' that is most likely to lead to crime.

The rebels may accept the goals of the society but resort to illegitimate means of attaining them because they are denied access to the legitimate means. They may accept that a large car is desirable (all the advertisements tell them so) but know that with their limited educational and social background they are unlikely ever to obtain one—so they steal one. Alternatively, they may reject the goals because they

Indictable offences: age groups and types of offence, 1974 (England and Wales)

	All ages	Under 14	14 and under 17	17 and under 21	21 and under 30	30 and over
				Age groups		
Percentage of males found guilty of indictable offences:						
Murder, manslaughter or infanticide	0.1	—	—	0.1	0.1	0.2
Other offences of violence	9.5	2.6	6.6	9.9	12.0	10.8
Sexual offences	2.2	0.6	1.1	1.3	2.2	4.8
Burglary	19.3	38.8	32.6	18.2	14.9	8.5
Robbery	0.8	1.3	1.0	1.1	0.7	0.3
Theft and handling stolen goods	50.5	42.2	46.8	51.9	49.8	55.2
Fraud and forgery	4.4	0.6	0.8	3.1	6.6	7.4
Criminal damage	10.6	13.6	10.7	12.9	9.7	8.2
All indictable offences (100%) (number)	321 566	22 954	69 898	82 412	80 841	74 461
	(293 414)	(19 278)	(49 784)	(75 059)	(78 247)	(71 046)
Percentage of females found guilty of indictable offences:						
Murder, manslaughter or infanticide	0.1	—	—	0.1	0.2	0.1
Other offences of violence	4.3	4.4	7.8	4.3	4.5	3.0
Sexual offences	0.1	—	0.1	—	0.1	0.1
Burglary	3.8	15.4	9.6	5.2	2.5	0.9
Robbery	0.3	1.0	0.8	0.4	0.2	—
Theft and handling stolen goods	78.4	72.9	72.5	74.2	74.9	84.7
Fraud and forgery	6.9	1.5	3.3	9.6	9.7	5.7
Criminal damage	3.9	4.2	5.5	4.6	4.1	3.0
All indictable offences (100%) (number)	53 352	2 362	6 665	9 867	12 666	21 792
	(46 621)	(1 850)	(8 374)	(8 374)	(11 687)	(19 660)

1972 figures in brackets

Source: Adapted from *Social Trends* 4 and 6, HMSO 1973, 1975

1   *At what age is someone most likely to commit a crime? What sort of crime is it likely to be?*
2   *Why do you think women are less likely to commit crimes than men?*
3   *Approximately how many males of ages twenty-one to twenty-nine were found guilty of murder or manslaughter in 1974? How many were involved in some sort of robbery, theft, or receiving?*

know they cannot achieve them, and set up their own status system, at least for a time. Albert Cohen showed that the gang boy was more concerned with showing prowess in his delinquent activities than in gaining from them materially: 'There is no accounting in rational and utilitarian terms for the effort expended and the danger run in stealing things which are often discarded, destroyed or casually given away.' [6]

For more than a hundred years there has been a well-documented connection between poverty and crime: in 1867 Von Mayr in Bavaria found that property-crime increased in direct ratio to the cost of rye.[7] In recent years poverty has become more relative, but there is still a clear connection between crime and poverty in adult criminals—even if the main reference point has changed from rye to unemployment.[8]

Most crimes are crimes against property, and for these the socio-logical aspect is likely to be the most important one; however, in the case of other crimes, such as sexual offences, personality factors are probably dominant. In many of such cases, indeed, we should look mainly for a psychological explanation.

From 1960 to 1965 known crimes of violence in Britain rose by 42 per cent and in America by 25 per cent, so that in 1965 there were about 185 known serious crimes of violence per 100 000 people in the United States and about 75 per 100 000 in England and Wales.[9] Other offences have shown similar increases, and all known indictable offences in Britain rose by 53 per cent during this period. These figures represent only reported crime, and studies in the United States show that the total figures are likely to be much higher: for example, bur-glaries may be three times as high, and rapes more than three and a half times the reported rates.

Although the crime rates have, in recent years, soared in Britain and America, it is unlikely that mental defects or child-rejection have markedly increased; and it is clear that poverty, even relative poverty, has not. So neither psychological nor the more obvious sociological changes seem to account for the increase. However, there have been increases in other causal factors. For example, the materialistic goals of society are constantly emphasized on television and in advertise-ments, and it may be that a consequent increase in illegitimate means of attaining these goals is to be expected. Other factors which may account for the increased crime rate are, first, the obvious one that there is more property lying about to steal (particularly unguarded property such as motor cars); and secondly, there are increased opportunities to steal from impersonal organizations such as supermarkets—people may well find it psychologically easier to steal from an anonymous victim, and 'fiddling' the income tax has long been regarded as a res-pectable pursuit by the middle class! Statistically, people under twenty-five are more likely to commit crime than their elders: for example,

Crime: types of offence known to the police (1974)

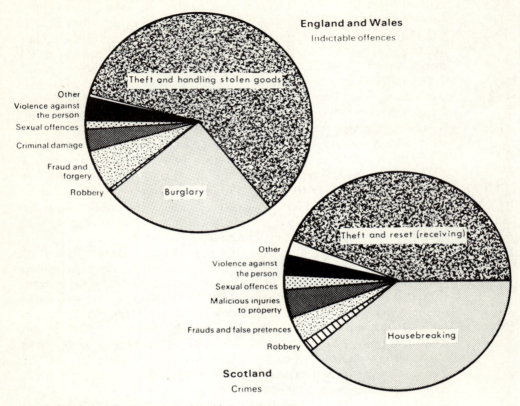

England and Wales
Indictable offences

Theft and handling stolen goods

Other
Violence against
the person
Sexual offences
Criminal damage
Fraud and
forgery
Robbery
Burglary

Theft and reset (receiving)

Other
Violence against
the person
Sexual offences
Malicious injuries
to property
Frauds and false pretences
Robbery
Housebreaking

Scotland
Crimes

Source: Home Office; Scottish Home and Health Department

the eleven to seventeen age group accounts for only one-seventh of the American population, but is responsible for nearly half the larceny and burglary. Thus the recent increase in the proportion of young people to the total population may also contribute to the overall increase in crime. The great structural changes in society, caused, for example, by increasing educational opportunities, may also have lessened social stability and increased status anxiety, throwing the responsibility for 'failure' more directly at the individual, who in turn may more emphatically reject the 'mores' of the society that has labelled him a failure.

An additional explanation for the increase in violent crime has come from research into animal behaviour. It has been found that a great variety of animals, including monkeys and apes, engage in serious fighting only when they run short of space. These animals need freedom of movement and opportunities to explore; for example, in 1965 Vernon and Francis Reynolds observed wild chimpanzees in the Budongo Forest in Uganda for 300 hours and saw only seventeen incidents involving anger or fighting—yet aggression is common among chimpanzees in zoos.[10] Experiments with rats have also shown that even when given ample food they will start fighting when their numbers increase above a certain level. In a ten-year study from 1950 to 1960 in London, F. H. McClintock found that violent crime was most prevalent in areas of high population-density. This sort of research suggests that there are limits to the crowding human beings can tolerate without strain, and that the amount of violent crime may be directly related to the degree of crowding.

It is clear that there are many reasons for crime and the ways we seek to punish criminals must, if they are to be effective, be various and flexible. If crowding encourages violence it may not be appropriate to crowd three prisoners into a cell intended for one: if a sense of failure is a causal factor in crime it may be foolish to increase it still more by sending a lad to Borstal.

The four motives for inflicting punishment are Retribution by society on those who have transgressed its code, the Prevention of the criminal from repeating his offence, the Deterring of others from engaging in similar conduct, and the Reformation of the criminal so that he will not wish to continue to commit crimes.

Retribution (or revenge) is a psychological rather than a material need and may lead people to demand such punishments for crime as flogging or capital punishment—even when these can be proved ineffective in influencing the amount of crime which is committed within a given category. Prevention, deterrence, and reformation can all be measured, and it would appear that up to now our methods of dealing with criminals have not been very successful in meeting these three requirements.

Obviously the structure of a society will have a considerable influence on the form that punishment will take in that society. In the law books of ancient Ireland there is no reference to a death penalty, and it is doubtful whether it was ever necessary to have recourse to extreme punishment—most crimes being dealt with by the payment of compensation. It is probable that there was very little ordinary crime, for the clan system was a tight-knit family one, and since most land and property were held communally by the whole clan, theft and murder in the furtherance of theft were unlikely. Attempts to gain more property were directed against other clans. In China, on the other hand, especially under the Manchu dynasty, capital punishment was very prevalent—strangulation, decapitation, and worse being the normal modes of death for robbery with violence, smuggling salt, and many other crimes. This may have been necessary in a country dominated by a few property-owners surrounded by a multitude of the very poor and yet possessing no efficient police system. It was thought necessary to be very severe on the few criminals caught, in order that others would be scared off from following their lead.

This detection-rate seems to be one important key to the prevention of crime, and we can greatly exaggerate the effect on criminals of severe punishments. 'Penal reformers, from Bentham and Romilly down to Lord Gardiner, have advocated that the cure for crime lies in making its punishment more certain rather than more severe. (Probably the only influence which deterrent sentences have is in inverse proportion to the gravity of the offence: they may have some effect on, for example, motoring offenders.) Research shows that 85 per cent of first offenders who are caught are not recorded as offending again; this is not only the highest, but virtually the only clearly established factor that is known to discourage crime.' [11] As most criminals think they will not be caught, the possible punishment is relatively unimportant; and when the criminal's personal belief in invulnerability is borne out by the fact that the conviction-rate for robbery in London gives the criminal an 8 : 1 chance of not being caught, the deterrent effect of punishment diminishes further.

Prison or the threat of prison is the normal way of dealing with criminals in our society, although the present prison system is comparatively modern. Until the late eighteenth century, criminals were usually sentenced to death, mutilation, or transportation—prisons being reserved for those awaiting trial, confined for political reasons, or detained for debt. John Howard was instrumental in establishing the principle of prisons as places of confinement combined with work: this attempt at reform was embodied in an Act of Parliament in 1778—although Pentonville, the first prison designed for this purpose, was not built until 1842. This aim of reformation was reiterated in the Criminal Justice Act of 1948 which laid a duty on prisons to prepare prisoners for their release.

Reformation in prisons has, however, been hindered by a number of factors. Overcrowding has meant that the available staff has been overworked when merely keeping the system operational and have lacked time to promote socially acceptable attitudes among prisoners. There are some 40 000 men and women in prisons in England and Wales at any one time (22 765 males and 1200 females in 1951 rising steadily to 47 788 males and 1207 females in 1971). Most of these are petty

Prisoners at Dartmoor occupy themselves and earn some pocket money.
It has been said that our prison system is essentially retributive rather than regenerative. *Do you think this is so?*
Photograph: Keystone

offenders who constantly return to prison. Many of these 'recidivists' claim actually to prefer the secure environment of prison to the outside world, where they are too weak emotionally to cope. Prisons in fact condition men to not working rather than motivating them to work, although some attempt has been made to reverse this process by releasing prisoners in the final stages of their sentences so that they can work in normal jobs 'outside'. Sexual problems are aggravated by the closed prison world—although in Russia wives may be allowed to live inside prisons with 'good conduct' men. It is often impossible for released prisoners to find an acceptable place to live, although some outside agencies are now helping. Merfyn Turner, for example, established the first 'Norman House' for homeless discharged prisoners in 1955. Finally, the fact that a man has been in prison will often make it impossible for him to obtain a job upon release, which virtually ensures his eventual return to prison!

Some attempt has now been made to provide an alternative to prison in cases where a simple fine or probation are not considered adequate. In 1968, suspended sentences were introduced (by the Criminal Justice Act of 1967); this meant that a court which passed a prison sentence

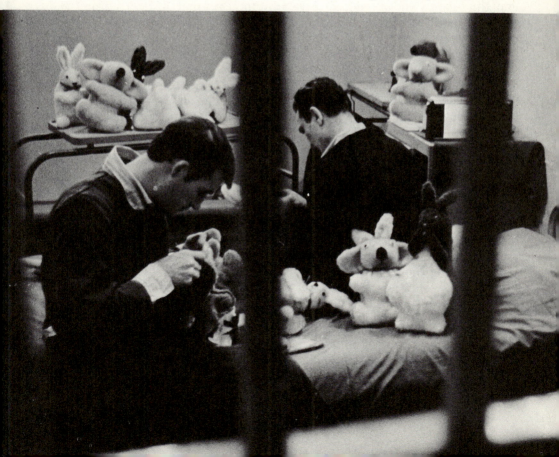

Public expenditure on justice and law (United Kingdom)

Figures in £ million	1951 −52	1961 −62	1966 −67	1971 −72
Police	73	156	255	474
Prisons	7	23	35	84
Legal aid	—	4	9	23
Probation and after-care ⎰	8	23	⎰ 9	17
Parliament and law courts ⎱			⎱ 34	69
Total public expenditure on justice and law	88	206	342	667

By 1974–75 expenditure had risen to £1081 million, mainly as a result of the increasing cost of police and prisons. Legal aid stabilized at £37 million but the cost of probation and after-care rose to £33 million.

Source: Adapted from *Social Trends* 6, HMSO 1975

Do you think that public expenditure on law enforcement and prevention is correctly allocated?

of two years or less could suspend it on condition that the offender did not commit a further offence within a stipulated period of between one and three years (now reduced to two by the Criminal Justice Act of 1972). Although it was originally intended that the courts should award a suspended sentence only to replace immediate imprisonment, it has been estimated that only about half the 98 080 people who received suspended sentences in the first three years of the Act's operation would have been imprisoned at all before the introduction of the Act. Nevertheless, even allowing for a substantial number of those awarded suspended sentences being reconvicted following a subsequent offence, it is clear that a considerable number of people have not been sent to prison who would have been in the past, and have committed no further offences as yet.

The Criminal Justice Act of 1972 also introduced a number of alternatives to imprisonment, as well as increasing the maximum penalty for certain offences (using a firearm to resist arrest now has a maximum penalty of life-imprisonment instead of fourteen years) and making a number of changes in court procedure. The first addition to the available punishments was to increase the courts' powers to order offenders to compensate their victims for 'any personal injury, loss, or damage' and to make criminal bankruptcy orders in respect of offenders whose crimes were worth £15 000 or more.

The second innovation was to set up a number of experimental 'detoxification centres' at which drunks could receive medical and social treatment. If, however, the drunken offender refused to accept treatment he could be charged with his offence in the usual way.

The 'non-custodial' penalty of 'deprivation of leisure' has been avail-

Population of prisons, borstals, and detention centres

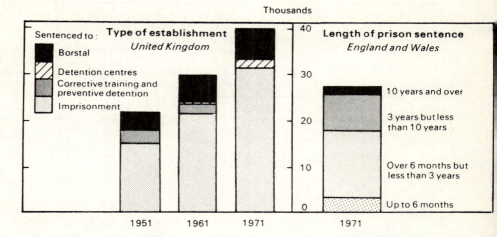

Male prison population: by age and marital status, 1971
England and Wales

	Prison population per 1000 population	Percentage of	
		prisoners who are single	population who are single
Age groups of prison population:			
15–19	6.38	97	93
20–24	5.68	68	63
25–29	4.31	40	26
30–34	3.24	33	14
35–39	2.26	31	11
40–44	1.57	30	11
45–49	1.05	32	10
50–54	0.61	33	9
55–59	0.34	30	8
60–64	0.18	37	8
65–69	0.12	44	8

Source: adapted from *Social Trends* 4 and 6, HMSO 1973, 1975

1   *From the figures given in the chart, what sort of people would you expect to constitute the bulk of the prison population?*
2   *What changes were there between 1951 and 1971 in the sort of punishments awarded by the courts?*

213

Ourselves and crime—who's guilty? (Opinion Research Centre Poll, 1966)

Although no two crimes are exactly the same, some kinds of crime are much worse than others. I would like you to say for each of the following how bad a crime you think it is (dreadful/very bad/fairly bad/not very bad/not bad at all)

Scores*	Sex			Age			Class		
	All	Male	Female	21–34	35–54	55 +	ABC1	C2	DE
Sample size:	824	396	428	211	332	281	260	305	259
Sexual assaults on children	98	97	98	98	98	97	99	97	98
Shoplifting	55	51	57	46	56	61	53	56	57
Taking stuff from work	58	54	62	49	60	64	60	58	59
Exceeding the speed limit	54	47	60	46	54	61	48	54	61
Fiddling the income tax	47	44	50	42	46	52	47	46	49
Fraud	72	70	73	69	72	72	72	72	71
Robbing a jeweller's shop	71	69	74	67	72	74	70	73	72
Knocking someone down in a pub fight	62	60	66	58	66	65	63	63	64

* Note: score calculated as follows: dreadful = 1; very bad = $\frac{3}{4}$; fairly bad = $\frac{1}{2}$; not very bad = $\frac{1}{4}$; not bad at all = 0 (i.e. maximum score where everybody says 'dreadful' = 100 and minimum score where everybody says 'not bad at all' = 0).

If you knew that a close friend of yours had stolen £10 from work, do you think you would report him or her, or not?

Figures are percentages	Sex			Age			Class		
	All	Male	Female	21–34	35–54	55 +	ABC1	C2	DE
Sample size:	824	396	428	211	332	281	260	305	259
Yes	32	34	31	26	34	35	30	28	39
No	45	43	47	52	45	41	50	48	38
Don't know	22	23	22	22	22	23	19	24	23

How about if your close friend seriously injured one of his children, would you report him or her or not?

Figures are percentages	Sex			Age			Class		
	All	Male	Female	21–34	35–54	55 +	ABC1	C2	DE
Sample size:	824	396	428	211	332	281	260	305	259
Yes	89	89	90	92	91	87	86	91	91
No	4	3	4	2	3	5	7	3	1
Don't know	7	8	6	6	6	9	8	6	8

Do you think that if things had gone differently for you, you could ever have become a criminal?

Figures are percentages		Sex			Age			Class	
	All	Male	Female	21–34	35–54	55+	ABC1	C2	DE
Sample size:	824	396	428	211	332	281	260	305	259
Yes	25	35	16	34	27	17	27	24	25
No	61	49	71	50	57	72	58	60	63
Don't know	14	16	12	16	16	11	14	16	13

There are many different reasons which people give to explain the increase in crime. I would like you to tell me for each one how important a cause of crime you think it is (very important/fairly important/not important/don't know)

Figures are percentages	Very important	Fairly important	Not important	Don't know
There is more about to steal	34	31	31	4
More people want to get rich quick	39	34	23	4
Lack of discipline in the home	71	23	5	1
Lack of discipline at school	47	36	16	2
Court sentences are not severe enough	74	17	7	2
The poor are envious of the rich	11	26	58	5
Too few policemen	53	28	16	3
People go straight from school into dead-end jobs	27	34	34	5
People do not show enough care about the young	37	34	23	5
People do not care what their neighbours think	12	24	58	5
People do not do enough to reform criminals	40	26	21	13

Where figures for percentages do not add up to 100 it is because they have been rounded up.

Source: New Society

1   What would your answers have been to the questions in this opinion poll? Can you give reasons for your answers?
2   Where answers are listed by sex, age, and social class, are the results those that you would expect from the respective categories?

able since the Criminal Justice Act of 1948, and the 1972 Act continues the provision of Attendance Centres which offenders may be ordered to attend, usually on Saturdays, instead of receiving some form of imprisonment; these have been compared with out-patient clinics in hospitals.[12] Most of these Attendance Centres are junior centres for boys between ten and seventeen, and the future of these centres is to be reconsidered if the new scheme of 'Intermediate Treatment' succeeds.

This Intermediate Treatment scheme has developed from the 1969 Children and Young Persons Act and is intended to cater for children who live in difficult home situations as well as those in trouble with the law. Under an Intermediate Treatment Order a young person can be required to live in a special place; to present himself to a specified person at given times; and to participate in a wide variety of specified activities—such as those provided by youth clubs and further education centres.

The 1972 Act also introduced an experimental scheme of community service as an alternative to imprisonment: courts in some areas can now order an offender, with his consent, to undertake between forty and 240 hours' community service over a period of twelve months as an alternative to imprisonment. The major difficulty with this scheme is likely to be a shortage of suitable community service work.

These experiments are not dramatic, but at least we are now moving away from the vicious circle of imprisonment leading to more offences with consequent further imprisonment. Once social causes rather than innate wickedness are accepted as the main source of criminality, a serious attempt can be made to prevent crime rather than depending upon punishment to cure it.

It may be appropriate to conclude this chapter by mentioning Durkheim's view that the criminal plays a definite role in social life by giving the society the opportunity to symbolically re-affirm its values by punishing those who do not adhere to them.[13]

More discussion or written work

1   The 20 per cent increase in crimes coming before the British courts in 1972 as compared with 1971 was the biggest increase ever. To what extent do you think that a decline in the ability or wish of parents to control their children is a cause of increasing crime?
2   'The more I see of these Indians, the more convinced I am that they all have to be killed' (General William Sherman, 1867). Give examples of behaviour in other societies (past or present) which we should now regard as criminal. Why do you think this behaviour was, or is, acceptable to the society concerned?
3   It has been suggested that a vicious and violent society is emerging because many people 'find soul-destroying frustration or ever-lasting boredom in their jobs'. Do you agree?
4   It has been suggested that the age of criminal responsibility should be raised. What do you think? (It was last raised in February 1964 from eight to ten years.)

Research

1   Find out how 'juveniles' are punished in two foreign countries, and compare this punishment with that used in Britain.
2   Relate the age and sex of offenders to the crimes they commit and suggest reasons for these variations.

Imagination

Think of some punishments that you consider more appropriate than those at present used in Britain. List these and say to which offences your punishments would refer.

Reading suggestions

* D. Morris, *The Human Zoo*, Corgi
† H. Jones, *Crime in a Changing Society*, Penguin
† D. West, *The Young Offender*, Penguin
  R. Jackson, *Enforcing the Law*, Penguin
  N. Walker, *Crime and Punishment in Britain*, Edinburgh University Press
  People in Prison, HMSO

Chapter 20

Death

In every society death is a constant fact of life and in most societies a great deal of attention is paid to preparation for death, ceremonials surrounding death, memorials commemorating death, and speculation as to what happens to a person after death.

The dominant religious beliefs in a society will have a strong effect upon the attitude that people have to death. If there is a generally felt conviction that there is a 'life after death', death may be a climax which calls for celebration, even though there is a strong element of personal sorrow over what is felt to be a temporary parting. Very often a party, called a 'wake', was held (and still is in parts of rural Ireland) on the night before a funeral, or a band would accompany the mourners to the graveside. In contemporary Britain much of the ritual surrounding death has been discontinued and it has been suggested that death has replaced sex as the 'taboo' subject; Geoffrey Gorer goes so far as to refer to 'the pornography of death'.[1] It may be that there is a general doubt that anything lies beyond the grave and that this makes people unprepared to face the fact of death; on the other hand, it may merely mean that death is being accepted stoically as something that is inevitable, carries with it no connotations of a future existence, and does not demand discussion.

'Rites of passage' exist in most societies to mark the different stages in a person's life. These (where appropriate) make it clear to the person immediately concerned what sort of behaviour is expected of him and also make it clear to others what their attitudes should be: these rituals help to give order to a society. For example, in Catholicism, 'baptism' acknowledges the entry of a new member into the society; 'first holy communion' accepts the fact that the person can now be held responsible for his actions because he can distinguish between good and evil; the onset of puberty is marked by 'confirmation'—the person is now a young adult and in the past would often be starting work. 'Marriage' formalizes the sexual relationships which will in turn perpetuate the society. Death is marked by a funeral. In Britain in the past, funerals were as elaborate as possible to show respect for the dead person and to emphasize the part that he had played in the society: a 'eulogy' would often be read cataloguing all the virtues that the dead person had dis-

Expectation of life (Great Britain)

	Males				Females			
	1901	1931	1961	1971	1901	1931	1961	1971
Further number of years which a person can expect to live:								
At birth	48.1	58.4	67.9	68.6	51.8	62.5	73.8	74.9
At age 5 years	55.5	60.0	64.9	65.2	58.0	63.0	70.5	71.2
10 „	51.4	55.7	60.1	60.4	54.0	58.7	65.6	66.3
20 „	42.7	46.7	50.4	50.8	45.4	49.7	55.8	56.5
30 „	34.5	38.1	40.9	41.2	37.1	41.0	46.1	46.8
40 „	26.8	29.5	31.5	31.7	29.2	32.5	36.5	37.2
50 „	19.7	21.6	22.6	22.8	21.7	24.1	27.4	28.2
60 „	13.4	14.4	15.0	15.1	14.9	16.4	19.0	19.7
70 „	8.4	8.6	9.3	9.4	9.2	10.0	11.7	12.4
80 „	4.9	4.7	5.2	5.5	5.3	5.5	6.3	6.9

Source: Adapted from *Social Trends* 4, HMSO 1973

1   *What sort of factors contribute to the longer life which most women can expect compared with men?*
2   *Compare the expectation of life figures for 1901 with those of 1969. What sort of reasons account for the increasing expectation of life for each age group?*

played (real or fictitious!)—virtues that were also those seen as the most desirable within the society ('thrift', 'honesty', etc.), for the death was an opportunity to encourage these virtues in others.

The decline in formal religion in Britain has resulted in a decline in the celebration of rites of passage, although many people avail themselves of the service of the churches in celebrating these rites even when they do not otherwise attend a place of worship, which seems to suggest that rites of this kind do satisfy a deeply felt human need. Geoffrey Gorer expresses the view that we need mourning rituals in order to express our grief fully and publicly, and believes that in holding back our expression of grief we may well increase our liability to neurosis.[2] The lack of ritual makes it more difficult for people to know how to behave when they are bereaved, or are faced with those who are.

It may be true that there is a growing reluctance to discuss all matters relating to death and that this may cause unnecessary fear. Many people are afraid of the process of dying rather than death itself, because they believe that it will inevitably be painful. In fact, the final illness of most people is rarely more than three months and is often only a few days; as people get older the likelihood of pain at death decreases. However, a number of reports do show that people suffer more than they need to, particularly when they die at home.[3] A reluctance to face death can also mean that people make inadequate preparations for it and that widows and children are consequently caused unnecessary hardship. Bereavement also involves psychological dangers: people should be aware that grief often persists over long periods and that those who experience such long periods of grief should not regard themselves as abnormal. Bereaved people often feel an awareness of the presence of a dead person, and it is important that they should realize that this is normal and that they are not going insane.[4]

Death may not always be the result of natural causes and in an earlier chapter it was seen how the doctrine 'thou shalt not kill' has been interpreted by various societies. One of the most noteworthy features of 'savage' society is the relative unimportance of the individual as compared with the community, and in these societies economic forces may make euthanasia and infanticide acceptable. For example, about half of all nomadic peoples, who depend on mobility for their livelihood,

have hastened the death of their old people: Eskimos, Lapps, North American Indians, Australian Aborigines, have accepted the necessity of euthanasia, while still respecting the old.[5] In modern times euthanasia is not usually advocated for economic reasons, but rather in cases where, it is felt, disease has made someone's life permanently painful, or where physical or mental defects at birth make it unlikely that the person will be able to lead a happy, useful life. Both these viewpoints have been expressed or practised in the past—both Plato and Aristotle advocated euthanasia and abortion for the 'children of inferior parents'; and among the Karens of Burma a sort of euthanasia/suicide was accepted as part of the social code—a man with some incurable or painful disease would hang himself.

Euthanasia is illegal in Britain, although a poll carried out in 1965 found that 75 per cent out of a sample of 1000 doctors agreed that 'some medical men do in fact help their patients over the last hurdle in order to save unnecessary suffering, even if that involves some curtailment of life'. In 1969 a Bill to legalize voluntary euthanasia was defeated in Parliament (forty-one for, sixty against). Views on euthanasia vary from that of the Voluntary Euthanasia Society: 'an adult person suffering from a severe illness for which no relief is known, should be entitled by law to the mercy of a painless death, if and only if, that is his expressed wish', to that expressed by the Pope in 1971 to the International Federation of Catholic Medical Associations: 'Nothing except self-defence ever authorises a man to dispose of the life of another.' However, even the Catholic Church has accepted the view that one can distinguish between 'ordinary' and 'extraordinary' treatment, and that in certain circumstances such treatment as artificial respiration and heart-massage might be justifiably discontinued.

Much of the debate over euthanasia has therefore now shifted from when to end life, to when to stop prolonging it. Modern treatment has resulted in a situation where a body can be kept living almost indefinitely, although the mind has permanently ceased to function. The cost of keeping people alive by artificial means is enormous, and could never be extended to everyone in a position to make use of the facilities; doctors therefore face the problem of deciding under what circumstances they are justified in discontinuing treatment. Modern treatment also results in a very considerable increase in the survival rate of babies born with congenital malformations. For example, the survival rate of babies born with spina bifida has increased from 10 per cent to 50 per cent in just over ten years.

A funeral procession in Chile accompanied by guitars and banjo players.
To what extent does religion influence a person's attitude to death?
Photograph: Camera Press

The opponents of euthanasia fear that if the principle of euthanasia is accepted in one sphere, it may gradually spread to others. They feel that it will damage the relationship between the doctor and his patient; that people may fear admittance to hospital in case their death is hastened in order to supply material for transplant surgery; and that people may agree to euthanasia because they feel it is expected of them although they do not desire it. Also, people may agree to euthanasia thinking themselves incurable, although medical knowledge might advance quickly to a point where they could have been cured.

It is interesting to note that if a patient asks a doctor not to prolong his life the doctor might be guilty of assault if he *does* take action to prolong it, but if he does *not* take action he might be guilty of aiding a suicide under the Suicide Act of 1961.

Suicide rates are greatly influenced by the social structure of the society and are a good example of the practical value of sociology. In 1897 Emile Durkheim produced his study on suicide which has been the basis for much of the subsequent investigation of the subject; Durkheim described three types of suicide, altruistic, egoistic, and anomic.[6]

Altruistic suicide stems from a regard for social or religious rules. One example is the Hindu *suttee* where the wife was burned alive on the funeral pyre of her dead husband; another is the Japanese ritual suicide 'hara kiri' (really called *seppuku*) where suicide was accepted as preferable to dishonour. Even in England a hundred years ago suicide was sometimes regarded as 'the gentleman's way out' of a disgraceful scandal.

Egoistic suicide occurs in a society where the individual is thrown back upon himself, lacking integration in the society. For example, Durkheim found that more single people commit suicide than married people and more Protestants than Roman Catholics: this he believed was the result of the Protestant ethic which leaves the individual more isolated emotionally compared with Catholicism which deals more in certainties.[7] It is certainly true that Southern Ireland still has the lowest suicide rate in Europe; but this may be as much a result of the Roman Catholic teaching that suicide merits damnation as to the greater social integration of Catholics. (A study in 1963 showed that social disapproval may lead to suicides being 'hushed up' in Southern Ireland, although the rate was still the lowest in Europe even when this had been taken into account.) It has also been suggested that many shoplifters are committing a sort of 'moral suicide' for egoistic reasons, for many of those who steal from shops are middle-aged ladies of unblemished character who face a crisis in their lives which may leave them feeling neglected and alone.[8]

Anomic suicide results from a state of 'anomie' in the society, a situation in which the society does not present a clear set of values,

222

Selected causes of death, 1969

Deaths per 100 000 population	All causes	Accidents, poisonings, and violence		
		Total	Suicide	Homicide
Males				
United Kingdom	1 252.0	56.2	10.3	0.8
Belgium	1 361.7	103.8	21.3	0.8
Denmark	1 075.8	92.4	26.6	0.8
France	1 206.6	122.7	23.4	1.0
Germany (Fed. Rep.)	1 302.4	106.6	27.7	1.5
Irish Republic	1 250.9	58.6	2.6	0.4
Italy	1 090.3	73.7	7.6	1.1
Luxembourg	1 393.1	120.8	22.9	0.6
Netherlands	927.1	70.4	9.1	0.7
Canada	854.2	98.8	15.5	2.5
Japan	757.5	84.9	16.4	1.9
USA	1 081.7	—	15.7	10.6
Philippines	768.5	62.8	1.0	30.6
Females				
United Kingdom	1 126.8	41.3	7.0	0.7
Belgium	1 140.7	64.3	9.3	0.9
Denmark	886.5	54.1	15.2	0.5
France	1 065.1	71.9	8.5	0.7
Germany (Fed. Rep.)	1 151.4	61.6	14.7	1.0
Irish Republic	1 058.4	34.4	1.0	0.1
Italy	906.0	29.6	3.3	0.5
Luxembourg	1 088.4	46.5	8.1	0.6
Netherlands	744.6	45.6	5.6	0.4
Canada	612.0	38.8	6.2	1.1
Japan	605.3	34.3	12.7	0.9
USA	796.1	—	6.1	3.2
Philippines	606.8	14.3	0.6	2.0

Comparative figures for motor vehicle accidents which are included in accident statistics above, 1967 figures (1973 figures in brackets): UK 21.2 (14); Belgium 38.6 (30); France 40.7 (32); Germany 43.9 (26); Italy 35.4 (21); I. Rep. 19.6 (20); USA 39.4 (35).

Source: Adapted from *Social Trends* **4**, HMSO 1973

1 *Which appear to be the safest countries in which to drive? Why?*
2 *What sort of reasons might account for the different numbers of people committing suicide in the countries listed?*
3 *Is murder a serious problem in any country?*

where relationships have become blurred, and where the individual lacks a clear sense of identity. Anomie may result from a war or revolution which overthrows an existing social order; or be the consequence of rapid technological and social change within a society. Durkheim ascribed anomic suicide to a general lack of standards resulting from the breaking up of a society. He found a greater incidence of suicide in urban areas than in rural, and more among the middle class than among the working class.

It could be said that egoistic and anomic suicide are the result of too little integration of the individual within the community, whereas altruistic suicide is caused by too much integration.

Japan continues to have a consistently high suicide rate. In 1971, 3944 people committed suicide in England and Wales (compared with 402 people who were murdered), but this figure represents only about nine suicides for every 100 000 people in the population, compared with about twenty-five suicides for every 100 000 people in Japan. (These figures will, of course, fluctuate annually.) All Durkheim's suicide types can be distinguished in an analysis of the reasons for Japan's suicide rate. Suicide is still ethically acceptable in Japan, and Japanese films and novels continue to link self-inflicted death with concepts of loyalty, honour, and self-respect (altruistic suicide).[9] The Japanese examinations systems is fiercely competitive, and the Suicide Problem Research Group at Kyoto University has shown a correlation between exam-failure and suicide: the young person is thrown upon his own resources to prove himself (egoistic suicide). (Although this may also be altruistic when the motivation is 'loss of face'.)[10] Traditional principles have disappeared in Japanese life—defeat in war and westernization have meant that the moral guides and goals of the society have been removed. This aimlessness and confusion increases the likelihood of suicide (anomic suicide).

In Britain, the best-known study of suicide is probably Peter Sainsbury's investigation into suicide in London.[11] His finding was that social isolation was the main cause of suicide and that suicide correlated with a lack of a stable social framework. For example, the highest suicide rates were in those districts of London such as Kensington and Bayswater which had a large proportion of houses broken up into bed-sitters: 27 per cent of all suicides lived alone, although only 7 per cent of the population as a whole did so. Loneliness has been described as 'a disease without physical symptoms',[12] and it is certainly a factor in suicide. It may itself by symptomatic of a society that is forgetting how to communicate and form relationships.

More discussion or written work

1 (a) Should a dying person be told of his approaching death? (b) Is it better to die in a hospital or at home?

2 Would you accept euthanasia in any of the following cases? Say why. (a) Malformed or mentally handicapped children. (b) Road-accident victims whose brains are 'dead'. (c) A young incurably ill

person in pain who requests it. (*d*) Low-grade mentally defective adults. (*e*) Senile people.

3 What are the arguments for and against abortion?

4 In later years, Freud divided the fundamental human drives into two classes, Eros (life) and Thanatos (death). Do you think there is a death instinct?

Research

1 (*a*) Find out the typical costs involved in funeral expenses and the methods available for disposing of the corpse. (*b*) How does one donate one's body for medical purposes?

2 Find out the major factors involved in suicide in Great Britain and suggest some action that could be taken to reduce the incidence of suicide.

Imagination

Imagine that you have the opportunity of inventing a new sequence of 'rites of passage' to replace those that have largely disappeared from our society. Explain the occasions on which these rites would take place and the ceremonials that you would attach to them.

Reading suggestions

* G. Gorer, *Death, Grief and Mourning*, Cresset Press
† J. Hinton, *Dying*, Penguin
† E. Stengel, *Suicide and Attempted Suicide*, Penguin

The Human Science

Further reading suggestions listed at the end of each chapter fit into the following categories:
* Books suitable for the general reader.
† Books that are not particularly difficult and are about O-level standard.
Other books are suitable for students who wish to develop their study of particular topics or for reference.

The Human Science

Men, like most animals, run in packs. They gather together in groups—families, gangs, political parties, tribes, nations. Most people will belong to, or have contact with, many different groups. It is the study of these groups, and their effect on the behaviour of individuals—in so far as they are within or outside such groups—that constitutes the subject matter of sociology. If groups and individuals developed and functioned haphazardly, there would be no sociology, no 'science of society'. Societies, however, and the groups within them, develop, function, and change in fairly orderly ways, and sociology seeks to describe and analyse these processes.

In so far as we are aware of why we and other people about us think, feel, and behave in the ways we do, we are more likely to be tolerant of other people, and more likely also to be able to assist the ever-changing structure of our society to adapt in ways which will bring lasting benefit to future generations.

The word sociology (*socius* = friend: *logos* = science) was first used by Auguste Comte in 1838 to describe what he called 'the science of the associated life of humanity'. Many other philosophers before Comte, from Plato in the fourth century before Christ to Montesquieu in the eighteenth century, had engaged in systematic studies of society and had accepted that the institutions of society do not develop merely by chance; but Comte was the first to try to establish sociology as a distinct discipline concerned with 'the positive study of the totality of fundamental laws relating to social phenomena'.

Comte placed sociology at the apex of a hierarchy of what he saw as sciences of increasing complexity: mathematics—astronomy—physics—chemistry—biology—sociology; some people, on the other hand, will not accept that sociology is a science at all. Sociology does not deal in certainties as do the natural sciences, nor are the materials that it investigates constant; and some sociologists may have made the mistake of expecting mathematical accuracy in sociology as in the mechanical sciences, speaking in terms of 'human physics' and 'laws of human behaviour'. No social science can achieve pure objectivity, and even natural scientists make frequent mistakes in interpreting their evidence and put forward theories that are later found to be without substance.

Discussing whether or not sociology is a science is a sterile pastime: what is certain is that sociology is a disciplined pursuit of a defined body of knowledge.

There have been various attempts to improve on Comte's description of sociology, just as we have seen that there are different definitions of law and religion; but because the borderline between sociology and the other social sciences is vague this does not mean that there is not a wide body of knowledge that can be categorized with certainty as sociology, just as the existence of doubt as to the precise definition of religion does not imply that religion does not exist! Other social sciences such as geography, history, psychology, and economics are all closely connected with sociology, and are also concerned with 'humanity', but sociology is the link between them all.

Psychology, for example, is the study of men's minds, which involves the study of the minds of other animals, and their relation to man's. Psychology is the study of the way in which individual men think and the way they act; but the way they act will influence the way in which other men in their society act, and the study of such interactions is called sociology. The psychology/sociology relationship is not, however, a one-way process; it is not just a question of individual men influencing the behaviour of the groups to which they belong, for the actions of these groups will also affect the thoughts and actions of the individuals within them. Many things which some people regard as 'human nature' are in fact the results of the social and cultural conditions under which men live.

History is also a study of society. Taking a more factual approach than sociology, it records the past actions of men and societies and comments on them. Not only does history record events but it also records the customs of societies in the past, so that, by examining the behaviour of our ancestors, we can see how our social institutions have developed and may be assisted in foreseeing future developments. Equally, history is often the outcome of social movements and cannot be understood without reference to them: any history of trade unionism would be incomplete without an examination of class structure.

Sociology is not an isolated science. Dealing as it does with society, anything which affects society is of interest to the sociologist—and almost everything affects society! But it should be stressed that sociology is primarily concerned with the study of organized behaviour. This organized behaviour develops from our basic biological needs—the needs for growth, shelter, reproduction, and health. These biological needs have a cultural response: growth will require food and lead to production and training; the need for shelter will lead to housebuilding and bodily comfort; reproduction will lead to kinship systems; and the need for health will lead to hygiene.

As our culture develops new cultural needs also develop. Television was regarded as a luxury a few years ago, but now it is regarded almost as a necessity. Without it the individual might be unable to join fully in the conversation and activities of his group, since these may often be based on television programmes.

We find that there are essential ingredients in all organized behaviour: there is the system of values which the group holds, the way the functions are distributed among the members of the group, the way in which people expect themselves to act, the materials and products the group uses, and the activities which it carries out. As the society becomes more complex there is a need for laws, ethics, and knowledge. The production of the society is controlled by economics; the behaviour of the members of the society is regulated by various means including law; new members of the society must be prepared for their roles within the society by education; and power is exercised by politics. Economics, education, law, and politics are, therefore, also related to sociology.

Functionalists would say that every action in a society is the result of a need in that society, but this is probably too neat and tidy to be completely true. Sociologists disagree among themselves, just as historians or economists do; in fact, one would expect more disagreement among sociologists than among other scientists. The sociologist is studying something of which he is a part, namely, society, and will have his own opinions, prejudices, and emotional responses. The fact that a sociologist has difficulty in being impartial brings us to the important point that (among adults) only the insane can be wholly influenced by events outside themselves, or entirely unmoved by them: normal adult behaviour is partially influenced by events and partially the result of detached thought, varying in proportion with different groups and individuals. As man places greater restraint upon himself in order to control natural forces, he becomes increasingly dependent on his fellow man and this has brought in its wake problems connected with man's reaction towards man.

It is obviously easier for the anthropologist studying the marriage relationship of Polynesian islanders to be a true 'scientist' (completely uninfluenced by personal opinion and able to judge purely on the basis of observable facts), than it is for the industrial sociologist surrounded by men similar to himself, who has a similar background of social and political thought to the subjects of his study. But both the theorist and the practical sociologist have important parts to play if man is to harness the present ungoverned forces of society to serve him and prevent the extermination of his society, as thousands of years ago the river dwellers of North Africa harnessed the natural forces of river-flooding to establish civilization as we know it.

Reading suggestions

* D. Morris, *The Naked Ape*, Corgi

† P. Berger, *Invitation to Sociology*, Penguin

† W. Sprott, *Human Groups*, Penguin

R. Aron, *Main Currents in Sociological Thought* (2 vols), Penguin

C. Wright Mills, *The Sociological Imagination*, Penguin

P. Worsley (ed.), *Introducing Sociology*, Penguin

A Short Glossary of Some Sociological Terms

Where term is marked with an asterisk, see also entry in index.

Acculturation	The changing of cultural behaviour by contact between cultures (sometimes used in the same sense as socialization).
Adaptation	Adjustment to the environment (either biological or social).
*Alienation**	An individual's feeling of separation from the values and norms of his society, leading to a feeling that his life is meaningless and that he has no power over his destiny.
Altruism	Putting the welfare of others above one's own welfare. An altruistic society is one in which the interests of the individual are submerged within the interests of the group.
*Anomie**	A lack or confusion of values within a society or group.
Anthropology	A comparative study of mankind, particularly the study of man in primitive societies.
*Attitude**	A consistent approach and a predictable response towards particular views and situations.
*Automation**	The replacement of men by electronic and mechanical devices.
Behaviourism	A school of psychology concentrating on definite, observable behaviour and the use of scientific techniques. Also used to describe a sociological approach emphasizing the individual and his interaction with other individuals.
Cognition	All the processes by which an individual comes to understand his environment.
Concept	A word or words expressing a point of view reached by concentrating on certain aspects of a subject.
Conformity	Behaviour that fits in with the expectations of a group.
Control group	A group similar to another group which is the subject of experiment, but not itself subjected to the variable under examination. It serves as a comparison with the experimental group.
Deviance	Behaviour that does not conform to the expected pattern.
*Delinquency**	The breaking of the legal code of a society.
Dysfunction	An action within a social system that prevents or hinders the stability or integration of the system.
Ecology	A study of the adaptation and relationships between man, animals, and environment.
Ego	A person's conception of themself. The Ego checks the impulsive drives of the Id (Freudian).
*Elite**	The most powerful group within a group or society—a group which has considerable control and influence.

233

Empiricism	An outlook based on experience rather than a set of values.
Endogamy	An insistence that marriage must be to people within one's own kinship or social group. (When social pressure is not so strong this is called 'homogamy', i.e. like marrying like.)
Exogamy	An insistence that marriage must be to people outside one's own kinship or social group.
Fixation	A compulsive attachment to a particular person, object, activity, or stage of development.
Gerontocracy	Rule by the old.
Hypothesis	A suggestion that there is a relationship between certain facts that can be tested later.
Id	Instinctive impulses that seek immediate gratification (Freudian).
Induction	Reasoning from specific facts to general principles (opposite of deduction).
Innate	Describing behaviour which has not been learnt.
*Matrilineal**	Descent through the female line (opposite of patrilineal).
Methodology	A study of the way in which knowledge is built up.
*Mores**	Normal standards of behaviour within a society that are regarded as essential to the group's welfare and are informally sanctioned. (Sometimes the term is also used to include official laws.)
Motivation	Stimulation of an individual towards a specific goal.
Negativism	A rejection of conformity by an individual because conformity appears to threaten his position, values, or conception of himself.
*Norm**	A standard of behaviour shared by a group and acceptable within it. (Normlessness, a lack of norms to guide an individual's behaviour, may be the result of too few norms within a group; or too many, so that selection is difficult.)
Objectivity	The quality of attempting to use an unbiased scientific technique.
*Peer group**	A group whose members have more or less equal status (often used to describe a group of people of similar age).
Positivism	A view that knowledge can only be gained by using the methods employed in the natural sciences and that 'laws' governing social behaviour can be worked out enabling 'social engineering' to take place.
*Role**	The part that a person appears to play in a group and the pattern of behaviour that is expected from a person in a particular position (may be 'ascribed', that is given, e.g. father; or 'achieved', that is chosen, e.g. doctor).
*Sanction**	A penalty or reward intended to encourage or discourage particular forms of behaviour.
Self-orientated	The placing of one's personal interests before the interests of the group.
*Socialization**	The learning of the values of the group to which one belongs and one's role within the group (sometimes restricted to the learning processes of childhood).

234

*Status**	A person's position within a given social situation (sometimes used in the same way as 'class' or as a position within a hierarchy).
Stratification	The fairly permanent way in which people are ranked within a society by virtue of their inheritance, power, and wealth.
*Value**	A general principle governing conduct within a given sphere in a society, generally accepted by the group as a standard by which conduct can be judged.

Text Sources

These text references refer you to the sources of points of fact or opinion given in the text, or to sources of further information on the facts or opinions quoted. Where only a page or a number of pages are relevant these are given. The publication dates given are not necessarily those of the latest editions but those of the editions to which the page references refer.

Chapter 1   The Family

1 D. and V. Mace, *The Soviet Family*, Hutchinson 1964, p. 205
2 J. Bowlby, *Child Care and the Growth of Love*, Penguin 1965, thesis and p. 76; *see also* W. Van der Eyken, *The Pre-School Years*, Penguin 1969 (first published 1967), pp. 56–61
3 Ministry of Health, *Children and the British Government Evacuation Scheme*, London 1948
4 As 2 above, pp. 39, 41, 77
5 D. Riesman, *The Lonely Crowd*, Doubleday (Anchor) 1953, p. 55; *and* M. Rutter, *Maternal Deprivation Re-assessed*, Penguin 1972, pp. 13, 14, 92, 97–99, 108, 123, 128
6 G. Schaller, *The Year of the Gorilla*, University of Chicago Press 1964, p. 138
7 L. Mair, *Marriage*, Penguin 1971, p. 154
8 As 7, pp. 144, 150
9 E. Craighill Handy, *The Native Culture of the Marquesas*, Honolulu Museum 1923, pp. 39–40, 101
10 F. Kay, *The Family in Transition*, David & Charles 1972, p. 124
11 As 9, p. 126
12 A. Kondos, *One Among Many: Living in Urban Australia*, Cheshire 1971, p. 39
13 S. Eisenstadt, *From Generation to Generation*, Routledge & Kegan Paul 1956, p. 180
14 C. Hutt, *Males and Females*, Penguin Education 1972, p. 136
15 N. Bell and E. Vogel (eds.), *A Modern Introduction to the Family*, Free Press 1960, pp. 80, 96; *and* M. F. Nimkoff (ed.), *Comparative Family Systems*, Houghton Mifflin 1965, pp. 163, 191
16 As 9, pp. 45, 48

Chapter 2   Education

1 W. and L. Kellogg, *The Ape and the Child*, McGraw-Hill 1933
2 A. Jensen, *Educability and Group Differences*, Methuen 1973
3 H. Eysenck, *The Inequality of Man*, Maurice Temple Smith 1973
4 R. Herrnstein, article in *Atlantic Monthly*, Sept. 1971; *and* R. Herrnstein, *I.Q. in the Meritocracy*, Allen Lane, the Penguin Press 1973
5 As 3

6 H. Skeels, *Monographs of the Society for Research in Child Development* 31, no. 3, 1966. Also H. Campbell, *The Pleasure Areas*, Eyre Methuen 1973, pp. 232–234, 248

7 J. Brierly, 'The crucial years of life', *New Society*, 4 Oct. 1973

8 T. Burgess, *Inside Comprehensive Schools*, HMSO 1970, p. 1

9 T. Monks, *Comprehensive Education in England and Wales*, National Foundation for Educational Research 1968, p. vi

10 As 8: p. 8, 'children do as well or better'; pp. 30–32, 'intelligence develops differently'; p. 5, 'not two different sorts of children'. *And* R. Pedley, *The Comprehensive School*, Penguin 1969 (first published 1963), p. 204

11 As 8, pp. 37–38

12 M. Carter, *Into Work*, Penguin 1966, pp. 200–204, 220–221

13 G. Pickering, *The Challenge to Education*, Penguin 1967, pp. 40–41; *and* N. Anderson, *Work and Leisure*, Routledge & Kegan Paul 1961, pp. 137–139

Chapter 3 Morality

1 M. Mead, *Sex and Temperament*, Routledge & Kegan Paul 1952 (first published 1935), p. 212

2 J. Calvin (translated by F. Battles), *Institutes of the Christian Religion* IV (trans. 1959), ch. XX, pp. 10–12

3 Rothe, *Theologische Ethik*

4 G. Gorer, *Sex and Marriage in England Today*, Nelson 1971, p. 39

5 G. Gorer, *Exploring English Character*, Cresset Press 1955, p. 96

6 As 1, p. 50

7 J. Flugel, *Man, Morals and Society*, Duckworth 1945, pp. 82–83

Chapter 4 Marriage

1 G. Mardock, *Social Structure*, Macmillan 1949, pp. 5–6; *and* M. Farmer, *The Family*, Longman 1970, p. 11 ('Marriage is the licensing not of sexual intercourse but of parenthood'—Malinowski)

2 E. Kay, *The Family in Transition*, David & Charles 1972, pp. 75, 74

3 As 2, p. 96; *and* for Victorian morality generally see R. Pearsall, *The Worm in the Bud*, Penguin 1969

4 *Britain 1973*, HMSO 1973, p. 11; *and Social Trends* 3, HMSO 1972, pp. 7, 63, *and Social Trends* 8 (all figures rounded up)

5 L. Mair, *Marriage*, Penguin 1971, p. 191

6 T. Parsons and R. Bales, *Family, Socialization and Interaction Process*, Routledge & Kegan Paul 1956, pp. 3–34

7 M. Young and P. Wilmott, *Family and Kinship in East London*, Penguin 1972, pp. 139–141 (Routledge & Kegan Paul 1957)

8 J. and E. Newson, *Patterns of Infant Care*, Penguin 1965, p. 147

9 As 2, p. 99

10 J. Dominian, *Marital Breakdown*, Penguin 1968, p. 97

11 *Social Trends* 3, HMSO 1972, p. 7

12 G. Rowntree, 'New facts on teenage marriage', *New Society*, 4 Oct. 1962

13 As 2, p. 12

14 As 10, p. 19

15 National Marriage Guidance Council, *Marriage Guidance*, Jan. 1970

Chapter 5 Occupation

1 Statistics given in this chapter are, unless otherwise stated, based on *Britain 1976* (HMSO 1976); *Social Trends 6* (HMSO 1975); *Dept of Employment Gazette*, Feb. 1976; E. Ferri, *Growing up in a One-Parent Family*, NFER 1975
2 S. Yudkin and A. Holme, *Working Mothers and their Children*, Michael Joseph 1963; P. Jephcott, N. Seear, and J. Smith, *Married Women Working*, Allen & Unwin 1962; and V. Klein, *Britain's Married Women Workers*, Routledge & Kegan Paul 1965
3 W. Van der Eyken, *The Pre-School Years*, Penguin 1969, p. 58 (*see also* p. 26—of 2 500 000 women with children under five, 314 000 had jobs, 140 000 of them full-time)
4 R. Fletcher, *The Family and Marriage in Britain*, Penguin 1973, p. 181
5 R. and R. Rapoport, *Dual-Career Families*, Penguin 1971, p. 299
6 S. Eisenstadt, *From Generation to Generation*, Routledge & Kegan Paul 1956, pp. 64–65
7 N. Dennis, F. Henriques, and C. Slaughter, *Coal Is Our Life*, Eyre & Spottiswoode 1956, p. 144
8 J. Tunstall, *The Fishermen*, MacGibbon & Kee 1962
9 As 7, pp. 130–170, 179
10 As 7, pp. 180–233, 146, 174
11 *Social Trends* 4, HMSO 1973, p. 105

Chapter 6 Religion

1 E. Taylor, *Primitive Culture*, 1903 (fourth edition)
2 J. Frazer, *The Golden Bough*, 1922 (first published 1890)
3 Church Information Office, *Facts and Figures about the Church of England* 3, 1965.
4 E. Durkheim, *Elementary Forms of the Religious Life*, English translation 1926
5 H. Gerth and C. Mills (eds), *From Max Weber: Essays in Sociology*, Routledge & Kegan Paul 1961, p. 271
6 N. Cohn, *The Pursuit of the Millennium*, Heinemann 1957, p. 13
7 K. Marx and F. Engels, *On Religion*, Foreign Languages Publishing House, Moscow 1957, p. 42
8 M. Argyle, *Religious Behaviour*, Routledge & Kegan Paul 1965 (first published 1958), p. 143
9 K. Marx, *The Class Struggles in France 1848 to 1850*, Foreign Languages Publishing House, Moscow 1958, p. 187
10 K. Wittfogel, *Oriental Despotism*, Yale University Press 1958, pp. 90–93, 95
11 H. Jones, *Crime in a Changing Society*, Penguin 1967 (first published 1965), p. 107
12 E. Krausz, *Leeds Jewry*, Cambridge University Press 1964
13 Gallup Poll for the *Sunday Telegraph*, 1973
14 J. Brothers, *Religious Institutions*, Longman 1971, pp. 34, 35
15 B. Rowntree and G. Lavers, *English Life and Leisure*, Longman 1951
16 'Television and religion', Social Surveys (Gallup Poll) Ltd 1965
17 G. Gorer, *Sex and Marriage in England Today*, Nelson 1971
18 Léon de St Moulin, 'Social class and religious behaviour in England', *The Clergy Review*, 1968
19 As 13, and Gallup Poll on same basis in 1967
20 R. Rose and D. Urwin, 'What are parties based on?', *New Society*, 7 May 1970
21 R. Robertson (ed.), *Sociology of Religion*, Penguin 1972, p. 143
22 As 21, pp. 160–161
23 As 21, pp. 148–150
24 As 14, p. 90

Chapter 7 Politics

1 R. Tawney, *Religion and the Rise of Capitalism*, Penguin 1948 (first published 1926)
2 D. Morris, *The Human Zoo*, The Literary Guild 1969 (also published by Jonathan Cape), pp. 42–53
3 J. Vincent, *Pollbooks: How the Victorians Voted*, Cambridge University Press 1967, pp. 61–63
4 J. Blondel, *Voters, Parties and Leaders*, Penguin 1972 (first published 1963), p. 52
5 M. Abrams, R. Rose, and R. Hinden, *Must Labour Lose?*, Penguin 1960
6 D. Butler and A. King, *The British General Election of 1964*, Macmillan 1965, p. 296
7 As 6, pp. 57–58
8 As 6, p. 74
9 Berwick by-election, 8 November 1973
10 Interim Report of the Labour Party Sub-committee on Party Organization, 1955
11 C. Brinton, *The Anatomy of Revolution*, Jonathan Cape 1953, pp. 16–19

Chapter 8 Trade Unions

1 *Industrial Relations Act*, HMSO 1971
2 G. Bain, *The Growth of White-Collar Unionism*, Oxford University Press 1970, p. 1
3 D. Lockwood, *The Black Coated Worker*, Allen & Unwin 1958
4 As 2, p. 132

Chapter 9 Leisure

1 N. Anderson, *Work and Leisure*, Routledge & Kegan Paul 1961, pp. 46–48
2 J. Brown, *Techniques of Persuasion*, Penguin 1972 (first published 1963), p. 317 (J. H. Plumb's comments on *Life in Georgian England* by E. Neville Williams)
3 *Social Trends* 4, HMSO 1973, p. 95
4 J. Calman (ed.), *Western Europe—a handbook*, Anthony Blond 1967, p. 453
5 *Social Trends* 4, HMSO 1973, p. 94
6 E. M. Symonds, Professor of Obstetrics and Gynaecology, in his inaugural address at Nottingham University, 20 March 1974
7 W. Beveridge, 'How worthwhile is retirement?' *New Society*, 3 June 1965; *see also* P. Townsend, *The Family Life of Old People*, Penguin 1963, ch. 11
8 T. Davies, 'A year on the dole', *New Society*, 21 Sept. 1972
9 North-West Sports Council, *Leisure in the North West, 1972*, 1972
10 J. Barr, 'Free time in Britain', *New Society*, 15 April 1965
11 V. Packard, *The Waste Makers*, Penguin 1973, pp. 57–58

Chapter 10 Pressure Groups

1 S. Finer, *Anonymous Empire*, Pall Mall Press 1958, pp. 108–109
2 P. Self and H. Storing, *The State and the Farmer*, Allen & Unwin 1962, p. 23
3 As 1, p. 133
4 H. Wilson, *Pressure Group*, Secker & Warburg 1961
5 A. Ryan, *Mutiny at the Curragh*, Macmillan 1956, pp. 128–146
6 C. Mayhew, *Party Games*, Hutchinson 1969, p. 175
7 'The Register of Members' Interests' as on 1 November 1975, House of Commons Paper HC 699 HMSO

Chapter 11 Government

1 *Hansard* 907, no. 66, col. 430, 1976
2 House of Lords Debates 17 May 1950—Viscount Cecil of Chelwood
3 I. Jennings, *Parliament*, Cambridge University Press 1948 (first published 1939), pp. 342–343
4 I. Jennings, *Cabinet Government*, Cambridge University Press 1951, p. 443
5 *Hansard* 757, no. 43, 22 Jan. 1968 (written answers); *Whitaker's Almanack*, 1973
6 H. Morrison, *Government and Parliament*, Oxford University Press 1956 (first published 1954), p. 335
7 A. Gardiner, *The Life of Sir William Harcourt* II, Constable 1923, p. 588
8 R. Kelsall, *Higher Civil Servants in Britain*, Routledge & Kegan Paul 1955

Chapter 12 Supranational Authority

1 A. Comte (translated by R. Congreve), *The Catechism of Positive Religion*, 1858

Chapter 13 The Welfare State

1 Royal Commission on Children's Employment—Report 1842
2 J. Foster, *Class Struggle and the Industrial Revolution*, Weidenfeld & Nicolson 1974
3 *The National Encyclopaedia* XII, William MacKenzie 1882, p. 119
4 E. Benn, *The State the Enemy*, Ernest Benn 1953, p. 25
5 J. Lively, *The Social and Political Thought of Alexis de Tocqueville*, Clarendon Press 1962 (summary of position—ch. 1)
6 N. Senior, *Historical and Philosophical Essays*, 1865
7 B. Abel-Smith and P. Townsend, 'The poor and the poorest', *Occasional Papers on Social Administration*, Bell 1965
8 M. Young (ed.), *Poverty Report 1974*, Maurice Temple Smith 1974
9 Central Advisory Council for Education (England), *15 to 18* (The Crowther Report), HMSO 1959
10 L. Robbins, *Higher Education* (The Robbins Report), HMSO 1963
11 J. C. Kincaid, *Poverty and Equality in Britain*, Penguin 1973, p. 21
12 R. Lister, *Social Security: the case for reform*, Child Poverty Action Group, 1975

Chapter 14 The Law

1 A. Radcliffe-Brown, *Structure and Function in Primitive Society*, Free Press 1952
2 B. Malinowski, *Crime and Custom in Savage Society*, Littlefield Adams 1959 (first published 1926)
3 R. Merton, *Social Theory and Social Structure*, Free Press 1957, pp. 368–384
4 Contribution by A. Radcliffe-Brown, *Encyclopaedia of the Social Sciences*, Macmillan 1933
5 C. Wright Mills, *The Power Elite*, Oxford University Press 1956, p. 145

Chapter 15 The Economy

1 L. Mumford, *The City in History*, Penguin 1973 (first published 1961), pp. 251–252, 254–255, 268
2 J. Banks, *Prosperity and Parenthood*, Routledge & Kegan Paul 1954
3 P. Brown, *Birds of Prey*, André Deutsch 1964, p. 76

4 D. Hay, *Human Populations*, Penguin 1972, p. 20. (Discussion of J. De Castro's theory, which is based on the fact that fertility depends partially upon oestrogens, and suggests that people suffering from protein deficiency often have fatty degeneration of the liver, which makes the liver less efficient at destroying excess oestrogens and therefore increases fertility among those with least to eat.)

5 As 1, pp. 75–76

6 K. Marx, *Capital* 1, ch. XXXII, Foreign Languages Publishing House, Moscow 1958 (first published 1867), p. 763

7 V. Packard, *The Status Seekers*, Penguin 1972 (first published 1970), pp. 257–258

8 P. Worsley (ed.), *Introducing Sociology*, Penguin 1972 (first published 1970), pp. 208–209

Chapter 16   Communications

1 *Britain 1973*, HMSO 1973, p. 434 (1970–71 figures)

2 *Report of the Committee on Broadcasting, 1960* (Pilkington Committee), HMSO 1962, p. 15, para. 42

3 H. Himmelweit, A. Oppenheim, and P. Vince, *Television and the Child*, Oxford University Press 1958: pp. 17–18, ch. 18–21 (impact if touches values of the child); ch. 17 (television drama upper middle class); ch. 10 (tastes developed)

4 H. Himmelweit, 'Television revisited', *New Society*, 1 Nov. 1962

5 J. Halloran, *The Effects of Mass Communication*, Leicester University Press 1971 (first published 1964), pp. 23–26

6 J. Brown, *Techniques of Persuasion*, Penguin 1972 (first published 1963), p. 153 (reference to P. Pickard, *I Could a Tale Unfold: Horror and Sensationalism in Stories for Children*, Tavistock)

7 As 5, p. 27

8 P. Madgwick, *Introduction to British Politics*, Hutchinson 1970, pp. 435–436

9 W. Belson, 'Television and family life', *Advancement of Science* 16, no. 64, 1960

10 M. Schofield, *The Sexual Behaviour of Young People*, Longman 1965, p. 9

11 R. Williams, *Communications*, Penguin 1971 (first published 1962), pp. 27, 28, 33

12 V. Packard, *The Status Seekers*, Penguin 1962 (first published 1959), p. 279

13 As 6, pp. 188–189

14 As 6, p. 205

Chapter 17   Class

1 *Social Trends* 3, HMSO 1972. (Figures based on 1966 census. The balance of 3 per cent of population consists of armed forces, 1.4 per cent, and inadequately described occupations.)

2 V. Packard, *The Status Seekers*, Penguin 1971 (first published 1959), p. 217

3 M. Weber, *Economy and Society* 1 and 2, Bedminster 1968

4 C. Wright Mills, *The Power Elite*, Oxford 1956

5 D. Lockwood, *The Black Coated Worker*, Allen & Unwin 1958, ch. 3

6 W. Runciman, *Relative Deprivation and Social Justice*, Penguin 1972, pp. 99, 102

7 As 6, p. 105

8 As 6, p. 187

9 As 6, p. 114

10 M. Kohn, *Class and Conformity*, Dorsey 1969

11 D. MacRae, 'Classlessness', *New Society*, 26 Oct. 1972

12 C. Harbury, 'Inheritance in the distribution of personal wealth', *Economic Journal* **72**, no. 288
13 J. Wedgwood, *The Economics of Inheritance*, Penguin 1939
14 'The meaning of class', *New Society*, 16 April 1964
15 As 5, p. 116
16 As 2, pp. 24–25

Chapter 18 Race

1 J. R. Baker, *Race*, Oxford University Press 1974
2 de Gobineau, *The Inequality of Human Races*, 1855 (translated in 1915 by Adrian Collins)
3 A. Barnett, *The Human Species*, Penguin 1957 (first published 1950), pp. 131–140
4 H. Chamberlain, *The Foundations of the Nineteenth Century*, 1899 (translated in 1910 by John Lees)
5 A. Jensen, *Genetics and Education*, Methuen 1972; *see also* 1
6 A. Shuey, *The Testing of Negro Intelligence*, Britons Publications 1958
7 O. Klineberg, *Race Differences*, Harper 1935
8 As 3, pp. 153–154
9 *The National Encyclopaedia* **IX**, William MacKenzie 1882, p. 475
10 P. Griffiths, *A Question of Colour*, Leslie Frewin 1966, pp. 13–14
11 As 3, p. 161
12 M. Banton, *Race Relations*, Tavistock 1967 (quote from A. J. Beveridge 1900)
13 J. Hoagland, *South Africa. Civilizations in Conflict*, Allen & Unwin 1973, pp. 27–45
14 K. Marx, *Marx–Engels on Britain*, Foreign Languages Publishing House, Moscow 1954, p. 506
15 W. Daniel, *Racial Discrimination in England* (based on the 1967 Political and Economic Planning Report), Penguin 1971 (first published 1968): pp. 226, 232–233, 244 (employment); pp. 234, 155–156 (accommodation); p. 238 (motor insurance)
16 *Britain 1973*, HMSO 1973, p. 147

Chapter 19 Crime and Punishment

1 H. Jones, *Crime in a Changing Society*, Penguin 1967 (first published 1965), p. 41
2 From speech at annual meeting of American Association for Advancement of Science published in *Sunderland Echo*, 29 Dec. 1972
3 As 1, p. 49
4 Gabriel Tarde, *La Criminalité Comparée*, Paris 1886
5 R. Merton, 'Social structure and anomie', *American Sociological Review* **3**, 1938; *and* P. Worsley (ed.), *Modern Sociology: Introductory Readings*, Penguin 1970, pp. 468, 672–680 (social theory and social structure)
6 A. Cohen, *Delinquent Boys*, Free Press 1955, pp. 25–27
7 T. Morris, 'The sociology of crime', *New Society*, 29 April 1965
8 Glaser and Rice, 'Crime, age and unemployment', *American Sociological Review* **24**, 1959
9 R. Sparks, 'America looks at crime', *New Society*, 15 June 1967
10 W. Russell, 'Aggression: new light from animals', *New Society*, 10 February 1966; *see also* D. Morris, *The Human Zoo*, Literary Guild 1969 (also published by Jonathan Cape), pp. 148–151
11 B. Whitaker, *The Police*, Eyre & Spottiswoode 1964, p. 69

12 H. Jones, *Crime in a Changing Society*, Penguin 1967
13 E. Durkheim (translated by G. Simpson), *The Division of Labour in Society*, Free Press 1947 (first published 1893), p. 102

Chapter 20 Death

 1 G. Gorer, *Death, Grief and Mourning*, Cresset Press 1965, p. 169
 2 As 1, pp. 14–15, 53, 132, 115–116
 3 J. Hinton, *Dying*, Penguin 1972 (first published 1967), pp. 15, 80–83
 4 P. Marris, *Widows and Their Families*, Routledge & Kegan Paul 1958
 5 As 3, p. 45
 6 E. Durkheim, *Suicide: A Study in Sociology*, Routledge & Kegan Paul 1952 (first published 1867)
 7 M. Weber (translated by Talcott Parsons) *The Protestant Ethic and the Spirit of Capitalism*, Unwin Books 1965, p. 117
 8 H. Jones, *Crime in a Changing Society*, Penguin 1967, p. 68
 9 E. Stengel, *Suicide and Attempted Suicide*, Penguin 1965
10 J. Barr, 'Death in cherry blossom time', *New Society*, 8 April 1965
11 P. Sainsbury, *Social Aspects of Suicide in London*, Chapman & Hall 1955
12 *Sunday Times* enquiry, S. Cooper, 27 May 1962

Index

248